Charley,

Given in honor of your many Past – and many Future Successes.... like me !!!

Happy New Year!

Tom Cannon

D0049296

TRUE
SUCCESS

TRUE SUCCESS

A New Philosophy
of Excellence

TOM MORRIS, Ph.D.

A Grosset/Putnam Book

Published by G. P. Putnam's Sons

New York

A Grosset/Putnam Book
Published by G. P. Putnam's Sons
Publishers Since 1838
200 Madison Avenue
New York, NY 10016

Library of Congress Cataloging-in-Publication Data

Morris, Thomas V.
True success : a new philosophy of excellence / Tom Morris.
p.   cm.
"A Grosset/Putnam book"—T.p.
Includes index.
ISBN 0–399–13943–5
1. Success.   2. Success in business.   3. Excellence.   I. Title.
BJ1611.2.M64   1994   93–38664 CIP
158′.1—dc20

Printed in the United States of America
1   2   3   4   5   6   7   8   9   10

This book is printed on acid-free paper.

*To my children, Sara Noël Morris
and Matthew Thomas Morris.
In every aspect of their lives,
may they enjoy true success.*

Contents

First, therefore, we must seek what it is that we are aiming at; then we must look about for the road by which we can reach it most quickly, and on the journey itself, if only we are on the right path, we shall discover how much of the distance we overcome each day, and how much nearer we are to the goal toward which we are urged by a natural desire. But so long as we wander aimlessly, having no guide, and following only the noise and discordant cries of those who call us in different directions, life will be consumed in making mistakes—life that is brief even if we should strive day and night for sound wisdom. Let us, therefore, decide both upon the goal and upon the way, and not fail to find some experienced guide who has explored the region towards which we are advancing; for the conditions of this journey are different from those of most travel. On most journeys some well-recognized road and inquiries made of the inhabitants of the region prevent you from going astray; but on this one all the best beaten and the most frequented paths are the most deceptive. Nothing, therefore, needs to be more emphasized than the warning that we should not like sheep, follow the lead of the throng in front of us, traveling, thus, the way that all go and not the way that we ought to go.

Seneca, "On the Happy Life" (c. A.D. 58)

Preface

It was late at night and there I was, a professor at the University of Notre Dame, standing toe to toe with nearly two and a half dozen of the biggest, toughest college football players in the country. A group that would power its way to the national championship the following year. At a bit over six feet tall and just their side of two hundred pounds, I was in about the best shape of my life. But for what confronted me, I needed to rely on my wits.

It was my job to make them philosophers. A daunting challenge. By early indications, Mission Impossible. I had called them together for this special nocturnal meeting because most of them were struggling at the bottom of a difficult class of three hundred students and digging themselves a deeper hole with each passing, or perhaps I should say failing, day. They were hugely successful athletes, but they were taking a pounding from the Big Questions.

Some cynic might say that I was just confronted with the most common version of the mind-body problem: The more you have of one, the less you have of the other. The better the one, the worse the other. Baloney. The greatest philosopher in human history, Plato, was also a big, broad-shouldered championship wrestler. As I thought about the problems and glories of my student-athletes that evening, I had an intuition, a hunch, an instinctive suspicion that some of the very same qualities and habits that were giving them such spectacular success on the football field would also be able to bring them to a mastery of the classroom challenge they faced. If I could figure out, and help them to see, the connections. Maybe some of the fundamental conditions for success were the same for philosophy as for football. If I was right, I should be able to help them transfer some of the strengths they already had into the academic arena.

I was right. And without giving away too much of the story, which I'll tell a bit later in this book, the Notre Dame football team made one of its greatest comebacks ever in Philosophy 101. That evening I was able to identify several fundamental conditions for success that applied to both athletics and academics; I was able to present these conditions in a simple framework that those struggling students could easily master; and they were able to apply them for the rest of the semester with astounding success.

As soon as I began to identify these basic conditions for success in such different fields as football and philosophy, it struck me that they were exactly the ingredients for excellence in business endeavors, for dealing effectively with personal challenges of any kind, and for building successful relationships of all sorts. When I later turned my attention to these other domains of daily living, I began to discover more fundamental conditions for achievement. My framework evolved. And I began to present the results of my thinking to audiences of all kinds—to community groups, church gatherings, businesses, conventions, and professional associations. At first I spoke locally, then regionally, and then nationally. In lively interactions all over the country, I tested and refined this fascinating, developing framework, and I came to appreciate its power. I also came to see the importance at the present time of thinking clearly about what success is and about how we can attain the most satisfying and sustainable forms of it in our lives. I came to realize that we all need to philosophize about success.

We all need help. We need guidance for our journeys through life. Even the most successful of us need reminders and fresh, crisp articulations of the truths we may only vaguely grasp that have, in one way or another, led us to whatever we have managed to accomplish. We need to rethink. We need to refocus. How can we get where we still need to go? And how can we best convey to others what it takes to get there together?

What is it to achieve success? In any activity? In life? How can we strive for excellence and at the same time thrive as happy, fulfilled human beings? This book presents what I have come to see as the one and only framework of truly universal conditions for genuine achievement, the fundamental conditions for sustainable and satisfying success in anything we do, as well as in life itself.

One of the most common maladies of our time is a misunderstanding of success. In a recent book catalogue of new titles sent to my house by a national bookstore chain, I noticed on one page a book about how to help elementary school–age kids start and run profitable businesses. On the next page there was a book about stress and young children. I remember thinking that these two volumes should come as a boxed set. We are in such a hurry to get the edge for ourselves and to give our children all the advantages. The Japanese have special cram schools for preschoolers. We take our little people to lessons, practices, games, recitals, and programs of enrichment, to launch them into a life of success. Yet for all our pushing, pressing, and positioning, we haven't thought enough about what success really is, what it actually requires of us, and what it offers in return. In this book I want to lay out the simple truth about success. What it is and how to have it.

The quest for success should be an exciting and fulfilling adventure. A desire for success in any activity should be refined and enhanced by a broader perspective on what it takes for success at life. Only then can we attain the sort of harmony and balance that is necessary for true happiness and true success.

The paradigmatic philosopher Socrates, the teacher of Plato and the original wise guy, is reported to have made it a habit of surprising any man he met in Athens by saying: "Good Sir, you are an Athenian, a citizen of the greatest city with the greatest reputation for both wisdom and power; are you not ashamed of your eagerness to possess as much wealth, reputation, and honors as possible, while you do not care for nor give thought to wisdom or truth, or the best possible state of your soul?" As reported by Plato in his famous *Apology*, Socrates was convinced that most of us approach life backwards. We give the most attention to the least important things and the least attention to the most important things. It was his firm belief that "wealth does not bring about excellence, but excellence brings about wealth and all other public and private blessings for men." It was the state of our souls that was most important to Socrates. The inner life of each person. Greatness of spirit. Wisdom. Inner excellence. When we give precedence to the inner, both inner and outer fall into place. When we follow the opposite course, nothing will give us what we truly need. Only emptiness will result.

Make wisdom your provision for the journey from youth to old age, for it is a more certain support than all other possessions.   *Bias of Priene*
(as reported by Diogenes Laertius)

The conditions for success I'll present and discuss in this book, the universal framework of conditions for genuine achievement, all begin with something in the inner life of thought, feeling, imagination, and judgment, and provide for our moving into a form of success in the outer world that will resonate deeply with our innermost needs and values. There is, I believe, no hint of Machiavellian manipulativeness or predatory power moves to be found in what is needed. And that's a good thing. "For what is a man profited if he should gain the whole world and lose his own soul?" we are asked in the Gospel of Matthew. We have here a framework for success that proves you don't have to sell out to move up. It is a framework that allows for the best possible state of our souls. And it works.

A piece of preliminary advice. A man I know recently told me about a friend of his who is addicted to success books. He buys every one he sees, reads them with great enthusiasm, learns a lot, underlines particularly powerful passages, and passes on all the great advice to his friends. The problem is, he never takes the time to actually apply any of this great advice in his own life. He's too busy reading. In fact, his work and his relationships are suffering. The only thing he is really successful at now is in finishing these books, finding new ones, and memorizing any particularly catchy aphorisms they contain.

Now, clearly, this is a little perverse. If you have already read one or two success books, of the business-tips variety, or of the general self-help sort, then please do go on to read this book. It's different. But then don't go read another one until you've changed something you do. Make this book make a difference in your life. It can if you will. If this is the first book you've ever read on success, I hope you'll benefit right away, and that the framework you master will help you interpret and assess anything else you read or hear in the future on this central concern for our lives. But most of all I hope it will give you, and help you give others, more of that sustainable, satisfying success we all need.

> At the day of judgment we shall not be asked what we have read but what we have done.   *Thomas à Kempis*

Introduction:
Our Idea of Success

I remember vividly the day, a number of years ago, when I was first asked to give a public talk on success. I was in my office at the University of Notre Dame doing what a philosopher typically does—thinking—when the phone rang. It was a call from the representative of a large business group, some very successful people, who wanted me to come talk with them about what success really is. I was certainly flattered by the invitation and I enthusiastically accepted. A few minutes later that very same morning, by some cosmic coincidence, a completely independent call came in from a publisher—would I ever consider writing a book on how we should think about success?

Well, I was feeling pretty good about all this and couldn't wait to get home to tell my wife. But when I came rushing through the front door and told her with great excitement about both these calls, she just looked puzzled and said, "Don't you have to *be* a success before you speak and write about success?" We do what we can to keep each other humble around my house.

Introduction

In what I remember as a very pained tone, I replied, "What do you mean?" I was thinking, Hey, I'm a Yale Ph.D. (and the letters, I insist, do not stand for either *"Piled higher and Deeper" or "Phony Doctor"*); the students here at Notre Dame enjoy my classes (well, at least, I think most of them do); I've written lots of books and articles (even if up until now, I must acknowledge, none of them have been exactly runaway best-sellers—but, gimme a break, they've been pioneering efforts geared to the profundity market, never a big slice of the commercial pie); I'm a licensed real estate broker in my home state of North Carolina (although I have to admit I've never actually sold anything); I'm the founder of a record company (OK, a very small record company whose total production has been only one cassette tape—pretty well marketed, though, I should add); I have at least some past success as a rock guitarist (on a modest scale and, admittedly, with only one recording contract, with a very small record company whose total production has been only one cassette tape); but I am a pretty darn good dad and I do have a great, successful marriage (or so, at least, up until that point I had thought). . . .

Perhaps picking up on my mental rehearsal of credentials, my wife quickly responded, "Oh, I don't mean that you're not a success *in your own way*"—the emphasis is important here, as, of course, I took it to mean *in your own small insignificant monumentally trivial way*—"but," she continued, "you've got to admit, you're not Lee Iacocca or Lou Holtz. I mean, you've never had your face on the cover of *Time* magazine or *Newsweek* or *Fortune* or *Sports Illustrated*"—it was clear that the list could have gone on throughout the entire inventory of the Publishers Clearing House—"your name is not exactly on the lips of America."

"Well, *not yet*," I both humbly and confidently conceded. From my response she could tell that I had at least the right attitude. What else could I say? She had a point. In our society nowadays most speakers and writers on the topic of success are well-known heads of major corporations, top-notch full-time hotshot "consultants," prominent politicians, former military leaders, ex–sports heroes, or head football coaches with highly successful teams. What would a philosopher have to say?

Plenty.

A PHILOSOPHER'S POINT OF VIEW

Making sense of it all is my job. Figuring things out. Shedding new light on old problems. And old light on new problems. This is what I do. I develop frameworks for understanding the most important things in life. And the less important things as well. And I have plenty of resources for my work.

As a philosopher, I'm a student of all the greatest thinkers in human history, the people from Plato to the present day who have given us the great ideas that lie behind the dominant forms of government in world history, the ideas that have shaped the culture we all share, with its political systems, business structures, and football teams. My extensive reading and remarkable personal experiences have given me a special perspective on success I'd like to share with you, a point of view toward which a great many people are now groping. As a philosopher, I think I can help show the way.

We live in a time of tremendous confusion—political confusion, economic confusion, cultural confusion, personal confusion. Many old, formerly reliable structures are breaking up or showing their age. The only constant in our world seems to be change.

We live in a time of tremendous opportunity. People are confused enough to begin to ask questions they have long ignored, to begin to search for answers they finally realize they need. When men and women realize they are lost in the woods without a map or a compass, philosophers, who have always been cartographers of the spirit, map makers for the human journey, can step forward and offer some assistance, however rudimentary, for finding the way forward. And that is just what I want to do in this little book. It's not a weighty treatise, a tome whose interpretation will be a matter for generations to debate and settle. It's not a volume you need a Ph.D. or an MBA to understand. It's just a small map with a few basic coordinates to help us get our bearings when we think about how to live a richly successful life. If it can help launch anyone in the right direction, or assist and encourage anyone already on the path, it will have enjoyed the only true success of which a book like this is capable. It contains powerful ideas. And it is my hope that they will have the powerful effect in your life that they have had in mine.

THE FIRST POWERFUL PIECE OF VERY GOOD NEWS

There are seven conditions of success. Seven components of a successful mind-set. Seven means to a successful life.

Of course, there are hundreds of books, tapes, and articles on success, many thousands of maxims, tips, and hints on success, but there are only seven basic simple conditions we need to satisfy in order to launch ourselves into a life of true success. In reading the world's great literature on human excellence and personal success from the ancient Greek thinkers to the current motivational best-sellers, in watching and talking with extremely successful people, and in analyzing my own experience using all the skills I have cultivated over the years as a philosopher, I have come to realize that the fundamental conditions of success are simple to specify, easy to understand, and straightforward to master.

These seven conditions are not, however, just Things to Be Done on Monday So That Success Can Be Had on Tuesday. They are conditions we need to incorporate into our lives every day. Or, at least, most days. They are not overly arduous, demanding, and difficult. But they do take some work. Regular application. Ongoing effort. Yet once we understand these conditions and see their effectiveness, we'll be highly motivated to apply them in our daily lives. And their simplicity greatly increases their ease of application.

I often call them "the Seven Cs of Success" because the main term in each condition coincidentally begins with the letter C. Alliteration. A string of words all beginning with the same letter or sound. Surefire mnemonics. A great memory device. As a long-time teacher, I love this. I must admit, though, that I was told many years ago that a writing program at my own university had clearly laid down rules against what were viewed by purists as artificial rhetorical devices. Like this. But they found themselves in a bit of a bind. They wanted the students to remember the relevant rule here, so they firmly advised: "Always avoid alliteration," a rule I remember to this day. So I say: "Forget phony formulas" and proceed full speed ahead. If alliteration we've been given, alliteration we'll use.

The seven chapters that follow will lay out each of the Seven Cs of Success in their most general form. At every point I hope you'll ask yourself "How does this apply to me?" Think about how each condition might relate to what you face at work, or to your family situation, to friendships, or to any personal challenges you confront. I guarantee you that at least one or two of these conditions will leap off the page as relevant to your life *right now*. Maybe a couple of the others will be vitally important to you a month from now. The whole framework of seven conditions will provide you with a complete and powerful tool kit for constructing the most satisfying achievements for your life in every way. Aristotle once said that it is advantageous to anyone to come to know the most universal principles, because this puts us in the best position for specific applications anywhere. The most universal principles for success will put us in the best position for making the most of any opportunity, and overcoming any difficulty, we ever face.

The power of ideas is to help us change our lives, and the world in which we live, for the better. And as a teacher I know that if you want to provide anyone else with a framework of ideas that will motivate them and help them make changes that are needed, you have to provide them with a framework that is simple, insightful, memorable, and powerful. I am convinced that the Seven Cs of Success are just what we all need to help us make our lives count, to give us all the most satisfying success of which we're capable. I'm absolutely certain that we have here a framework that will work for you, if you will just work with it.

OUR IDEA OF SUCCESS

What is it that we seek? What exactly, or even approximately, is success? What is our idea of success? I believe that millions of people labor under false ideas of success. Because of this, they chase illusions and suffer needless frustration. Before we go on to examine the seven conditions of true success, we need to remind ourselves of a few important distinctions and, by doing so, sharpen our focus.

Nowadays there are a number of prominent ideas associated with the concept of success, and often confused with it. The idea of wealth, for example. Many people seem to think that success is the same thing as material wealth, that to be wealthy in this sense is just the same thing as being successful. But these things should not be confused.

It is certainly possible to be wealthy without being a successful person. The guy who happens to win the state lottery is not typically thought of as having thereby lived a successful life. We have another word for him: Lucky. And how about the person who inherits wealth without necessarily doing a thing to earn it or even to use it well? A total goof-off can be wealthy through inheritance. Or vice versa. And maybe *especially* vice versa. A person wealthy through inheritance can be easily tempted to a life of sheer indulgence, utterly devoid of any true personal success. You can have money in the bank without having any real success to your credit. It's certainly possible to achieve the one without the other.

> Riches get their value from the mind of their possessor; they are blessings to those who know how to use them, curses to those who do not.   *Terence (163 B.C.)*

And it's clearly possible to be successful without being wealthy. Mother Teresa is a good example. So is my wife, for slightly different reasons. My wife is a very successful gardener and volunteer helper in two elementary schools. No one pays her a penny for this. A successful neighborhood organizer will not necessarily be rolling in the dough. But if it's possible to be successful without being wealthy and wealthy without being successful, then success and wealth are just different things. Our idea of success should never be confused with our idea of wealth.

Something else commonly confused with success nowadays is fame. To be successful is to be famous. To be known is to be a success. Or so people seem to think.

It's really no surprise that these first two ideas are often mixed up with the idea of success. Whenever I ask a roomful of people for examples of successful men and women, I typically hear names of the rich and famous. But of course as with wealth, fame is no guarantee of success in any meaningful sense. There certainly are people who are known for their great successes. But some people these days seem to be famous for nothing more than being well known. And, of course, it's possible to be a famous bungler. A notorious screwup. Fame is not the same thing as success.

> Fame, we may understand, is no sure test of merit, but only a probability of such: it is an accident, not a property of a man.
>
> *Thomas Carlyle*

And success is not the same as fame. Suppose you have made it your goal in life to be the nation's most generous anonymous philanthropist. By definition, success at this can't make you famous. Any renown blows your goal of anonymity. But we don't need any such cooked-up example to make the point. Plenty of individuals succeed at meeting private goals, at overcoming personal challenges, and in accomplishing worthwhile tasks known only to a very few other people. There are many extraordinarily creative and accomplished people who never attain any level of public recognition remotely approaching fame. And there are great inventors, great thinkers, and, notoriously, great artists who attained fame only after their deaths. But that doesn't mean that they succeeded at their respective tasks only after their deaths. Success is one thing, fame another.

And power is something else altogether too. Yet it is also often confused with success. But by now it should be clear how this is indeed a mistake as well. Power doesn't always arise out of success. And success does not always accompany power. They are not the same.

And there is one other thing commonly confused with success:

the widely prized goal of high social status. Many people who think of themselves as pursuing success are really seeking status in the community, in the workplace, among friends and acquaintances, or in their professions. A person's status is roughly his or her standing in the community, or in a profession, or among some other group of people, where that standing is thought of, or determined, in connection with a sort of hierarchy, or ascending scale, of respectability, honor, or importance. Status is an external social position, as perceived by others.

There is a strong tendency in American society to think of wealth, fame, and power as conferring high social status. In connection with this, we have come to speak of "status symbols" and those who seek to accumulate these symbols, as well as the standing they symbolize, as "status seekers." The pursuit of status is deep down a quest for approval, deference, and privilege. Insofar as wealth, fame, and power are perceived to bring with them approval, deference, and privilege, a pursuit of status can become wholly tied up in a quest for these externals. But there is a more subtle yearning for status that need not involve a money chase, the fame game, or any sort of obvious power trip. In an institutional structure, like a modern large business, volunteer organization, university, or church, an *official position* is capable of conferring some level of positive status to some extent distinct from any specific considerations of money, fame, or power. Such a position can even be largely or entirely honorary and need not necessarily involve any additional financial compensation, scope of renown, or even ability to get things done, though such perks most often do come with the territory. But if an official position, office, or title is utterly devoid of these accompaniments, and in addition has no connection whatsoever with approval, deference, or privilege, it is altogether empty.

There are of course a great many people who aspire to the sorts of official positions in organizations that they see as conferring status. Many times they also aspire to certain positions because these roles bring with them additional money, recognition, and power. But the people I have primarily in mind here are those who seek status mostly for its own sake. They feel they need the honor, the approval, the deference, and the sometimes subtle privileges that such status confers.

There are great numbers of middle managers in American business today who have always aspired to a corporate vice presidency, but in our current institutional climate there are relatively few such positions of status to be had. A good many of these managers are coming to realize that their last few career moves were basically horizontal at best, and that their chances for the status they have always sought are diminishing. But a vice presidency has always been their standard for career success and, unfortunately, for personal success as well. So they are confronted with two possibilities. They can come to think of themselves as likely failures, or they can rethink their standard for success. I recommend course number two. Success and status are not the same thing. Having gained some long and fervently sought status will not guarantee that a person will thereby have lived a successful life, in the broadest and deepest sense of "success." Some perceptive individuals of high status realize this. But it is difficult for many people to appreciate this truth. That's why it often requires so much courage for a person to leave a promising career trajectory within the confines of an organizational hierarchy where some significant status is ready made and nearly guaranteed, and launch out on his or her own to follow a personal dream wherever it might lead. That's one of the difficulties, nowadays, of working in the home. It often takes a special person to be able to do it. Some such people's lives demonstrate that the natural human quest for success is not always a drive for status. Success and status are different, though often related, aspirations. We should not confuse one with the other.

It is easy to be captivated by the images of famous people, wealthy people, and powerful people. These are often people of high social status in America, as well as in international circles. Wealth draws admiration when it is used for great good. It draws attention when it is enjoyed on a grand scale. Fame can be dazzling. Power can be fascinating. Status can be very attractive. Wealth, fame, power, and high social status are often the companions of success on a broad scale. They are sometimes the results of success. But they are not themselves the heart of success. By failing to see this, many people chase the wrong things.

Now, don't get me wrong. I'm not saying that there is anything wrong with money or even with wanting a more than ample supply. It's long been said that money can't buy happiness. And this is true. But with it you can be unhappy in much more comfortable surroundings. And, of course, money can be used to do great good. For this purpose, the more the better. Likewise, there is nothing wrong with wanting to be acknowledged by other people. Yet it has been pointed out that many people who have spent their lives seeking fame end up wearing dark glasses so they won't be recognized. And power is not evil. It can tend to corrupt, but so can the lack of power. A pursuit of power, though, always leads to one question: Power *for what purpose?* And status is the same. There is certainly nothing wrong with it, or with wanting it, but the question inevitably arises as to why it should be desired.

EXCELLENCE, FULFILLMENT, AND HAPPINESS

It is possible to seek wealth, to seek fame, to seek power, and to seek status. People do it all the time. And it's possible to pursue these goals successfully. But wealth, fame, power, and status do not often come to a person through her own efforts if these are her only goals. They more typically come as the by-products of the successful attainment of other goals. A football player becomes wealthy because he is a great runner. A business person becomes famous because she is a successful entrepreneur. A dancer becomes a powerful member of the world of performing arts because he is an extraordinarily creative, accomplished artist. A volunteer worker attains high social status in the community because of all the good she has done to alleviate poverty, or to care for the homeless. Wealth, power, fame, and status are sometimes the social results of success. And they can in turn enter into expanding that success, raising it to a higher level, or giving it broader impact. But they are never the heart of the success. That's one reason why chasing these things, first and foremost, is chasing the wrong things.

> Why do I not seek some real good—one which I could feel, not one which I could display? *Seneca*

Our idea of success should be more closely related to our ideas of excellence and fulfillment. And to our idea of happiness. A careful look around the world will show us something in this connection that's very interesting. The happiest people in the world are people who love what they are doing, regardless of whether wealth, fame, power, and elevated social status ever come their way. The most fulfilled people are individuals who delight in their work, whatever it might be, and strive to do it well. They are people who derive rewards from the intrinsic enjoyment of what they are contributing to life, come what may. And they are people who relish the challenge to pursue excellence in their activities, as well as in themselves. The people who attain true success in their lives are people who enjoy a good measure of both fulfillment and happiness as they invest themselves in worthwhile pursuits.

The kind of success I am most interested in is the sort available to every human being living, breathing, thinking, and doing things on this earth. It does not require wealth, fame, power, or high social status. It need not involve aspiring to any of these things. But it does require making the most of what we are, for the benefit of others as well as ourselves. It means making a difference and experiencing the deep satisfaction that that brings. It means using *your* talents and following *your* heart. It involves being true to yourself and being good to others.

To be a success in the way that counts, we need not all seek high-paying, high-ranking, high-visibility positions carrying impressive titles and privileges. The seven conditions of success can be applied to achieve whatever we want. However, one of the most elusive keys to satisfaction in life consists not in focusing on getting what we want, but in truly wanting what we get. Are we mapping out a course for our lives that is right for us, and are we progressing along that course in a way that brings us real satisfaction?

The framework for success I want to lay out and discuss in this book can be used just as effectively by a custodian, a carpenter, an auto mechanic, a college professor, an electrician, an artist, a machine operator, a schoolteacher, a grocer, and a salesman, as by an entrepreneur, a supervisor, a lawyer, a small-business owner, a venture capitalist, a corporate vice president, a physician, a CEO, a senator, or a recording star. True success is not limited in its potential scope. It's not restricted to any particular social or economic class. It is multiform and variable. It can be manifested in different ways by different people and at different times in one person's life. But it always consists in making the most of who we are and being the best that we can be, in the fullness of our personalities, in accordance with the conditions I will present.

Fame is to some extent up to other people. So is wealth. So is power. And so is social status. The happiest people are people who realize that true success is up to them. They are people who launch out in a meaningful journey, keeping their eyes on the road and yet often pausing along the way to enjoy some of the sights. They are people who don't confuse personal success with any of its some-time accompaniments. And, ironically, they are very often the people who end up with all the wealth, the fame, the power, and the status they need. They are people who most fully satisfy the seven conditions of success.

1

A Conception of
What We Want

Condition One: We need a clear conception of what we want, a vivid vision, a goal or set of goals powerfully imagined.

The quest for success always begins with a target. We need something to aim at, something to shoot for. Too many people seem to wander through life like sleepwalkers, meandering from day to day, week to week, year to year. Each day they get up, get dressed, eat, fall into some familiar routines, engaging in various forms of activity or inactivity, eat again and then again, filling the time between, undress, go back to bed, and then hours later begin the whole cycle once more, over and over and over, without ever really waking up to ask "What am I doing with my life?" and "Why am I doing it?" So many people really don't know what they're doing because they have no idea where they are going. They lack a road map. They lack clear direction. They have no overall goals to steer by.

Many people in this condition seem frenetically active, rushing, pushing, making things happen. But ultimately they're shooting

35

in the dark, not at any clear target they've set themselves. This can go on for only so long without producing frustration and weariness, or even despair.

> The soul that has no established aim loses itself.
> *Michel de Montaigne*

Our lives are full of change. Things happen. We act. But we have no way of counting any of this as progress unless we have goals, standards against which we can measure these daily developments. An old nautical proverb tells us "No wind blows fair for a ship without destination." And without a vision for where we are going, without a clear conception of what we want to accomplish, we have no idea of how to initiate real progress in our lives, or even of how to control change productively. As Yogi Berra once said, "You've got to be very careful if you don't know where you're going, because you might not get there."

> Men were born to succeed, not to fail.
> *Henry David Thoreau*

We human beings are programmed for success. We are meant to flourish. You and I are here on this earth because generation after generation of our ancestors succeeded in various ways, in sometimes harsh and terrible conditions. And we are their legacy. We are their inheritors. We were created to accomplish. We have what it takes. But we must learn to use what we have or we risk squandering our vast potential.

SETTING CLEAR GOALS

The first condition of success, any kind of success, is that we develop a clear conception of what we want. An idea of where we want to go, what we want to accomplish. A conception of what we want to become. It should be both clear and specific. Vague goals can't motivate specific behavior. Vague goals can generate vague, positive emotions. But success requires more than fuzzy dreams and warm feelings. The warm fuzzies alone never got anyone very far. Lily Tomlin once recognized this and confessed, "I always wanted to be *somebody*. I should have been more specific."

Everybody wants to be somebody, but not just anybody. We want our lives to count. We want to accomplish something in this life. But what? How about you? What do you want to be? What do you want to do? Are you becoming it now? Are you beginning to do it already, in some small way? If not, why not? What are you waiting for? If you are moving in a general direction you feel good about, are you making the sort of progress you think is appropriate? And where will you end up? Or are these questions for which you have no clear answers at the moment?

Do you ever stop to ask yourself things like "Why am I in this job?" or "What am I doing in school?" or "Where is this relationship going?" or "How would I like to see my family life develop?" In our professional lives and in our personal lives, we need specific goals. We need answers to questions like these. We need a clear conception of what we want.

> Without some goal and some effort to reach it no man can live.
> *Feodor Dostoyevsky*

All the success books of recent vintage talk about goals and goal setting. In formulating the first universal condition of success, I've used the word "conception" in part because I like its reproductive associations. We need to give birth to a vision to guide our thoughts, efforts, and activities. But of course, giving birth is not an easy task. It can be very difficult. What exactly do you want in life? What precisely do I want? It's not always self-evident. We may have to dig deep into ourselves to find the resources to define a conception of what we really want in a relationship, in an activity, for a business or an office, or in our lives.

It's an exercise in self-knowledge. We don't always know what we want. It may take a bit of effort to find out, but it's well worth the trouble. Knowledge is power, and as the prominent television producer Norman Lear once pointed out to me, self-knowledge is the greatest source of personal power on this earth. When we begin to know ourselves, to aim our lives and target our energies appropriately, we dramatically empower ourselves. When we start to define clear goals, we begin the exciting task of discovering and defining ourselves. It's certainly not a once-and-for-all event. Like everything else, our goals may change or evolve over time. But we must begin the process of setting ourselves targets right away and shooting for those targets or we are wasting some of the opportunities that each new day brings. We need the target practice, and we need it now.

1. Thinking and Doing

But how do we come to know exactly what we should pursue? What does it take to gain the sort of self-knowledge required for powerful personal goal setting? The first part of an answer to these questions is very simple: We need time to think. Some time to reflect on who we are, where we are, what we are doing, what we enjoy, what we value, what we love, and what we really want to accomplish. We need time to ask ourselves some questions and time to formulate some answers. This is almost too simple. It should be obvious, but we live in an action-oriented world where doing takes precedence over thinking, a world whose pace seems constantly to increase, leaving us few opportunities and little time for probing, reflective thought. And yet nothing is more important. We must take time to sit and think.

The New York Times not long ago quoted one prominent British business executive as having said, "Some people feel uncomfortable just sitting at a desk thinking. They should be doing it, and they should be doing it for a more significant part of the day. Otherwise, how do you say to yourself that you're giving the right direction and the right emphasis to the things you're doing?" After five years in a monastery and a year studying philosophy at the Sorbonne, this unusual business leader had come to appreciate the importance of contemplation and reflective thought for every human life.

Have you ever seen Auguste Rodin's famous sculpture *The Thinker*? Most of us have seen photographs of this classic nineteenth-century work of art, or small-scale reproductions in the form of bookends or paperweights. A nude man is sitting on a rock, his chin on his fist, deep in thought. What *is* he thinking about? Countless kids around the world have asked this question throughout the years, and, of course, one of their most common guesses is: "I wonder where I left my clothes. . . ." The lack of clothing shows something significant that I only recently noticed for the first time as I walked through an art museum in Helsinki, Finland, where one of the larger, original bronze versions of the statue is displayed. Looking it over carefully, I suddenly became aware of the striking musculature of the figure. This is not some flabby, sedentary guy who lives only within the confines of his cranium, but rather, quite clearly, a strong man of action who is pausing to ponder something of importance. This one sculpture, which has come to be the standard symbol of what Aristotle and most other philosophers consider the highest prerogative of human beings, clearly represents thinking as positioned within a life of doing, and that is just as it should be. Thought is not opposed to action; it is rather its proper foundation and guide.

We all need time to think if we are to be able to come up with a clear, powerful, and appropriate conception of what we want and what we should pursue. We need to use our heads. But then we also need to use some other parts of our anatomy as well.

> The unexamined life is not worth living.　　*Socrates*

> But then, of course, it's also true that: The unlived life is not worth examining.

When my wife was a student at the University of North Carolina, Chapel Hill, she was once in a physical education class where the exasperated instructor said to his assembled students, "You all need some goals. You need to examine where you are and where you're going. What each and every one of you ought to do is sit down, get out a piece of paper and a pen or pencil, and *write down* some goals. Lots of famous and accomplished people have reported that their lives began to turn around and change for the better only when they made a list of their goals in life. In fact, I *guarantee* you that if you'll just write some goals down on a little piece of paper, no matter how big they are, they *will* come true."

Well, my wife tells me that when the instructor said that, the students looked at each other and rolled their eyes. Some laughed out loud. The pen is not that mighty. But she said that despite all the evident skepticism, at the end of class she did notice several students scribbling on little scraps of paper things like "BMW" and "Rich blonde." Just in case. No sense taking any chances.

There is of course nothing magical about writing down goals. But what is almost magical in a way is the distinctive mental effect of physically articulating your goals in simple language. Forming them in the mold of linguistic expression. Putting them into words. Writing is just a particularly powerful form of articulation.

It's truly amazing how vague and sketchy our ideas sometimes can be before we try to articulate them. Have you ever experienced going into an exam or into a meeting thinking you were clear on some subject, only to discover that when you were called upon to write about it or speak on it your mental focus was surprisingly blurry and confused? You weren't clear at all. You can feel quite familiar with a subject, even very comfortable with it, but until you are called upon to articulate your views, your own ideas may remain very ill formed and vague.

William Faulkner once said, "I never know what I think about something until I read what I've written on it." Well, I've read Faulkner and often still don't have a clue what he thought. But his point is an important one. A philosophy professor friend of mine in Texas puts it a little differently: "Sometimes I don't have clear ideas on a topic until I write about it."

At first this can be a bit perplexing to hear because we most often suppose that thinking and writing work like this: First you think of something, then you write about it, expressing what you've already thought. But that's not always the way it works. I believe both Faulkner and my friend were onto something important.

41

Writing is a form of thinking. Or at least it can be. At its best, the act of writing is not just a form of communication. It's not just an expression of thought. It is a way of thinking. A mode of cogitation that conduces to clarity. And the same can be true of speaking. The contents of our minds don't always just spring into existence already well formed and clear apart from any attempt at articulation. It's more often true that only in the effort of writing or speaking do we come to form crisp, clear, well-defined thoughts. It may be that one reason so many people seem so confused nowadays is that so few of us write regularly or carry on conversations with each other about things that matter to us. We have lost the culture of conversation and correspondence that was once America.

As recently as a few decades ago, I believe many more families sat down at meals together and talked. And there was conversation after dinner. People sat on front porches or front stoops and shot the breeze. Neighbors talked out windows, across fences, and when they met in local markets. Barbershops and beauty parlors were as much for conversation as for hair care. And people at work had the time to talk with their coworkers. Casually. Personally. This does seem like ancient history, but traces of it are still to be found in a few small towns and isolated neighborhoods around the country. It's just lamentably rare.

In addition to all this talk, people once wrote letters. Long letters to good friends. Short letters to relatives. Notes to acquaintances. Postcards to all sorts of folks. And some people, a great many more than nowadays, I suspect, even wrote to themselves in diaries and journals. People recounted their days and ruminated over their lives. They wrote about their hopes and dreams and fears. By doing all this, people I knew as a boy were interpreting to themselves the directions of their lives, their pasts, presents, and futures. Small details and big developments. They were attaining clarity about their own hearts. They were arriving at self-knowledge as well as knowledge of the world. Their goals for work, for family life, and for personal development naturally grew out of this knowledge, as a powerful by-product of their habits of articulation.

Let diaries, therefore, be brought in use.   *Francis Bacon*

We are now no longer as accustomed to articulating and clarifying our thoughts, our beliefs, our hopes, and our goals on a regular basis. So much in contemporary culture seems to militate against this. We're in such a hurry. We're too busy. We're on the go. But what's the hurry? Where are we going? We obviously have some bad habits, habits of inarticulateness about who we are and what we really want out of life, patterns of neglect that urgently need to be changed.

We need goals to motivate and guide our progress in any area of life. Specific, clear goals because, as we have noted, vague goals cannot adequately motivate and direct specific behavior. Success always arises out of specific actions, the right actions at the right times. So if we want to move toward success, we first need clear goals. And if it's true, as I think it is, that we are most likely to arrive at a clear conception of what we want if we talk it out with someone else or write it out for ourselves—exploring the possibilities and establishing our targets with conversation, or at least pen and paper—we need to begin to articulate our aims.

But at this point a warning is in order. If we plan to aim especially high and take on some great challenge, or accomplish something particularly grand, we may not find it helpful to talk about our dreams with just anyone, especially early on. Some people may resent what they'll consider our "presumptuousness," dismissively label us as "dreamers," or just laugh at our ambition. There is a lot of competitiveness in the world, and a great deal of jealousy. If you suddenly begin setting yourself high goals, it may sometimes be best to keep them to yourself for a while. In certain company. Others around you will not want to be left behind in your vapor trail as you launch yourself beyond your present circumstances, or your present achievements. And it could be that in setting yourself new and different enough goals, you will be perceived as abandoning and rejecting values, assumptions, and expectations that many of the people around you continue to base their lives on. This can be very threatening to them, and can occasion resentment. It can also cause perplexity. It may be that in following your own heart, you find yourself setting goals that are higher in your estimation than your present course and that are more important to you, but that seem just totally puzzling to the people around you who have heard no such calling in their own lives, and whose values are to some extent different from yours. This can result in a great deal of interpersonal awkwardness. So for some personal goals, particularly lofty goals involving tremendous change, it's sometimes best to do your articulation exercises in private.

Other goals must be shared. Community or group goals, for example. A goal for the family, or a goal for the office, any goal whose best realization requires the explicit cooperation of other people, must be shared in the right way, in the right spirit, and at the right times. And some very challenging personal goals may need to be shared as well.

Suppose you have smoked cigarettes for years and have recently decided to stop. Years of habit are not often peeled away overnight. Mark Twain once put it like this: "Habit is habit, and not to be flung out of the window by any man, but coaxed downstairs a step at a time." And a habit like smoking is particularly difficult to break, since it involves some clear measure of chemical dependency. Even coaxing it downstairs a step at a time is going to be difficult. It's going to take tremendous willpower and persistence, for a time—that length of time it takes to cleanse your system and to establish new habits. Which can take a while. Bad habits are not usually just uprooted. They have to be replaced with better habits. To replace a habit like smoking with new habits takes time; it takes determination, and very often it takes the support of other people. If you share your goal of a smokefree life with well-disposed people around you, you make it possible for them to help and encourage you toward realizing that goal. It's amazing how important the help of other people can be in the struggle to attain any difficult objective. We need others, as they need us.

And another thing. Every time you say to another person something like: "I've quit smoking. I'm a nonsmoker now," you recommit yourself to your goal, and in a public way. There is more at stake. If you let yourself fail, you not only disappoint yourself, you fail in the eyes of the other person. Your own desire to succeed in the eyes of others—a desire, by the way, that we all naturally have—will support your persistence in progressing toward your goal.

2. The Satisfaction Audit

But whether you talk with other people about your goals or keep them to yourself, a good place to begin your articulation of a clear conception of what you want is alone in a room, at a desk or table, with a pen and some paper. Sometimes it helps to start by doing a simple little written self-evaluation exercise I like to call *The Satisfaction Audit*. In order to be able to identify and set clear goals for the future that will be the right goals *for you*, you may need to begin by first assessing your satisfaction with the present.

Here's a good way to start. At the top of a piece of writing paper make a heading: WHAT I DO NOT LIKE ABOUT MY LIFE RIGHT NOW (THINGS TO CHANGE). And then make a list. Loosen up. This is not for publication or public circulation. It won't appear on the front page of the local paper. Write whatever comes to mind. Brainstorm. Stream of consciousness is fine at this point. Just write it down as it comes to you. It may be "Finances—not enough income, too much outgo," or "Too many unresolved business decisions," or "I don't feel my talents are really being used at work now," or "Too little time with the kids," or "There's too much noise in the neighborhood," or "The guy next door is a total jerk," or "I've got to handle anger better." Some entries may be very general, others very specific. Remember, the goal here eventually is specificity. But it's fine to warm up to that gradually.

When you run out of things to put down under this category, and hopefully you will, make a second heading: WHAT I DO LIKE ABOUT MY LIFE RIGHT NOW (THINGS TO PRESERVE). You might write here "Friends," or "Great relationship with my children," or "A job with flexible hours," or "Working for a company I can really believe in," or "Living in a part of the country where I can afford the kind of house I want," or "Life in the city where there's so much to do." You get the idea.

Now make a third heading: WHAT I DO NOT LIKE ABOUT MY JOB RIGHT NOW (THINGS TO CHANGE), and a fourth: WHAT I DO LIKE ABOUT MY JOB RIGHT NOW (THINGS TO PRESERVE). We're just trying to get more specific in our focus now. If you basically like your job but find that there are problems with how some things are done, or not done, in your office or department, add the headings: WHAT I DO NOT LIKE ABOUT THE WAY THE OFFICE WORKS RIGHT NOW (THINGS TO CHANGE) and WHAT I DO LIKE ABOUT THE WAY THE OFFICE WORKS RIGHT NOW (THINGS TO PRESERVE), or whatever precise headings are appropriate for your work environment.

Maybe some quick listing will end up focusing on problems you have with a coworker or colleague. You now need two more headings featuring your relationship with that person.

These twofold lists, two kinds of headings, can be written up for any aspect of your life, going from the most general to the most specific. Working through this kind of articulation exercise can put any of us into a position to realize clearly what goals we want to set for ourselves, what changes we want to make, and what aspects of our lives now we want to preserve.

Improvement always involves preserving and enhancing the good while getting rid of or changing the bad in our lives. Too many people who are frustrated in their circumstances or disgruntled with their lives tend to think only in terms of dramatic change. The temptation is to go overboard in fantasizing that what's really desirable is just quick, radical, and complete metamorphosis. A total break with the past and present. But in every person's life there are some goods that need to be retained and built on, nurtured and enhanced, even if they are to be found only in the innermost recesses of the soul. Positive movement in a life never requires the utterly radical surgery of obliterating the past, totally reversing the present, and launching out into the future by just starting from scratch. Some things may need radical alteration. But others will require protection and retention. Change and preservation are both important in the right sort of goal setting.

I've just mentioned in passing "the soul." Whenever you do a satisfaction audit of your life, it's important to ask yourself a question. Look over your lists. Do they mention your own qualities very much, or are they geared mostly toward external circumstances—other people and things that happen, or tend to happen, to you? If your own inner life, your qualities of heart and mind, your capacities, personality traits, and behavioral tendencies hardly show up at all on the lists you've made, then perhaps you need an additional double list focusing directly on yourself: WHAT I DO NOT LIKE ABOUT MYSELF RIGHT NOW (THINGS TO CHANGE) and WHAT I DO LIKE ABOUT MYSELF RIGHT NOW (THINGS TO PRESERVE). If you find it easy to make entries in the first of these categories, make sure you write down items for the second list too. If we're honest with ourselves, most of us will find it fairly easy to specify things about our personalities, or our habits, or our tendencies, that we would really prefer to be different. And if we're not honest with ourselves, well, that little fact itself should be a starting point for the negative list.

Some people find it very difficult to be self-critical. Others get easily carried away with negativism. What's important to stress here is that for the vast majority of us, it is vital that we give equal attention to the question of what within ourselves needs to be changed, and what it is about us, in our personalities or characters, that should be preserved and enhanced as we set goals for the future. Ideally we want to build on our strengths while correcting our weaknesses. But in order for our goal setting to be sensitive to each of these tasks, we need first to make sure we identify clearly exactly what our strengths and weaknesses, our virtues and vices, our basic positives and negatives are.

> A happy life is one which is in accordance with its own nature.
> *Seneca*

Self-examination is not always easy. Many of us know more about heaven and earth than we do about our own hearts. But getting to know our hearts is a task that's necessary if we want to chart out the most appropriate paths for our lives. Once we are more in touch with what we like and dislike about ourselves and our current conditions, we are in a much better position to begin setting clear goals whose pursuit and attainment will bring us genuine satisfaction. As we come to understand better what we love and what we most deeply desire, we also discover where our most fundamental tendencies, capacities, and talents lie. We begin to discern how we can best live in this world, and what we have to contribute to it.

This little articulation exercise I've outlined is just an example of what it may take for us to be able to put ourselves in the position where we can come up with a clear conception of what we want. It is a way of following the advice of the oracle at Delphi in ancient Greece, that famous, much-repeated injunction "Know thyself!" It is an exercise in self-knowledge, self-discovery, and self-definition.

Some people may become impatient with an articulation exercise like this. They may want to list for themselves goals such as:

1. I want to be self-employed.
2. I want to be financially independent by the age of forty-five.
3. I want to write songs for popular country-music singers.
4. I want to establish some sense of community among my neighbors.
5. I want to be able to give at least $10,000 a year to charity.
6. I want to learn to handle stress better.
7. I want more time with my wife and children.
8. I want to run a 10K race.

But not everyone simply knows, off the top of their heads, what goals they want to set for themselves. And even for those who seem to, the sort of exercise I've described can be very helpful, because

49

any initial goal list will need some fine-tuning. And for every remote or difficult goal, we need some subgoals, some preliminary
targets, some specific ways to get to where we eventually want to
be. To know how to get from here to there, we need to know what it
is about our circumstances, or our selves, right now that we want
to change, and what it is that we might feel is important to
preserve. We need clear goals that are right *for us.* Goals we can
believe in. Goals from the heart.

3. Our Values and Our Hearts

Behind every goal you set yourself there will be some value or
cluster of values. You seek that goal because you embrace those
values. If you set as your goal financial independence, that will be
because you value a certain kind of personal freedom. If you have
as one of your goals providing as fine an education as you can for
your children, that is because you value both your children and the
benefits of a good education. Personal goals don't just drop out of
the blue. Goal setting is not an exercise in a vacuum. Our values
give rise to our goals.

Sometimes the values behind your goals will be directly related
to those goals. And sometimes you will discover that the relation is
indirect. Are you pursuing any goals that were just given to you by
other people? If so, why? If a student is pursuing the study of
medicine because her parents always wanted her to be a doctor, it
may be just because she places a high value on pleasing her
parents. If a salesman takes on certain sales goals just because
they've been given to him by his sales manager, it is likely because
he values pleasing his boss and keeping his job. These values are
only indirectly related to the goals themselves. If the parents had
insisted on law instead, or the boss had set different sales targets,
the secondhand goals in either case would have been different.

We often inherit goals from other people around us. And that's fine. But we work best toward goals only when we have truly made them our own. If the young student genuinely comes to value helping the sick, then she can come to own the goal she received, and has otherwise merely borrowed, from her parents. Likewise, if the salesman comes to see the importance of his new sales goals and personally values the benefits their attainment would bring, they become truly his own. The greatest efforts and deepest satisfactions of which we are capable can be experienced only in connection with goals we genuinely take for ourselves as our own. As long as the values backing them up are only indirect, we will be unlikely to attain the highest success of which we're capable. Our goals must either come from the heart or at least resonate thoroughly with what our hearts tell us. They must appeal to our deepest instincts and to our most fundamental values in the most direct way possible if we are to pursue them to our greatest possible benefit.

One of the worst things that can happen in connection with goal-directed behavior is for a person to take on goals from other people just to please them, or to benefit from their favor, despite the fact that the values and desires behind those goals are alien to his own value system and destructive for him to embrace. This is always a prescription for disaster. And it's too commonly encountered in our world. To avoid any possibility of a situation like this, we should always contemplate carefully the goals others would have us pursue, and ask ourselves if we can wholeheartedly embrace the underlying values behind those goals. If we cannot, then any pursuit of those goals is bound to cause trouble in our lives.

And there is, of course, the other side of the story. If you are in a position to set goals for other people, you should do whatever you can to make sure that those goals have behind them values that those other people can in good conscience embrace. And help them to see the connections so that they can take up those goals as fully their own. Only then can they attain complete ownership of their goals.

We all need ennobling goals, goals that inspire us because of the values they embody. And we all need to understand how the goals we are given connect up with the values we most deeply embrace. The most powerful possibilities for accomplishment reside in a situation where a goal is shared by a number of people who all embrace it from the heart and genuinely believe in it because they are committed to the values they know it expresses.

Many businesses are beginning to discover that strong profits, high salaries, and material benefits are not alone the great motivators they were once thought to be. Everybody likes to be rewarded. But what is even more important is to be doing a job that is felt to be, in itself, rewarding. Deep down, most people want to do good in the world. They want their lives to make a positive difference. They need to be able to work toward goals consistent with their noblest tendencies and aspirations. Purely materialistic or narrowly self-centered goals are typically insufficient to inspire and sustain deep commitment, enthusiasm, and loyalty of effort over the long run. Whenever we set goals for others, we need to keep this in mind.

But before we even begin to think about setting goals for others, we have to be careful to set the right goals for ourselves. What do we wish for? What do we want? What do we need? What can we accomplish?

A friend of mine likes to say: "Be careful what you wish for— you might get it." Whenever I hear him give this advice, I'm reminded of a Calvin and Hobbes cartoon strip. As I recall it, the little boy, Calvin, is in a field playing by himself. He hits a baseball high into the air, drops his bat, grabs his glove, and tries to catch the ball before it falls to the ground. He misses. Too late. He tries again. No luck. And again, going for a nearly vertical hit. Finally he makes the catch. Success. But then he looks at the reader with a perplexed expression on his face and says, "I'm out." He didn't realize the implications of his goal until it was too late. A cute way of making an important point recognized throughout human history. We are sometimes pretty careless with our wishes, our fantasies, and our daydreams. But we'd better not be cavalier when it comes to real goal setting.

4. Desires and Goals Are Different

A goal is not the same thing as a desire, and this is an important distinction to make. You can have a desire you don't intend to act on. But you can't have a goal you don't intend to act on. This is a purely conceptual point, but it's a very important point as well. There can be plenty of targets in the world you never aim at, but once you've taken a target as your own, that just involves your having formed an intention to shoot at it. Goal setting is not an activity of fantasy or wishful thinking, and it's not just an intellectual exercise. It is a serious directing of the will, a setting of your intentions, the making of a real commitment to move in a certain direction.

Drawing a clear distinction between desires and goals has a liberating result. We need not be bullied by our desires. You can have a desire and not set yourself the goal of satisfying it. Desiring is not always up to us. It is not always within our control. But goal setting is. Once we see this distinction we can clearly see that an unsatisfied desire is not the same thing as a failure. You can be happy with many unsatisfied desires as long as you don't embrace them and set their fulfillment as a goal.

Let me give an example of what I mean. You may be a person who sometimes finds arising within yourself some measure of physical desire for about one out of every twenty people you pass on the street. If so, I recommend a regimen of vigorous exercise and cold showers, as well as the cultivation of some additional interests. But not even this frequency of desire is necessarily problematic unless you set as a goal romantic involvement with 5 percent of the people you see. You may have had fantasies and desires of fame as a rock guitarist, or a fashion model, or a film star. And this is fine. But that doesn't mean you have to pursue a high-profile career in one of these areas. And it doesn't mean that living your life without any fame, or even involvement, in these fields will amount to some sort of failure. Anyone with a rich fantasy life will live with some unsatisfied desires. Most of us live with a great many. But this is completely natural and fully compatible with living a very happy life. A desire is one thing; a goal is something else altogether. An unsatisfied desire is not the same thing as an unattained goal. And it's not the same thing as a failure.

> Of our desires, some are natural and necessary; others are natural, but not necessary; others, again, are neither natural nor necessary. *Epicurus*

Many of our desires, on the other hand, do properly prompt goals. It is by consulting the deepest desires of our heart, our most fundamental and most continuing longings, that we often find our own distinctive path of excellence in the world. But many of our desires are most properly left alone. Some fleeting desires may be inconsistent with our overall values and commitments. Some recurrent wishes might take us places we really wouldn't want to go.

Desire can be a very powerful thing. And it's important for us to understand its power. In my years of analyzing the human condition as a philosopher, one of the simplest but most useful insights I've had can help us here. This is captured by what I call *The Double Power Principle:*

The greater a power anything has for good, the greater the power it also correspondingly has for evil.

I believe that this little principle expresses a fundamental and universal truth. Consider, for example, modern science and technology, where great power for tremendous good is clearly accompanied by enormous potential for horrific disaster. How they are used and where they lead is in the end up to us. And precisely the same thing is true of human desire. It has great power for good. If there were no such thing as desire, human beings first of all wouldn't have lasted very long on the earth. And there never would have come into existence any of what we know as the marvels of civilization. But desire also just as obviously has significant power for ill. A great many of the problems of humanity can be traced to desire out of control. War, murder, theft, social injustice, and squandered lives are some of its consequences. How the power of desire is used and where it leads, though, is in the end up to us.

We don't have to act on desires we have, even when they come over us powerfully. We are free to choose whether a particular desire should give rise to a goal, or should instead be left alone, perhaps to be enjoyed in the imagination, but not to be pursued in the world. We can even choose to set ourselves the goal of doing everything within our power to avoid satisfying a specific desire we have, however strong it might be, if we judge this to be the better course to take. It is up to us. Desires don't automatically become goals for anyone trying to live sensibly and well, for anyone pursuing true success.

How do we decide what to do with our desires? By considering the consequences of acting on them. And asking ourselves if we really want to structure our lives in the direction they would take us. One important thing to keep in mind is this. As strong as various desires we experience might feel when they first come upon us, that power can be greatly magnified by the process of goal setting. The whole psychology of goal setting, with its engagement of intention, commitment, and action, provides a conduit through which desire can flow and increase in momentum. Any desire we have can present us with a possible goal or set of goals. But the question we have to ask ourselves is whether the pursuit of those goals and the consequent potential magnification of those desires would be a good thing or a bad thing for us.

Goal setting is a serious business of personal commitment. It is never to be undertaken lightly. We need to think through possible goals before we commit ourselves to them, and before we begin to act to see them through. Do we really want all the likely consequences of attaining those goals? Suppose I have a vision for my life. I need to ask myself: Is this exactly what it is that I want? Do I understand what will be changed and what will be preserved by the attainment of this particular goal or set of goals? Again, working through some written exercises can help us to think through the needs and desires we have, the values that matter to us, and the real-life implications for us and those around us of the various goals we might set ourselves. We might also talk with people who have pursued and attained similar goals. They can tell us about their experiences. And we should read. One of the functions of great literature has always been to trace out all the hidden implications of basic human choices. Even popular biographies, memoirs, and magazine articles can help. The more broadly we read, the better positioned we are to evaluate the various goal-setting possibilities that come our way. We can draw wisdom from other people's experiences and thoughts as well as from our own. With activities like these, we are doing everything within our power to assure ourselves that in pursuing a particular goal, getting what we wish for will be even more enjoyable and satisfying than merely wishing for it.

No man is wise enough by himself. *Plautus*

One more philosophical point should be made as we tie up our brief reflections on the connection between having desires and acting on them through the procedure of goal setting. It is a realization repeated in one form or another by the wisest people in every century. The desire to have, to acquire and possess, is in principle insatiable, and rarely generates the sense of fulfillment and happiness it promises. By contrast, only the desire to do, to produce, to contribute, or to give can reliably, when acted on, yield the true sense of satisfaction we all deeply need. The conclusion I draw from this is that each of us should be guided in our goal setting by the simple question: "How can I best make my contribution to the world?" In our own priorities, doing should always precede having. Only then will we have what we most truly need.

By writing down some of your hopes, dreams, desires, frustrations, and sources of contentment in the form of a satisfaction audit, you can begin to sort through various areas of your life in such a way as to increase the likelihood that your goal setting will be altogether proper and fulfilling for you as a person. Any articulation exercises like this should culminate in a clear recording of specific goals toward which you have decided to work. The simple act of writing down your goals can become not just an act of clarification but also one of commitment. A thought captured by ink on paper can take on a life of its own. Keep the piece of paper around to look over every now and then as a reminder. Some people may need to do this every day. Some may find it helpful to do it weekly. Others, less frequently. When you begin to doubt, or even to forget, the written word can act as testimony to your resolve. Yes, you did think these thoughts. You did set yourself these goals. It is written. You have a commitment.

Put the most important of your goals on a small piece of paper or a three-by-five-inch card and tape it up where you'll frequently see it: on a closet door, beside a mirror, over your desk. I have a five-year plan and two focal goals for that plan written simply on a small card, posted on my refrigerator door, where I'm often to be found. Sometimes I find myself glancing at it and saying to myself, "Oh yes, that's right. Keep these things in view."

Self-talk. Silent, inner self-reminders. Mental affirmations. Articulation within. Psychologists tell us that nothing is more important than how we talk to ourselves. Do we remind ourselves of our goals? Do we tell ourselves that these goals are right for us? We should use our written articulation exercises and posted notes to set off clear self-talk on a regular basis. Life is full of distractions. We need to remind ourselves of where we are headed. We need to keep our targets clearly in view. So talk to yourself about these things. And listen.

THE POWER OF IMAGINATIVE VISION

Do you vividly envision your goals? Do you use the power of your imagination? The first condition of success involves having not just a clear conception of what we want, but also a *vivid vision*.

The book of Proverbs in the Bible gives a profound and powerful diagnosis of our current cultural malaise. It says: "Without a vision, the people perish." Many people lack a vision for their lives.

What do I envision for my family life? For what I do at work? Do I have a vision for my community? Do we have a vision for America? For what we human beings can be accomplishing as global citizens together on this earth? Without a vision, we perish.

From the workplace to the world, many people seem to lack a vision for what they can contribute and for what they can attain. But that need not be the way it is. We can conceive a vision for our lives and envision our purposes vividly. We can use the power of inner vision to structure our lives—our thoughts, actions, feelings, and attitudes. An inner vision gives guidance. An inner vision yields energy. An appropriate vision can enhance our lives with meaning and power.

For a lot of people life is a treadmill. No matter how fast they go, they get nowhere. And they *feel* they're getting nowhere. Every day is a whirlwind of activity, and yet the only discernible results of the frantic pace are exhaustion, confusion, frustration, and pain. But there is an alternative. As Mary Wollstonecraft Shelley pointed out more than a hundred years ago: "Nothing contributes so much to tranquilize the mind as a steady purpose—a point on which the soul may fix its intellectual eye." The power of an inner vision is healing, tranquility, new life, efficient direction, and real accomplishment. Off the treadmill and onto the path of true success.

We need a clear conception of what we want and we need this conception, this purpose, this goal or set of goals to be firmly rooted in the fertile soil of the imagination. Albert Einstein once said that "imagination is more important than knowledge." And I think he was right. In fact, this claim of his has for years been my motto for teaching at Notre Dame. If I can excite my students' imaginations, their minds will follow. Knowledge is a grasping of what is. Imagination reaches out to what can be. And imagination lures us along with a powerfully attractive force.

> Imagination is not a talent of some men but is the health
> of every man.   *Ralph Waldo Emerson*

I still vividly remember seeing the first *Star Wars* movie. As I was walking out of the theater afterwards, I recall commenting to my wife that this movie and others like it may mean more for the future of science and technology than any number of unimaginative educational reforms and normal classroom experiences. This is what it takes to get the kids' imaginations into gear. Then, with the right guidance, they'll want to learn. I decided that when I became a teacher I would bring into the classroom whatever it took to engage the imaginations of my students.

The great Harvard philosopher Alfred North Whitehead thought of all education first and foremost as "the imaginative acquisition of knowledge." Any learning that fails to engage the imagination is mere memorization. Any personal goals that we fail to envision vividly within are mere abstractions. People intellectually set goals all the time that they never attain, that they eventually give up on, because those goals are for them just remote, abstract aims. Only the imagination has the power to engage the emotions, the attitudes, and the will over the long run. Only the imagination can really motivate us and sustain us with the energy we need to achieve difficult and worthwhile goals.

A vivid story of greatness can powerfully motivate us. A dramatic tale of tragedy can deeply move us. They touch the imagination. Have you ever tried to motivate someone with generalities? With abstractions? With numbers? With statistics? Only the imagination can really inspire us, put us into gear, and start us down the road.

1. Fighting Fire with Fire

For many years I was afraid to fly. I couldn't get on an airplane. I couldn't even consider getting on an airplane. The very thought of it horrified me. Friends constantly filled me in on all the relevant statistics contrasting air and highway safety. They reminded me how many flights each day make it safely and without incident to their destinations. They claimed I was statistically more likely to choke on a chicken bone at a barbecue restaurant while wearing plaid shorts and speaking French than to go down in flames on an airplane. And on and on and on. No good. The statistics and numbers made no difference whatsoever. They were directed at my intellect. Where I needed help was in my imagination.

Years earlier I had read too many articles and books describing air-crash scenes in detail. I had allowed myself to try to imagine what it must have been like for the passengers. I had imagined these scenes vividly and repeatedly. By doing so, I had programmed myself, without realizing it, to stay off planes. I had closed my mind to any contrary statistics and generalities.

Then one summer I had the opportunity to fly to a very famous resort on a private plane with friends. I didn't want to miss out on a great vacation trip, so for two weeks, many times each day, I busied myself imagining happy smiling people on a plane, looking out the windows into a beautiful sunny blue sky, a smooth flight, an easy landing, a great day at the beach, and an equally pleasant return trip. Vivid pictures were frequently brought to mind. Pictures that elicited positive emotions. Detailed pictures. Powerful emotions. When the day of the trip arrived, I was eager and ready to go. So, to everyone's surprise, I got on the plane and flew the friendly skies.

At the end of the return trip, as we climbed out of the small plane and jumped down onto the runway, one of the other passengers, a psychiatrist, could not contain herself any longer and said, "Look, I know you've had a strong fear of flying. So, how did you like this experience?"

I said, "It's the greatest form of transportation I've ever taken. I loved every minute of it, and I'll never do it again."

She said, "What?" I went on to explain how my fear had arisen and what I had done to undermine it for two weeks. She told me I saved myself a lot of money. For nearly a hundred dollars an hour, that's just what a good psychiatrist would have had me do.

You fight fire with fire. Negative thoughts with positive thoughts. Negative imagination with positive imagination. But why, this student of the mind wanted to know, had I said I'd never do it again? Simple. I had engaged in negative imaginings for years. I had countered all this with intense bursts of positive imagination for only two weeks. With two flights, one to the resort, the other back, I had used up my new stock of confidence and optimism for the time being. The imagination is powerful, but we must use it habitually, over the long run, in service of our goals if our goals are big and challenging. A day's imagination, a week's worth, will not always give us all we need. We need to use the power of the imagination on a regular basis.

2. Using Our Imaginations

We also must use our imaginations properly. It has often been said that losers visualize the penalties of failure, but that winners visualize the rewards of success. And as a report on habitual tendencies, this is true. I've seen it among athletes. And actors. And among entrepreneurs. And public speakers. Among people of all sorts. We must be careful with the power of the imagination. All of us. It is a two-edged sword. As my fear-of-flying episode shows, it can help us or it can hinder us. If we want the boldness to pursue new goals, we should not allow ourselves to dwell imaginatively too much on the possible risks of failure. It's not that we should blind ourselves to the costs or risks in any endeavor. We should make any new decision or take any new path with eyes wide open. Whenever we are considering the pursuit of very new goals, it can be extremely beneficial to ask "What is the worst that could happen if I try my best to make this go and it doesn't work out?" Because, most times, the worst that can happen is not so bad. And we need to realize that. Once. It is just as important not to continue needlessly to think about it. By seeing that we could live with the consequences of failure, that they would not destroy us or anything we value deeply, we can free ourselves from the fear of them and free ourselves from dwelling on them in our minds. We then free our imaginations to focus instead on the goal we are pursuing and on all the possible rewards of attaining it. We allow our imaginations to serve us, not hinder us.

The power of the imagination must be respected. But this means that if my imagination firmly says no to a goal, I'd better be prepared to listen. If a perceptive, well-informed use of my imagination to discern the possible costs and risks of adopting a particular goal, or of pursuing a specific way of attaining that goal, turns up a strongly negative result—the lively prospects or significant likelihood of consequences I could not live with in good conscience, or that I would not want to be responsible for—I need to be prepared to set aside that goal, or abandon that particular way of pursuing it. If I have imaginatively counted the costs, assessed the risks, and determined that they are too great, I'll probably not be able to attain the level of confidence or commitment I need for a good shot at success, at that goal. Nor should I want to try. If we cannot imaginatively embrace a goal, or a path to a goal, we should chart ourselves another course, one that we will be able to embrace at the level of the imagination, and thus believe in wholeheartedly.

> Imagination decides everything.   *Blaise Pascal*

The goals we want to set ourselves must be firmly planted in the fertile soil of the imagination. If they blossom there, we should pursue them. If they grow dangerous thorns, or wither and die, we should uproot them immediately and plant other seeds, setting ourselves new and different goals instead. It's always a mistake to neglect to test our goals, and the means by which we intend to pursue those goals, with a vivid use of the imagination. We need either the warning or the energy a perceptive, vivid use of imagination can provide.

Let me tell you about a time long ago when I failed to assess imaginatively the possible risks and costs of a course of action. At about the age of seven or eight, I saw a television show about a boy who found a wounded deer in the woods, took it home, and nursed it back to health. The deer became the boy's loving companion until the day he finally had to set it free. He was its savior, a young hero. While watching this drama, I felt a stirring, a deep need for this sort of heroism and returned love in my own life. I wanted to do what the boy on television had done. But in the city neighborhood where I lived, there was no wounded deer to be found. There *were* lots of birds. But no wounded birds. Not one to be thwarted by inconvenient happenstance, I decided that I could wound one myself, shoot it in the wing with my trusty BB gun, take it home, and nurse it back to health. It would become my friend and loyal companion because of all the loving care I would devote to it. I would heal the wounded bird. And be a hero. I was,

of course, completely oblivious to the inherent moral contradic-
tions in my creative plan.

I got my gun and went out into the backyard, seeking to prepare
the way for my intended mission of mercy. I saw a bird and, with a
trembling anticipation running through my body, took aim and
shot. The bird dropped. I ran up to it, thrilled at the chance to save
it from its new wound. Progress toward the goal had begun.

But the BB pellet had missed its intended target. By just an inch.
It had gone straight through the little bird's heart. I was stricken
with shock and sudden inner panic. In an instant I was utterly
miserable. I was stunned. I had not anticipated even the remote
possibility of this terrible turn of events. I had neglected to
imagine the possible costs and risks of the course I was pursuing.
My narrowly limited use of imagination had locked in on a
remotely possible outcome that I considered positive; it had completely short-circuited my conscience about means and ends, and I
had rushed into the sort of messy misadventure young children
often get themselves into.

I was a sensitive boy. Five seconds of good, imaginative risk
assessment would have been enough to veto this misguided little
plan. But children don't often think of these things. They don't
reliably use their imaginations to evaluate costs and risks. They
have not matured enough to have well-informed imaginations and
to have the understanding of how to use their imaginations to
gauge the appropriateness of goals and of particular paths to those
goals. Adults have no such excuses. A suitable employment of the
imagination to assess cost and risk would save a great many people
from pursuing inappropriate goals, and many others from chasing proper goals with altogether improper means.

Bring your goals into the realm of the imagination. Consider
consequences, costs, and risks. If your imagination says no, then
you should let go. Back to the drawing board. Chart a different

course, one you can commit to. One whose pursuit and attainment you can imagine positively, vividly, and energetically. A goal, and a path to that goal, you can embrace without the worry of real fears, or imaginary fears, standing in your way.

We should never let groundless or inappropriate fear stop us from being true to ourselves and stretching ourselves to set the highest goals of which we're capable. I think it's important to aim high in whatever we do. During his life I enjoyed very much reading the syndicated columnist Sydney J. Harris. He expressed one insight in particular that I think may encourage us to try things we otherwise might hesitate to attempt. He said, "Regret for the things we did can be tempered by time; it is regret for the things we did not do that is inconsolable." Don't miss the opportunity. Don't pass up the chance. Be the best that you can be. Be all you can be. Do the best you can do. Give it everything you've got. Then you can live a life of inner satisfaction, not inconsolable regret.

> For what is most choiceworthy for each individual is the highest it is possible for him to achieve. *Aristotle*

Ultimately, only you can decide what it means to be the best you can be. You can't let other people dictate to you. As you discover your talents and meet with opportunity, *you* have to decide what to do. But you should make your decisions wisely. Success is not the same thing as "lifestyles of the rich and famous." Stretching yourself and setting high goals need not mean that you have to join the bumper-to-bumper traffic in the fast lane. One of the best motivational speakers in the country often says, "See you at the top!" But would it ever be even possible for everyone to end up "at the top" in terms of income, prestige, and power? It's easy to think we can imagine an inverse pyramid, a top-heavy structure that's admittedly not at all stable and that would easily topple. But of course it's literally impossible for everybody to be at the socioeconomic top. There is a no top without a bottom and a middle.

By contrast, it is not impossible for everybody to be a success. Setting high goals is not necessarily a matter of striving to become a company president, CEO, or governor of your state. It doesn't require planning to be the number-one salesman in the country or to write a runaway best-seller book. Stretching yourself doesn't have to mean increasing your income, fame, power, or social status at all. It means digging deep into your own heart, finding what you're capable of and what you love, and not settling for anything less. It means not narrowing yourself but exercising and enjoying every aspect of who you are. It involves discovering your own personal excellence, your own best path to fulfillment, and walking that path every day. These are what I think of as high goals.

In the long run, men hit only what they aim at.
Therefore . . . they had better aim at something high.
Henry David Thoreau

Have high goals for yourself. Stretch. Strive. But strive with patience. Lofty goals take time to reach. For many years I lived in an old house. Whenever I turned up the thermostat in that house on a cold South Bend day, the ancient furnace had to work hard for quite a while before the temperature in the house reached the setting. And I noticed something else. The furnace never just kept going. When it got to the set goal, it stopped. No higher.

We human beings are just like that. We tend to get no higher than the goals we set ourselves. And when we set them high, it may take quite some time to get there.

How high are your goals? If life is leaving you out in the cold, do something about it! Turn up the heat! Strive. And wait. It's worth it.

THE IMPORTANCE OF RENEWAL

I've come to believe that resetting goals is just as important as setting them in the first place. For one thing, we may want to make adjustments, improvements, and clarifications in our goals as we work toward them and discover new information relevant to their specification and precise fit with our developing talents and enjoyments. The exact details by which we first state our goals are not carved in stone, although as I have indicated, I think they should at least be written in ink. Don't abandon initial goals prematurely, but do always be ready to refine, redefine, and renew.

Date your articulation exercises on paper. If you come to realize that a goal you have listed should be redescribed or replaced with a better goal statement, keep this original list in a goals file and make any corrections on a fresh sheet of paper, also dated. It's important to keep track of the progress of your thinking about what you want for your life. This is another exercise in self-knowledge.

When you make an important step toward a goal you have set yourself, have a celebration. It doesn't need to be anything elaborate. It can be a family trip to your favorite fast-food place, buying a coworker a cup of coffee, treating yourself to a small indulgence, almost anything fun and positive to mark the moment and rekindle the vision. Remind yourself: I have done this to get there. I'm on the way. It feels great.

> I celebrate myself, and sing myself.   *Walt Whitman*

Prior to this book, I have written or edited eleven others. When I finish a manuscript I often take the rest of the day off. I goof off. I go walk my dog, or play with my kids, or bother my wife. I wander a great bookstore. I go home, hook up my electric guitar, and play real loud. Whatever I feel like. It's a celebration. And we have a family ritual. Whenever a book is accepted for publication, we go out to dinner. At some place fun, but at some place cheap, so the advance will at least cover the bill. We celebrate. And I make sure to tell the family what we are celebrating, and how it's another step along the path to my goals. This is an act of renewal. A renewal of energy. A renewal of the spirit.

One of the most common problems in a goal-oriented society is the failure of successful people. What I mean is this: We set goals, we attain them, and then we ease up. After a big project is completed, after a high goal is reached, we coast. Not just for a day, or a week, but for the long haul. And that's when the competition moves in. This is the human tendency that on a smaller scale allows for dramatic comebacks in sporting events. It's a very dangerous habit.

Now, I believe that everyone deserves a rest after successfully striving for a goal and making it. So take the afternoon off. But don't have an off year. Too often today's excellence is tomorrow's mediocrity. And not just when the standards have changed. That is one problem. People highly successful in one context, at one time, can become stuck on one conception of what it is to achieve, of what it takes for excellence, which may not fit a later time or a different context. We need the flexibility to change with a changing world. We can't just put our lives or careers into cruise control, stuck on one setting. If we do, we'll eventually crash.

This year's top sales agent can become next year's has-been. This year's hottest companies can cool real fast. Have you ever noticed how the *Fortune 500* has changed over time? Highly visible people, highly visible companies seem to drop out of sight. They are often people and they are sometimes companies that do not understand the importance of renewal, of resetting their goals.

A lofty goal is something that, by necessity, you work toward for a long time, organizing your time and energy around it, thinking about it, hoping for it. And then you attain it. At the initial culmination of your efforts, you're flying high. And then before you know it you're flying off a cliff.

Postpartum blues. After the birth of a baby, nine months in coming; after the awarding of a Ph.D., years in the making; after a big promotion, a major recognition, any significant attainment, long awaited, there can be a letdown. There is a vacuum. The philosopher Bertrand Russell once wrote: "Unless a man has been taught what to do with success after getting it, the achievement of it must inevitably leave him a prey to boredom." One thing we must do with any success we attain is to use it to launch ourselves onto the next quest for a new success. Whenever you attain your goals, you need new goals. Right away. Otherwise you risk the near certain ennui of literal aimlessness.

Get out a sheet of paper from the goal file. Check off the goal you've met. Describe briefly the circumstances of its accomplishment. Say how you feel. Date it. Get out another piece of a paper. Set new goals. And visualize anew. The importance of resetting cannot be exaggerated. Our lives are made for success. And not just for enjoying it, for seeking it. As a matter of fact, those people who are most likely to enjoy success are those who most enjoy seeking it. There is satisfaction to be found in the search, not just at the end of the road. We are wired to pursue goals. So any success deserves a new quest. You've earned a long lunch, or a week's vacation. But you've also earned the right to turn the heat up a bit. Notch up those expectations. Go to the next level. Set new goals. You won't be happy without them.

Human beings need renewal. We need celebrations. We need reminders. We need meaningful work. We need to be on a quest. We need targets to aim at. We need a clear conception of what we want, a vivid vision, a goal or set of goals powerfully imagined. And we need to renew our vision regularly. This is the first condition of success.

2

A Confidence to
See Us Through

Condition Two: We need a strong confidence that we can attain our goals.

Not long ago I went to the gas station a few blocks from my house for my normal fill-up, and I was confronted with an unusual spectacle. Right across the street in a typically empty parking lot there were hundreds of noisy people standing around a tall yellow construction crane. I asked the station attendant what was going on. "Bungee jumping," he replied with a skeptical look.

I had heard about this. Bungee jumping. People, screaming like maniacs or praying like crazy, leap off high bridges over rivers, attached to the bridge by a long elastic cord tied around their ankles or hooked to their waists. They sail through the air like acrobatic suicides and then, right before contact with earth or water, are snatched back into flailing security by the cord. In theory. When everything works right. The jumper is lowered down carefully into a waiting boat and untied. A few inches taller and a few years older.

Not everybody lives conveniently near a tall bridge over a deep gorge, so bungee jumping companies began bringing large cranes into big parking lots to lift adventurous souls on metal platforms high above the asphalt for their daring dives. That's what was going on here. I sat in the car and watched for a few minutes. But nothing happened. I yelled over to the gas guy, "Hey, how come nobody's jumping?"

He explained, "They forgot to bring the cord." No cord, no takers. Nobody there quite that crazy. No thanks, we'll wait for the cord.

But when they got the cord and hooked it up, people began to line up to pay their sixty-dollar fee and get on the platform. This was interesting to watch. Especially first-timers. You could see on their faces the transition from bold to tentative to terrified. Hoisted up into the air, peering over the edge of their little perch, these folks confronted something the likes of which they had never done before. And most froze. But the bungee pros, the operators, were prepared. A companion on the platform spoke reassuring words of encouragement, a little pep talk. A guy with a microphone and PA system blasted out over the crowd "Three, two, one, *bungee!*"

And on the count, most people jumped. But some stood there with jelly legs, shaking, trembling, realizing that this might not be such a good idea after all, willing at this point to offer a lot more than sixty bucks just to get back down to solid ground the slow, safe way. But their platform partner said something like, "Hey, you can do this. You'll be fine. It'll feel great. *Just do it!*" At this point, the crowd was chanting "Jump, jump, jump!" Easy enough for them to say, feet planted firmly on the ground. And then over the loudspeakers came one more booming, authoritative "Three, two, one, *bungee!*" With a roar from the crowd below, the novices dove. Some took three countdowns, nonstop pep talks, and lots of cheering from the multitude. But all I saw took the plunge.

This is a metaphor, isn't it, for those times in our lives when we face something new and are tempted to lose our nerve. We've set ourselves new goals, we've been given a new assignment, we face a new challenge, and, peering over the edge, we experience a bit of anxiety. We think about turning back. We ask ourselves, "What am I doing here?" or "Who am I to be doing this?" or "What if I fall on my face?" or "What if I crash and burn?"

One thing I learned from watching the ambivalent bungee jumpers that day was the role cheerleading can play in our lives. We all need support when we confront something new. We all need cheerleaders. And we all need to be cheerleaders for the other people around us. Family members. Friends. People at work. Professional colleagues. When we support others, they are a little more likely to be able to do what it takes to succeed. And they will appreciate our encouragement, which will make them a little more likely to support us in turn. And with the confidence that comes from having the cheerleaders we need, we will be a little more likely to be able to do what it takes to succeed. Support builds confidence, and confidence is a vital condition for succeeding with any difficult challenge.

> Self confidence is the first requisite to great undertakings.
> *Samuel Johnson*

It can be hard to leap out into something new. It can take a lot of reassurance. It can take pep talks. It can sometimes take a great deal of cheerleading. But with enough support, with enough confidence, and with the momentum that brings, we can do it. When we set ourselves high goals, we always face a challenge. Fear can lead to failure, confidence to conquest. Which will we choose? It's really up to us, whether we find ourselves surrounded by cheerleaders or not. We can become our own best cheerleaders. We can give ourselves the great gift of believing in ourselves.

THE CONFIDENCE GAME: FAITH UP FRONT

Life is risk. Now, I'm not just talking about bungee jumping, skydiving, open-heart surgery, or vacations in the Middle East. Everyday life is risky. But the risks are so common, we're so accustomed to them, they hardly ever cross our minds. Until we contemplate something new. A new job, a new relationship, a new strategy, a new set of goals. Then we worry. "What if I fail?" "What if I make a fool of myself?" What if . . . What if . . . There are few guarantees in life. There are lots of opportunities—if you're willing to take a chance, if you're willing to run the risk.

"I've never done this before." The world is run by people who have never done it before. Of course it shows, but don't worry. There's a first time for everything. Run your own life and do it right.

"But how do I know I *can* do this?" How do you know you *can't*?

"Maybe I don't have what it takes." Maybe you do. Give it a shot and find out. Nothing ventured, nothing gained. As the first-century Roman philosopher Seneca pointed out: "No one knows what he can accomplish except by trying."

When we talk to ourselves within the privacy of our own minds, what do we say? Are we our own best cheerleaders, or our own worst critics? Do we give ourselves encouragement, or wallow in the worst of our worries?

Whenever we set ourselves new goals we believe in, higher goals we aspire to, and whenever we face new opportunities for growth and development, it is easy for doubt to rush in and catch up with us. It grabs us tight and tries to hold us back. Fear of the new. Fear of the unknown. Fear of change. Fear of risk. Fear of failure. Fear of embarrassment. It's been said that fear is the darkroom in which negatives are developed. "Maybe I can't." "Perhaps I shouldn't." "Guess I won't." Negatives. Once we've set our course with goals that are right for us, negatives get us nowhere we want to go. Never have, never will.

Yet nothing is more common in this world of ours than negative thinking. And negative comments. If it suddenly became impossible for anyone to say anything negative about anybody else, an amazing hush would descend upon the world. We have to be careful about how we think and how we talk to ourselves in the intimacy of our innermost thoughts, but we also have to be very cautious about how we listen to the negative pronouncements of others. Have you ever given voice to a deep-felt wish or shared an important goal only to be told in the most authoritative of tones that it was completely impossible, that it would never work, and that you should wake up to reality? Walt Disney used to say that whenever he had a new idea that absolutely nobody thought would ever work, he knew for sure that he was onto something big and went after it full speed ahead. Now, maybe this is a little extreme, but Jonathan Swift once claimed that "when a true Genius appears in the world, you may know him by this sign, that the Dunces are all in confederacy against him."

> Nothing will ever be attempted if all possible objections must be first overcome. *Samuel Johnson*

Some ideas won't work. And sometimes we should proceed with caution. But most often the naysayers around us would not have us proceed at all. Even people who care for us can sometimes be inappropriately negative in reaction to our plans and dreams. And there is one simple reason. They may be taking into consideration all the evidence they can muster about the likelihood of our success, and it may look insufficient to them because there is always one piece of evidence we ourselves can have that they must of necessity lack—a full knowledge of the fire in our hearts, of the determination and drive within us that can sometimes overcome tremendous odds and make all the difference in the world.

Always remember this: Whenever you have thought long and hard about a new idea or plan for action, working out lots of details and preparing for all sorts of contingencies, and you first tell someone else about it, they are hearing it *for the first time*. It will be nearly impossible for any newly informed person to be as enthusiastic or as confident as you are. And it's natural for your own confidence level, like water running downhill, to settle at the lowest point nearby. That's why it is so important to be very careful about how you share your plans with others, and limit your exposure to the negative thinking and negative comments casual disbelievers can produce.

> I will listen to anyone's convictions, but pray keep your doubts to yourself. *Johann Wolfgang von Goethe*

It's easy to underestimate the power of negative thinking. It has tremendous power for ill in our lives. A great many people live in the self-imposed imprisonment of low expectations about life. Their negative thinking robs them of the wealth of experience and accomplishment that should be theirs. And an increasing body of literature from physicians, psychologists, and careful observers of the human condition warns us that negative thinking can rob us of our health, and even our lives. A friend of mine who is an epidemiology professor at a major medical school once told me that he has seen shocking examples of negative thinking with literally fatal results. In one tribal society he visited, he watched an otherwise healthy man weaken and die over a short period of time as the result of a curse put on him by the revered shaman, or medicine man, of the tribe. It is known that fear and worry can produce twitches, rashes, and ulcers. Under the stress of persistent doubt, we can weaken, and sicken, and perhaps even die. The attitudes and emotions we cultivate determine in large part the quality of life we live.

1. William James and Winnie-the-Pooh

The great Harvard psychologist and philosopher William James once said that one of the most important discoveries made by his generation was that by changing our attitudes we can change our lives. On the inside. And on the outside as well. We need to learn to banish unhelpful doubts and cultivate beneficial self-confidence. Sometimes we need faith in ourselves that runs ahead of the evidence available to us. We need to create the positive attitude that will see us through to success. We need a strong confidence that we can attain our goals.

Most of us don't want to be deluded or duped as we go through life. We want our beliefs to be rational. We want our convictions to be true. Often we want proof, or at least good evidence, before we'll believe in something, especially when the stakes are high. But what about believing in ourselves? If we want more out of life than we have been experiencing, if we want to give much more to this life than we have yet been able to give, then we need a new vision for our lives. Even having these desires can mean we are already reaching out toward a new vision. We need new goals, higher goals. But we can never expect to stretch ourselves to reach those goals unless we believe in ourselves. Do we have any proof that we can make it? Is the evidence compelling, or conclusive?

Typically the answer here is no. Since we want something new for our lives, we will not be able to find in our pasts any sort of absolute proof that we can make it. We will lack sufficient evidence for an objectively grounded confidence. Because of this, many people are afraid to stick their necks out and follow their dreams. They decide to keep on living as they always have. But there are times when playing it safe is the most dangerous thing you can do.

William James coined a term. Sometimes, he said, we need *precursive faith*, faith that runs ahead of the evidence (from Latin roots: "cursive" means "running" and "pre" means "ahead of"). James thought that it was altogether proper and rational to launch out in believing beyond the objective evidence you have when so doing is, in his words, a *genuine option*. He went on to specify that believing beyond the evidence is a genuine option when: (1) It is possible for you to form the belief. Nothing you know proves the belief couldn't possibly be true—it is what James called a *living option;* (2) By waiting and not committing yourself to the belief you would run the risk of losing what might be gained by having the belief—it is what he called a *forced option;* and (3) What is at stake and may turn upon your having or lacking the belief in question is of great value, or of tremendous personal importance—it is what he labeled a *momentous option*. If an option to believe beyond the presently available evidence is *living, forced,* and *momentous*, then, James held, it is altogether appropriate for you to go for it: Take up the belief and march boldly forward.

> Confidence is that feeling by which the mind embarks in great and honorable courses with a sure hope and trust in itself.
>
> *Cicero*

This can all sound a bit abstract. Just the sort of thing a professor might say. But it's extremely important and liberating. Suppose you want to change careers, propose marriage, turn a hobby into a business, go for a major new client or promotion, or take on a huge, exciting new project. It is unlikely you'll succeed unless you believe you will, unless you believe in yourself and in the rightness of what you're doing for yourself. Yet the bigger and newer and more important the task is that you're facing, the less likely it is that you'll find in your past history sufficient evidence or proof that you can do it. But I bet that if it's something you really deeply desire or want to accomplish, you'll have nothing in your background that proves you can't do it, either. The option of confidence is living. And we know that without confidence you won't get moving the way you should, you won't keep moving the way you should, and you are likely to lose the benefits that confidence would most probably bring. The option of believing in yourself is forced. And in addition, there are few things more important to you than your own future, which is what's at stake here. So the option of confidence is momentous. According to William James, this is just the sort of situation in which it is right for you to adopt the belief you need, establish your confidence, set your will, and chart your course. Forget the nagging doubts. Turn around and move forward. Focus. Tell yourself you can do it. Become your own best cheerleader. Make yourself believe in yourself. Take charge of your attitudes and take charge of your life.

One Notre Dame football story. Several years ago I was talking on the telephone for the first time with the great former Notre Dame football coach Dan Devine. I asked him what was most memorable to him about his time with the Fighting Irish. He said January 1, 1979. Notre Dame was playing the University of Houston at the Cotton Bowl in Dallas. The windchill was six degrees below zero, a bizarre near-arctic temperature for Texas. At the half, Houston was far, far ahead and the Irish quarterback was a sick young man. His body temperature was ninety-six degrees. He was ordered to stay in the locker room and was fed hot chicken soup. The team was told he was not coming back. They thought it was over.

And so Joe Montana missed most of the third quarter. Another quarterback had to be put in. But Montana later described his own personal determination at the time, and said, "I was coming back no matter what." An attitude that would have made William James proud. With just seven minutes, thirty-seven seconds left in the game, Houston led 34–12. The sick and shivering quarterback got back into the game, focused a laser-intense confidence onto his goal, and led what most people consider the greatest comeback in Notre Dame football history, finally throwing his last touchdown pass of the game that was caught just as time expired on the clock: Notre Dame 35, Houston 34.

> Skill and confidence are an unconquered army.
>
> *George Herbert*

Precursive faith. The power of belief. The conquest of confidence. What was the evidence with seven and a half minutes remaining? Not good. Was it impossible? Close, but no. Was it momentous? For those involved, you bet. Forced? Absolutely.

Most of us rarely face such extreme conditions. But all of us face challenges where we have to stretch beyond what we've ever done before if we're going to make the most of the opportunity we have. We need confidence. And we can't wait on the evidence. We can't always wait for the people around us to give us that confidence, either. We need to take matters into our own hands. We need confidence up front, and we need to do whatever it takes to give ourselves that confidence. And especially when we face something we've never quite faced before, we need to create within ourselves a strong initial confidence, a precursive faith in our abilities and in our prospects.

Let me give you a vivid example of this from my own life. First, a little background. One day I received a phone call from one of the largest advertising agencies in the country. The lady I spoke with said that she had been engaged in a nationwide search to find a philosophy professor to make some network TV commercials and act as the national spokesperson for the Winnie-the-Pooh series of Disney Home Videos. She said she had been searching the country for a philosopher with personality and, so far, had not been able to find one. She was ready to give up when she heard about me. I thanked her with all the warmth and enthusiasm of personality I could muster and told her I would indeed be interested. I love Winnie-the-Pooh. When my wife and I were dating in college, we often read Pooh stories to each other. We even owned a dog named after a Pooh story character, Kanga's little offspring, Roo. And, lest this interest on the part of a philosopher seem strange, I should assure you that I see Pooh bear and his friends as true philosophers, in their own way.

The ad agency people wanted to come to campus and get me on video to see whether I was sufficiently telegenic, but when I told them I had lectured for The Learning Channel, they flew a person from Chicago to the Washington, D.C., area that very day to pick up one of my tapes. The man flew back to Chicago, watched the tape, decided he wanted me for the commercial, and the next day flew out to Los Angeles to show video clips of me to the Disney people. They said, "We like this guy. But is there a problem with his southern accent?" They detected my Carolina roots. The ad agency representative, who was originally from Asheville, North Carolina, said, "What accent?" and I was hired.

The talent coordinator called and explained that they would fly me out to LA first class and put me in a nice room in a hotel in Beverly Hills. My family and I had never been to California, so I asked if I could bring my wife and two children, who were eight and ten years old at the time. Yes, I was told, that would be fine, and we'd be given a suite of rooms in the hotel. We would also be picked up at the airport by a limousine. At this point, I knew I was pushing my luck, but I asked, "Can it be a white limousine?"

A moment of silence. "Why do you ask?" I explained that my ten-year-old daughter had always wanted to ride in a white limousine. My generous talent coordinator said she'd call me back in a few minutes. I feared she must be wondering at this point whether there might not be a philosopher out there with just as much personality but a lot fewer requests. She called back and said they'd had to switch limo companies to do it, but they got me a white limousine.

Well, we flew out there and, yes indeed, we were met by a gracious driver in a white stretch limousine stocked with our favorite snacks and sparkling waters. We were driven around for a little preliminary sight-seeing and then were taken to the studio for some wardrobe consultations, which would all have been very enjoyable except for the fact that during the flight out I had come down with the worst case of flu in my life. I could hardly breathe, my eyes were watering, my ears were stopped up, I was dizzy, and I was losing my voice by the minute. When the producers first saw me they were stunned. We weren't planning to shoot a commercial for any kind of medication. I promised them with great confidence and authority that by the next day at the scheduled time of the shoot I'd be symptom-free, completely healthy, and ready to roll. By the time I finally got to the hotel, I was swathed in a cocoon of my own misery. In the midst of it all, I decided not to be conquered by this sickness, but rather to conquer. At birth, my mother and father had given me the middle name Victor, and I was determined to live up to it.

> The honor of the conquest is rated by the difficulty.
> *Michel de Montaigne*

I did more positive thinking and praying that afternoon and evening than I've ever crammed into a twelve-hour period in my life. I said to myself over and over, "I have to do this. I can do this. I will do this. I'll be symptom-free." I visualized myself in front of the cameras looking fine and doing well. Over and over. All night long. I also took lots of cold and flu medication.

The next day I was symptom-free for the entire six hours of the shoot.

But there was a second test of my confidence and resolve. People I talked to on the set told me in tones of awe how Disney had hired all the best people for this shoot: the best director from New York, the best makeup artist, from Aspen, Colorado (they knew they had a challenge here), the best lighting people, camera crew, and so on. I could tell they were good. The director and the makeup woman stood in front of me for what seemed like five minutes just looking at my face, in silence. It wasn't respectful reverence.

Finally the director pointed at my nose and mouth and said, "Get him natural-looking." It took her an hour and a half.

The third assistant producer told me he had produced music videos on top bands for MTV and that the Disney budget for incidentals on our shoot was greater than his typical entire budget. The set itself was pretty impressive. They had asked me to take twenty-four pictures of my office at Notre Dame before I left, had sent someone for the film, and had reproduced the office in amazing detail on a soundstage there in Hollywood. Even the guitar I kept in a corner. And the mess it had taken me ten years to make they had created in a matter of days. In response to my amazement, they said, "This is Hollywood—we can do anything." Actually, their reproduction office was a lot nicer than the original. I was tempted to ask them whether I could take twenty-four pictures of that office and send the film back to Notre Dame. Impressive. A very big budget, a beautiful set, a crew of dozens of experts, and me. Standing on the mark (as we say in the 'biz), I looked around the room and saw for the first time all these accomplished, highly professional people, all looking *at me.* Suddenly a phrase imprinted itself on my brain: *weak link in the chain.*

> When you are a Bear of Very Little Brain, and you Think of Things, you find sometimes that a Thing which seemed very Thingish inside you is quite different when it gets out into the open and has other people looking at it. *Winnie-the-Pooh*

I had never done this before. I had never made network TV commercials before. And I wasn't a face in the crowd, or a member of an ensemble. It was just me and the camera. Pooh would be added later. But not in my shots. Every worry and fear appropriate to the moment came flooding into my consciousness. I suddenly felt a bit nauseous. But in a moment, in a matter of seconds, I chose to reject all negative thinking, banish all doubts, and plunge forward. "I can do this," I told myself. "No problem." "This is going to be great."

And it was. All day long, no matter what I was asked to do, I'd hear myself saying, "No problem, I can do that," even when I had no previous evidence in my life to go on. I just manufactured the confidence I needed. With willpower and imagination. With positive affirmations. I took charge of my consciousness and focused my energies in a completely positive way. I created the up-front confidence I needed. The precursive faith. I thought of old William James and mentally thanked him. I surfed on a wave of strong self-confidence and completed my assignment to everyone's satisfaction, including my own. Now, wherever I go, I am "the Pooh philosopher," or as my children put it, "the Poohlosopher." I was able to rise to a new challenge. A very new challenge. And if I can do it, so can you.

2. The Action Approach to Attitude

If I can do it, so can you. I say this again because it deserves repeating. I am no master of self-confidence. It doesn't come easy to me. I often battle with doubt. Lack of self-confidence stalks me. At Notre Dame I've taught as many as twelve hundred students a year. A typical semester involves a freshman class of two to three hundred students and a senior class of a couple hundred. I've done this for many years. But with every new semester, I face a new group of students, students who are often not so sure about what a philosophy class is going to be like. Before the first class meeting, I always recall the old saw that you never have a second chance to make a good first impression. Aware also that well begun is half done, I want to get off on the right foot with the new students. I want to spark in them a love for ideas. And for that to happen, they have to like what we're doing together. For about three hours before walking over to the large auditorium where we'll have that first class session, I almost always have a very upset stomach. I feel extremely nervous. My legs sometimes actually start to tremble. Now, remember, I've done this sort of thing many, many times before; the students and I have always had a wonderful experience together in the past, but somehow I am usually tied in a knot in dread of that first meeting. In a typical semester, out of three hundred students, two hundred and ninety-eight will have a very good time and will feel like they've learned a lot. Two will hate the course and feel like they've wasted their time. This used to bother me immensely, until I realized that the very things that make it work for most people will be the things the others can't stand. This is the human condition. You can't please everybody. Don't even try. And don't let it bother you.

Why am I often such a nervous wreck on that first morning of the semester? Do I think it's possible to have a class of all disgruntled misophiacs (a term I just made up, etymologically, to mean "haters of wisdom") who think that philosophy is bogus and that I'm a total jerk? I don't know why, but I am a wreck. I pace the office, reread teaching awards I've received (kept in the office for just such times as these), trying to convince myself that I can still do it, and flop unconvinced into my desk chair to listen to my heart race. I get up again and walk over to the bookshelves. I gaze upon a statue of the Buddha I was once given by a student. A strange adornment for the office of a Southern Baptist–born-and-bred professor of philosophy at a great Catholic university. The big-bellied statue has both his arms raised in a manner often seen among football referees indicating a score in Notre Dame stadium, across the street, and like the famous, huge mural of Christ on the side of the library facing the stadium, the picture long known as "Touchdown Jesus." The bulging stomach of my little statue is adorned with the felt-tipped-marker inscription "Touchdown Buddha." I pat his tummy for luck. Nothing changes.

I'm desperate. I consult with a figurine of Pooh. Nothing. I approach a very large ashtray formed in the shape of the football stadium. A bronze plaque on the front says:

FOR WHEN THE ONE GREAT SCORER COMES

TO WRITE AGAINST YOUR NAME

HE WRITES NOT THAT YOU WON OR LOST

BUT HOW YOU PLAYED THE GAME

And a statue of The Coach, Knute Rockne, stands tall over the little press box, holding a football and smiling on me. I rub his bald metal head and say out loud, "Come on, Coach, let's go in there and do it. Let's win one for Notre Dame."

At this point I feel so silly, embarrassment starts to displace nervousness. I begin to give myself a pep talk, I visualize a huge room full of eager smiling faces, and I start to do deep-breathing exercises. After all this I'm usually ready to go. I walk out of my office and across campus to where I'll be teaching, breathing deep and using the power of my imagination, creating for myself a vivid vision of success in the classroom. Somehow, as if by magic, this begins to reinterpret and redirect the nervous energy that had been tying me in knots.

That's one thing I've learned about nerves. Nervousness involves energy. It's great to have it if you know what to do with it. Don't let it power negative thought. Take control of it with positive thought and, with the power of the imagination, make that energy work for you. It can give you just the edge you need.

On the first day of one fall semester, none of this worked for me. I could not shed the dread. I couldn't rout the doubt. I could not overcome my fear. But it was just ten minutes until class time, so I had to pick up my briefcase and leave. I walked on slightly trembling legs down the stairs and out of my office building. I was headed to the large auditorium in the Theodore Hesburgh Library. It was pouring rain, and at the same time all the in-ground sprinklers around campus were on full blast. Water was coming at me and all the students on the walk from all directions. I had my umbrella open, but I was still feeling a spray. I was dressed in a dark blue sportcoat, khaki dress pants, and new "dirty buck" suede shoes. The sidewalk was a half inch deep in water from the rain and the sprinklers, which were gushing like fountains. Outside the library, on my way to class, there is a large reflecting pool surrounded by a one-foot-high, one-foot-wide marble wall. As I approached the pool, I was busy worrying about this first class session and I was feeling my stomach flutter. I was tight as a drum. Noticing that my new shoes were getting wet and discolored, I decided to jump up on the wall of the pool, where there didn't seem to be nearly as much standing water. I didn't stop to think what even a little water on marble will do. I know now.

In a split second I was in the reflecting pool. Soaked. Drenched. Sputtering. I looked at my watch. Two minutes till class. What could I do? I was a total disaster. I laughed out loud. And all my nervousness disappeared. That very moment. No turning back. With a huge smile on my face, I sloshed into the auditorium of three hundred astonished freshmen, who had never seen a philosopher before. I reached down and pulled off a shoe, held it up high and poured out what seemed like a good pint of water. A tremendous laugh erupted from the class. And we got off to a great start.

My point in telling this story is a simple one. When you face a new situation with goals you believe in and self-doubt begins to take you over, when your nerves begin to tie you up, when fear starts to grab you by the gut, do whatever it takes to gain control of your emotions and attitudes. Tell yourself: "I'm all wet with these doubts. I can do this." Try positive self-talk. Remind yourself of past victories. Recall to mind the values lying behind your goal. Phone home for encouragement. Go through any rituals that help. Pray. Cheerlead for yourself. Breathe deep. Visualize. Picture yourself doing well. Imagine success. Feel the emotions you know it will bring. And even if nothing seems to work, take charge and do what real confidence does: March forth. You'll be taken care of. Precursive faith. Believe, and then do. Or at least do. Sometimes acting as if you have confidence will bring you the real thing. Go for it. Take the plunge.

This is what I call *The Action Approach to Attitude*. Sometimes we find ourselves lacking an attitude that it would be good, beneficial, or important to have. We're never just stuck; we can take action to make a change. Confidence is an attitude—an attitude tinged with positive emotion. A lack of confidence is also an attitude—an attitude tied to negative emotions. I believe that we all have some degree of control over our attitudes, but usually the control we have is only indirect. We can't very often just directly *will* a change in our attitudes. Instead we have to take action and *do* something that will bring about a change of mind or a change of heart. Walk into the classroom. Speak up in the meeting. Pick up that telephone. Begin writing that proposal. Lace up those shoes and step up to the starting line.

Let me use a simple chart to show how this can work. Ordinarily we seem to think that human experience works like this (beginning from the bottom and reading up, the arrow is to be interpreted as meaning "gives rise to"):

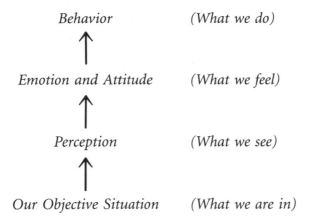

Behavior   (What we do)

↑

Emotion and Attitude   (What we feel)

↑

Perception   (What we see)

↑

Our Objective Situation   (What we are in)

Note that there is a specific, one-way directionality represented here. The objective situations we are in are responsible for what we perceive to be true. And what we perceive our situation to be in turn influences how we feel. It calls forth one sort of attitude rather than another, and one set of emotions rather than some other. Then these emotions and attitudes feed into our behavior, influencing us along certain avenues of action. To do one thing rather than another. To take action in one way rather than another. What we do is affected by what we feel, and by how we feel.

Suppose you're in a new work situation. This causes you to perceive yourself as an inexperienced, unproven novice, compared to the other people you're working around. This perception can give rise to a measure of anxiety and a hesitant lack of confidence that may be a new experience for you. And these attitudes and emotions in turn can generate a very cautious, conservative behavior that doesn't feel right because it's not really you. It's not your style. You're usually confident, creative, and very innovative, always trying new things. What do you do in this situation? What should any of us do?

If our perceptions are valid and our emotions and attitudes are appropriate, then going with the flow of experience in this direc-

91

tion, for at least a while, can often help get us in touch with reality and keep us in touch with the particularities of our situation. Sometimes we should proceed with caution. But there may indeed come a time when we sense that our behavior is not what it ought to be. Our emotions and attitudes are not right. Our perceptions aren't accurate. And the objective situation we're in could use a little work.

It's at times like these that we can turn the chart of experience around and run it in the opposite direction:

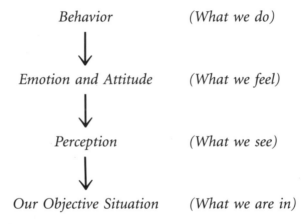

Behavior	*(What we do)*
Emotion and Attitude	*(What we feel)*
Perception	*(What we see)*
Our Objective Situation	*(What we are in)*

By taking the actions that ought to be taken we can very often bring about the emotions and attitudes we need to have. They in turn can open us up to seeing things we otherwise would have missed. And the whole process can end up altering our objective situation in ways that it needed to be changed.

Too often we stand still waiting for confidence to descend upon us, or for opportunity to knock loudly on our door, when what we need is to launch out and take the action that alone can generate that confidence and position us to perceive that opportunity to succeed that's already out there. In human life, the flow of experience goes in both directions. When we take The Action Approach to Attitude we just divert the flow to where it needs to go. We launch ourselves in the right directions.

RESILIENT FAITH: HANGING IN THERE

In any new enterprise, for any new goals, faith up front is vitally important. A strong initial confidence that we can achieve our goals is an extremely important condition for sustaining any pursuit of them and actually getting there. But as important as it is to have initial confidence, precursive faith, it is every bit as crucial to have resilient faith, persistent confidence that can take its lumps and keep on going.

1. Striking Out with Confidence

Nothing worth doing is easy. The road to genuine personal attainment is not smooth asphalt laid straight, wide and downhill. It's often tough, rough, twisting, narrow, and steeply climbing. But it's worth all the work to get to your goal. The problem is, you have to be prepared for setbacks along the way. It's often hard enough to pump up your confidence at the start of the trek. What do you do when you face obstacles, hurdles, failures along the road? Do you give up and stop trying? Does your confidence come unraveled? I hope not. One of the biggest differences in this world between the people who succeed and those who do not is resilient, persistent confidence that refuses to give up.

Making my first TV commercial, I was told at one point, "This time, smile not with your mouth but with your eyes." I thought I knew what that meant, but I had no idea how to do it. I said, "No problem. I can do that." But the first time I tried, I didn't quite manage to pull it off. The second effort didn't seem much better. After a few more takes, the director got up and came over to show me what he wanted. He stood right in front of me, by golly, and smiled with his eyes. They sparkled. I was beginning to feel just a twinge of panic.

What do you do when you hear someone say "Smiling with the eyes, take thirty-seven"? Terror in the eyes is not what they're looking for. You can't give up. You need a kind of confidence that can rebound. In any effort, initial failure can be a tremendous learning experience. By learning how not to do it, you are beginning to position yourself in such a way that you'll be able to do it. Successful people realize this. Successful people depend on it.

A lack of failure in a person's life often indicates a lack of effort, a policy of playing it safe. It usually signals a lack of risk taking, a dearth of innovation and experiment. People who are stretching themselves, trying new things, and setting high goals will try some dead-end streets along the way. At least they're out there moving, searching, testing, and learning. A lack of any failure can even be the greatest failure—in the life of a business or in the life of an individual.

The gem cannot be polished without friction, nor man perfected without trials.   *Confucius*

Now, of course, I don't mean to be extolling failure for its own sake. To face and overcome failure is both educational and character-building. But it would certainly be more efficient, and it would likely be more profitable, at least in the short run, to do everything right the first time. If that were possible, which it's not. But even in falling flat on our faces we learn. How to land. And what not to do the next time. Or at least how not to do it. To confront and overcome failure is to be promoted in the most public of schools, the famous school of hard knocks.

The key in dealing with difficulty is most often just a matter of perspective and attitude. One day recently I was throwing a Frisbee with my ten-year-old son, Matthew. We were standing a little farther apart than usual, and my first throw was a bit off. No big deal. But I grimaced. My second toss veered to the left. I shook my head. The third effort was no improvement. "Sorry," I said, "bad throw." Once more. "Oh, no. Bad throw again." And again. "Sorry, Matt, it looks like nothing but bad throws today."

Matthew held the Frisbee, stood perfectly still for a moment, and looked at me thoughtfully. He said, "Dad, don't say 'bad throw'; it's just a good chance for me to make a great catch." A new perspective. And an admirable attitude. I immediately loosened up and got on target.

How we handle difficulty is a result of how we perceive it. How do we interpret setbacks? The way we view the feedback we receive from the world goes a long way toward determining how resilient, how strong and flexible our confidence in ourselves will be. Let me tell you my favorite story about this.

A little boy about eight years old is standing in front of his house with a baseball bat over his right shoulder and gently tossing a ball in his left hand. He is saying out loud, "I'm the greatest baseball player in the world. The world's greatest baseball player," over and over, louder and louder. After several repetitions, he seems to become a little self-conscious and, looking up and down the street, walks down the driveway into his backyard. There, in a large open space, he says again, "I'm the greatest baseball player in the *world*," while tossing the ball up and swinging at it. He misses.

He bends down, picks up the ball, and without any hesitation says much louder, "I *am* the greatest baseball player *in the world!*" He throws the ball up and takes a bigger swing. He misses again. He coughs, looks around, and picks the ball up, rubbing his thumb over the seam. After a few seconds, he thunders, "*The world's greatest baseball player,"* while tossing the ball up again and taking his biggest swing yet. It falls to the ground once more without any contact with the bat.

At this point our young athlete just stands and stares at the elusive ball. He sighs and says aloud, but in a lowered voice, "Three strikes." Then, in a moment, a big smile breaks out on his face: "Wow, what a pitcher!"

What an attitude! That's resilient confidence. If we could have even a measure of that resilience in our self-confidence, we could be almost anything we wanted to be.

Your life is what your thoughts make it. *Marcus Aurelius*

Notice what the little boy did. He reinterpreted a negative situation into a positive one. He found the silver lining. He asked for the moon and refused to take no for an answer. He displayed philosophical equanimity. He showed undefeated optimism. He proved that he had what it takes—the most important resource in the world: a positive attitude of great resilience, a confidence that would not fold.

But of course it was Mark Twain who once said: "If at first you don't succeed, try, try again. And then give up. There's no sense being a damn fool about it." Very funny. And partially right. If you try something new, do it a certain way, and find that it doesn't work, don't give up; try it again. Maybe circumstances just weren't right the first time. Maybe you just needed some practice. But if you fail again, or yet once more, maybe you should rethink your strategy. Give up the way you tried it. Try a different way. Let your failures teach you and lead you to a new plan of action or a new technique. Give up a method that doesn't work. But don't give up the ghost.

Don't lose your spirit. Don't give up your goals and your confidence that you can attain those goals. Go at it in a different way.

When faced with setbacks, too many people too quickly change their minds, not their methods. Our hold on our goals should not be so tentative and fragile that a little trouble derails us altogether. We should be optimistic realists, or realistic optimists. I like to say that I'm usually a short-term pessimist and a long-term optimist. I'm prepared for any crazy thing to happen in the short term, but in the long run I'm absolutely confident that everything will work out well.

When I was growing up my mother used to comfort me in times of difficulty and apparent failure by saying, "Whenever you're disappointed, tell yourself there's something bigger and better for you ahead." Keep the faith. Forge ahead. Think long term. My mother's long-term optimism has proved itself again and again as I have applied it in my own life. When our dreams seem to be going down the drain, we need to transcend the present moment and bet on the future. One reason we have so many pessimists in the world nowadays is that we have so many short-term thinkers, people who can't see beyond their immediate situation and any difficulties it may contain.

> Endure and persist; this pain will turn to your good by and by.   *Ovid*

My first book was turned down by thirty-six publishing companies. I was a senior in college, and I was determined to keep on trying. I circulated letters about it and sent out copies of it to any company that would agree to take a look at it. Finally one publisher liked it and sent me a contract. At the age of twenty-two I

97

was a real author, a published-author-to-be. I had kept the faith and it paid off. It paid off again and again as people read the book and wrote me to say that they had benefited, as positive reviews appeared, and as royalty checks began to show up in my mailbox. I remember all the good those royalties did while I was in graduate school, but I can't remember the names of many of those companies that turned me down.

The history of achievement is the history of rejection, failure, persistence, and conquest. Human history is full of best-selling books, extraordinary works of art, important inventions, long-running Broadway plays, smash-hit movies, and chart-topping songs that were turned down, overlooked, rejected, and even ridiculed time and time again before they achieved the recognition and acceptance they deserved and were to have. Merely knowing this helps us to prepare to overcome the hurdles we'll inevitably face along the way to the success we seek. Too many people give up after numerous setbacks, only a step or two before they would have had success. And this is indeed a tragedy. We need resilient faith, strong flexible confidence, and a persistent will to succeed that is both realistic and optimistic at the same time.

> The greater the difficulty, the greater the glory.   *Cicero*

When we do hit a wall, we sometimes need to engage in a little confidence-restoring exercise. Take out a piece of paper and make a heading: THINGS I HAVE ACCOMPLISHED ALREADY. Then make a list of past personal achievements. Big things. Small things. Anything will help. Just seeing past successes in ink on paper can act as a powerful reminder and confidence builder. Remember those accomplishments. Savor their memory. Draw a breath of confidence from each one. Recall the effort they took. Remind yourself that nothing worth doing comes easy. Review why it is that your new goals are worth working for. Remind yourself that a strong confidence that you can attain those goals is a tremendously important condition of success, and that an attitude like confidence is finally up to you. You can take control of your attitudes. You can take control of your life. Stick with it. Don't give up.

2. Don't Worry About Worry

And don't feel guilty about going through little crises of confidence. Doubts are natural. We all have them. Second thoughts are normal. They are often testimony to your sanity. A healthy dose of caution is good for anyone. But, to borrow an image from the sixteenth-century theologian Martin Luther, who used it to characterize temptations, our worries are a bit like the birds of the air—you can't prevent them from flying around your head, but you can keep them from building a nest in your hair. If doubts or worries are standing in the way of your own best interests, you have to learn to acknowledge them, put them behind you, and move forward. Having attended to them, you put them aside and do what you need to do to move on.

Whenever we launch out into something new, we can expect to experience a bit of anxiety. Even some measure of fear can be quite normal. Fear of the unknown. Fear of what we've never experienced, or of what we're insufficiently accustomed to. Fear of the worst-case scenarios our imaginations can dream up, without much help.

When I was a teenager, I was more than a little nervous about elevators. I guess I had a degree of anxiety you might without undue exaggeration call "fear." It wasn't claustrophobia, the fear of enclosed spaces. It was just a version of acrophobia, the more general fear of heights, an anxiety connected to my occasional fear of flying, which we've already discussed. I don't want to sound too phobic, but I think I should be honest about some of the weaknesses I've had to overcome in my own life. Despite the fact that I've also already admitted to a fairly regular bout of anxiety on the first day of classes each semester here at Notre Dame, I am not a person full of fears and worries. I hasten to point this out, of course, fearing that you might think otherwise.

Is it because I'm a philosopher? I don't know, but some of the great thinkers of the past have admittedly been even greater worriers. The influential nineteenth-century German philosopher Arthur Schopenhauer, for example, was known to say that he was almost always worried about something. In fact, he said, whenever he caught himself not worrying about anything, that really worried him. He explained that the dangers we know about are bad enough, but those we haven't even yet thought of are surely much worse. The pinnacle of anxiety.

But back to my confessions. At the age of seventeen or eighteen, whenever I thought of elevators, I imagined a ridiculously thin elevator floor only tentatively supporting its passengers and undependably keeping them from plunging into the abyss of the empty shaft below. I grew up in a fairly small town. Before graduating from high school, I had ridden on elevators only a few times, and then only to the second or third floor of a department store. But even on such short vertical excursions, I remember concentrating on making myself as light as possible, as if a little mental levitation would surely decrease the stress on that joke of a floor, which in my imagination might as well have been a trap door. Mid-trip, however, I would find myself remembering the few skinny cables that held the whole thing up and I would vow to live a ground-level existence in the future.

The first day of my freshman year at the University of North

Carolina, I discovered that my new room was on an upper floor of a high-rise dormitory. Standing in the dorm lobby with my room assignment clutched tight in my sweaty hands, I nervously stared at the elevators I would have to take every day, many times a day. I was a bundle of anxiety. I imagined free-fall in the long, dark elevator shaft. Just then I was roused from my daydream by a loud *ding!* and the elevator door opened. One guy stood alone in the middle of the elevator, wearing an orange jumpsuit and, I swear, a parachute. A sight to behold. I said to myself, "Now, there's a guy who doesn't trust elevators." I laughed out loud, and I got on board. I've ridden elevators ever since free of fear in even some of the tallest buildings in the country. The silliness of what I saw, or of what I interpreted myself as seeing, pointed out to me vividly the silliness of my fear. And that's all it took to free me from its hold.

Sometimes humor is the best antidote to fear, or worry, or doubt. Sometimes it's the thought that, however bad off you think you are, there's someone out there in even worse shape. And sometimes the only way to get rid of your fear is just to get on board. Again, The Action Approach to Attitude. Go for the ride. Start doing what you need to do, accustoming yourself to whatever might be unfamiliar in the path you need to take, and the fears you have will most likely disappear. But first and foremost, be re-assured that you are not the only person struggling with doubt, anxiety, or fear. Many other people have managed to fight through these negatives and find the confidence they needed. You can too.

Of course, in all my comments about doubt and confidence, I am assuming that you are pursuing goals you really believe in, goals you feel are right for you and that are worth your seeking to attain. Sometimes what appears to be a crisis of confidence can really be the mask of a crisis of conscience. Strong and persistent doubt about your abilities or chances for success can be a way for your subconscious moral conscience to slow you down. Is this goal right

101

for anyone to pursue? Is it right for you? Does it connect up with values you truly embrace? Is it consistent with the self-knowledge you've already attained, the knowledge you have about who you most deeply are? If your most honest answers to these questions are in the negative, then what feels like nothing more than a battle with doubt or fear is actually something else altogether. You don't really have a crisis of confidence after all. You have a crisis of conscience. You need different goals, or you need better connections between the values you embrace and the goal you face. Think through your situation carefully and make sure you are launching yourself out into a journey you can believe in. It is only when you have goals you believe in, backed up with values you embrace, that you can draw on your deepest resources of willpower to defeat all self-doubts that stand in your way and march forward with all the precursive faith you need. In the end, your confidence in yourself cannot be separated completely from how your conscience judges your goals. When the conscience is satisfied, the confidence will come. If you take action. If you take control.

THE COMMUNICATION OF CONFIDENCE

It's important that you communicate confidence to yourself through positive self-talk. Frequently. On a regular basis. And also by launching out and acting the way confidence would act. By so doing, you strengthen and deepen both your confidence and its grip on your life.

It's also important that you communicate your confidence to other people in the right way. There are many books available on how to do this. How to speak with confidence. How to dress for success. How to project poise and control through body language. It is crucial that a proper form of confidence be communicated to the people around you. But a few words of caution are needed about when and how this is done, with a little bit of background.

Philosophers have always said "Know thyself." We should have also been saying "Value thyself." One of the most elusive treasures in the modern world is a proper self-esteem. The human race seems to divide into three categories: (1) people with far too high a view of themselves, (2) people with far too low a view of themselves, and (3) those who vacillate between the two. It is the hardest thing in the world to attain and hold onto an accurate and consistently appropriate self-image. When it comes to self-esteem, we are prone to err. That being the case, it makes the most sense to do everything you can to err moderately on the high side. Franklin Roosevelt once said, "Never underestimate a man who overestimates himself," and even though this piece of advice can be given a cynical reading, I believe it hits the mark in a completely positive way. Self-esteem is the fuel that powers the engine of accomplishment. The more we have, the farther we can go. So if you have to err, err in overestimating yourself. But to the extent that you do, it's sometimes best to keep it to yourself.

No one likes a braggart. No one is attracted to arrogance. No one admires presumptuousness. It's important to tell yourself repeatedly that you can achieve high goals, that you are worthy, that you are a success, if even in just preparing yourself for other success, that you're every bit as good, as capable, as worthy, and as deserving as the other person who is your competitor, or perceived superior. But such positive self-talk should be your own private cheerleading, not shared with other people, except for perhaps a spouse or a best friend who understands what you are doing in making such affirmations.

Of course, we often engage in joint projects with other people. Group goals require group efforts, and every team benefits from the confident participation of everyone involved. To build up team confidence, interpersonal cheerleading is necessary, within the team. The group equivalent of positive self-talk is required. But this then becomes a new level of privacy. You will say positive things within the team, the office, or the company, that are not necessarily appropriate for a general public audience.

We can call this *The Privacy Principle of Positive Self-Talk.* Praising yourself to yourself can build confidence. Praising yourself to others can breed resentment. For members of a team to praise the team to each other, or to praise each other to each other, can build confidence. For the team to praise itself to others outside the team can breed resentment.

There is, however, one interesting twist to a proper application of The Privacy Principle. Sometimes praise builds the confidence of another person most effectively when a third party is brought in carefully, and direct praise is supplemented with indirect compliments. What I mean is this. Typically, if you want to build Mary's confidence, you praise her directly on her abilities, or on her accomplishments, and you indicate to her your belief in her. Sometimes it is of great extra effect to praise Mary's abilities or accomplishments to another person, within her hearing, and to express to that third party your belief in Mary and pleasure in working with her. Also, on the team level, it can be very effective for team morale if a team leader, a coach or executive, praises the team to some other group or individual outside the team, and the team knows about it. This is one reason why a corporation's advertising that praises its people can be as effective inside the company as it is with the general public. But whenever any third party is brought into the confidence-building enterprise in this way, care must be exercised so that there is no problematic perception of braggadocio on anyone's part that could end up somehow generating consequences detrimental to the group's progress.

Establishing the strong personal confidence you need is like hammering a long nail. One hit won't do it. To sink it and seat it well you have to hit it again and again. Your repetitively positive self-talk is like this. To cause the confidence you need to sink in, you need to hammer it in again and again. But to share these regular self-affirmations with other people would be a serious mistake. Confidence is properly communicated to them in a completely different way.

We appropriately communicate our own self-confidence to other people in four ways: (1) how we look, (2) how we act, (3) what we say, and (4) what we do.

Good posture, a relaxed demeanor, and a pleasant expression communicate confidence. Appropriate clothing that expresses your own individuality can send the same message. A firm hand-shake communicates confidence. Eye contact while speaking does the same. When you know the answers, give the answers clearly and crisply, with an absolute minimization of colloquial vocal delay and hesitancy signals such as "um," "well, uh . . . ," and "well, let me see . . ." as if you're desperately searching the contents of a largely empty mind for filler. A moment to compose your thoughts can be a moment of reflective silence. There is no law against silence. A pregnant silence beats an empty noise any day. You may even cultivate honest, intelligent time-buying phrases such as: "I've never thought about it just like that, but it seems to me that . . ." Such prologues give you extra time to organize your thoughts. But if you know, say. If you don't know, say so. Don't be afraid to admit that you need a little time to check out a fact, to mull over a decision, or to consider a situation from a new vantage point. Bluffing in the dark is rarely a very advisable strategy. A candid straightforward admission of a temporary lack of sufficient information expressed in the right tone, without embarrassment, can powerfully convey to others a solid overall self-confidence. You are not rattled. You are not shaken. You're on solid ground.

105

If you want others to believe in you, you have to believe in yourself, and you have to communicate that attitude to them in the proper ways. Other people don't need elaborate, explicit assurances of your own self-confidence. Anything more than "Yes, I can do that" will sometimes raise questions and worries, not the other person's confidence level.

Prepare for meetings. Prepare for important conversations. Write out brief notes for phone calls that can make a difference. Nothing builds your own confidence like the hard work of good preparation. And nothing communicates confidence like the content of what you can say when you are well prepared. When your thoughts are well organized.

Finally, you communicate confidence to other people by what you do. Do you act as confidence acts? Do you take the measured risk? Do you move forward? Or do you procrastinate, hedge your bets, and bury your head in the sand? Everything you do, or fail to do, that is available to public view will communicate to the people around you. What we do with our time when a decision needs to be made, and when an opportunity presents itself, sends signals to the other people around us. What we do had better be consistent with what we say and how we otherwise present ourselves if we want others to perceive us as confident and, in turn, to believe in us themselves.

In order to achieve anything of value in this world we need at some point to have other people believe in us. They will believe as we achieve and they see our accomplishments. But it can happen even sooner. They will believe as we believe if we have a strong enough confidence in ourselves and communicate that confidence to them in just the right ways. It's human nature. And that's a very good thing.

We need a strong confidence that we can attain our goals. This is the bottom line. Condition two for true success.

3

A Concentration on
What It Takes

Condition Three: We need a focused concentration on what it takes to reach our goal.

There are success slogans around that seem to indicate that only one or two conditions are necessary for attaining success. One well-known slogan shouts out "Name it and claim it!" as if you only have to know what you want in life in order to get it. It seems to imply that our first condition of success, a clear conception of what we want, is alone sufficient for reaching our goals. Another snappy aphorism acknowledges the importance of our second condition, the need for a strong confidence that we can attain our goals. It proclaims: "Believe it and achieve it!" This is just a shortened version of a very famous slogan coined decades ago by the popular writer Napoleon Hill, a statement that in its entirety recognizes both of our first two conditions, but also can seem to imply that nothing else is needed for success. Hill announced: "Whatever the mind of man can conceive and believe, it can achieve." Among people pursuing goals with potential financial payoffs, Hill's threefold slogan has generated a further fourfold staccato mantra for making it: "Conceive, believe, achieve, and *receive!*"

I love these little rhymes. These catchy slogans. They can be fun, but they can also be dangerous. The other members of my family have a particular favorite they live by: "Spy it and buy it!" *The Call of the Mall.* So I'm glad there are all those other compensating success slogans. I need something to help me pay the bills.

But things are not quite as simple as they appear in all these little slogans and rhymes of success. I've known dreamers who lived within the confines of condition one and never got out to accomplish anything in the real world. Their imaginations were in gear. Their visions were vivid. But they never took the first step from their dreams toward their goals. And I've known visionaries who seemed to be people of great confidence, with no doubts whatsoever about the appropriateness of their goals, or about the inevitability of their eventually attaining those goals, who nonetheless never amounted to much and never came near to where they wanted to be. In a great many cases, they were people who failed to understand the third condition of success, or at least failed to act in accordance with it. And it is a condition whose importance cannot be overemphasized.

We need a focused concentration on what it takes to reach our goal. How do we get from here to there? How do we get from where we are to where we want to be? A lot of people do seem to think that in this life you can just "name it and claim it," that you can simply jump from *A* straight to *Z*. But that's not the way it works in our world. Anyone who's lived long enough and who has reflected sufficiently on their experience really knows this. To get from *A* to *Z*, you have to go first to *B* and then to *C*, and then to *D*, perhaps jumping ahead a little, then plodding again, then leaping once more, walking, running, tripping, falling, picking yourself up, setting off again, and finally, with enough persistence, arriving at your destination of Z.

The quest for success is a journey, sometimes difficult, sometimes easy, occasionally brief, but often long, a journey of effort, frustration, and joy. At its best, it is a journey of the heart, mind, and body. It's an adventure of challenge and triumph. Most people who fail in life just fail to prepare themselves for the journey. They lack any focused concentration on what it will take to reach their goals. Or, as another catchy aphorism has it, they don't plan to fail, they just fail to plan.

> If there is any merit or importance attaching to a man's career, if he lays himself out carefully for some special work, it is all the more necessary and advisable for him to turn his attention now and then to its *plan*, that is to say, the miniature sketch of its general outlines. . . . If he maps out important work for himself on great lines, a glance at this miniature plan of his life will, more than anything else, stimulate, rouse, and enable him, urge him on to action, and keep him from false paths.
>
> *Arthur Schopenhauer*

Planning. Focusing on how to get from here to there. Concentrating on what it takes to reach the goal. For some people this seems to come naturally, like breathing. Others have to learn how. If you can indulge me one more piece of contemporary sloganeering, another adaptation of that ancient rhetorical device of linguistic patterning known as *chiasmus* (pronounced "kye-*as*-mus"; from the Greek for X, indicating a crossing pattern of words, as in "Ask not what your country can do for you; ask what you can do

109

for your country"): If you want to enjoy success in any endeavor, you have to *plan your work and then work your plan.*

Plan your work and then work your plan. Think it through in advance. Strategize. Organize. Take care to engage in a preliminary, advance concentration of thought. And then embody your plans in your actions. Step by step. Move by move. Maintain an ongoing concentration in action. The more difficult, challenging, complex, or elusive a goal is, the more important this condition is.

A MASTER OF CONCENTRATION

I've known people who were masters at concentrating on what it would take to reach their goals. People who intuitively knew how to plan their work and then work their plan, bit by bit, piece by piece, until every piece of the pattern fit into place. Let me give you just one example from my personal experience. But it's a fairly spectacular example.

When I was in junior high school, I was a pretty good rock-and-roll guitar player. I had a friend named Don who also considered himself a musician. His instrument was the tambourine, and by my recollections, he wasn't very good at it. He also thought of himself as a singer. He made Bob Dylan sound like Frank Sinatra. When he was in the sixth grade, his church announced the formation of a new choir for which no singing experience was required. He attended the first rehearsal with great enthusiasm, but afterwards the choir director took him aside and explained as nicely as possible that some minimal shred of talent was necessary, and that he should try to find another way of serving the Lord. His father used to ask, "Don, can you sing 'By the Window'? If you can, I'll help you out." An old southern joke. He couldn't carry a tune in a bucket. Or hit a note with a shotgun. But he persisted in thinking of himself as a musician-singer-songwriter and envisioned an exciting rosy future in the entertainment world. So far as I could tell, he was a young man devoid of any real musical prospects whatsoever. But he was my friend.

Many days after school Don and I walked home to my house for a little time of music making. I would play my guitar and he would shake his tambourine and "sing." He asked me a number of times if I wanted to start a band. I didn't. But he was my friend. So I'd say, "Let's just play some today and talk about a band later." He was determined. The next day, same question. Same response. Over and over. Finally, without me, Don managed to put together a band of equally talented people. They were called The Back Porch Majority. Cacophony with attitude. But no future.

Years passed. Don still nurtured the dream. We drifted apart and lost touch during high school, when I was playing lead guitar in some regionally successful rock and soul bands. I went to the University of North Carolina, Chapel Hill, and Don went to Duke in our home town. After two years he dropped out to pursue his dream. He knew that Durham, North Carolina, was not the place for becoming a great success in the music business. For that he would have to go to New York, Los Angeles, or Nashville. New York and Los Angeles were too far away, so he decided to move to Nashville. Focusing every step on what it would take to reach his goals, he got himself a bus ticket and set off for Music City, USA, the Country Capital of the Cosmos.

Once there, Don had to find a cheap place to stay. He had to make the most of limited resources as he worked toward his dream. He bought a used car, and for months he slept in it. The original motor hotel. He needed a job at night so that during daytime business hours he could visit the record companies and music publishing houses there in Nashville to show them his stuff. So he took on a job working the night shift at the Vanderbilt computer center. During this time he came to realize that he probably wouldn't be able to ride the tambourine to fame and fortune in the music world, so he decided he'd better learn how to play the guitar. And he realized that some vocal work might in addition be in order. He was a man concentrating on what it would take to get where he wanted to go. He was planning his work and then working his plan. As many months passed, he kept at it, hanging around the clubs where he could meet the working musicians, writing songs, practicing, knocking on doors, and taking his lumps.

> Diligence is the mother of good fortune.
>
> *Miguel de Cervantes*

Meanwhile, I graduated from Carolina and went to graduate school at Yale. One day I got a phone call up in New Haven from a friend in Durham who also knew Don. He said, "Tom, listen to this." He held the phone to his stereo speaker. I heard a few seconds of a very good song. Good singer. Good music. My friend came back on the line and said, "That's Don. Capital Records. It's on the country charts. Can you believe it?"

I couldn't believe it. A song Don had written and recorded. Capital Records. On the radio. On the charts. My friend Don had made it. He was a success.

The next time I was in Durham on vacation I asked around about Don. I'd hoped to be able to see him at some point and congratulate him on his surprising, gratifying, against-all-odds success. He had gambled big and won. A friend told me Don was still in Nashville and, by the way, had I heard about the recording of one of his songs by Kenny Rogers? I asked what the song was called. My friend said "The Gambler."

Country Music History. "The Gambler." It was the title song for one of the best-selling country music albums ever. It was the basis for three of the most-watched made-for-TV movies in history—*The Gambler*, Parts One, Two, and Three, starring Kenny Rogers and Linda Evans. My old friend Don Schlitz has since that time had one huge hit after another, at least *fifty* top-five chart busters, has won more awards than I can count, and has been financially rewarded far beyond his wildest teenage dreams. As a result of his focused concentration on every step it took to reach his goal. A dreamer. A believer. A master of focus. A master of success.

I have just one question that, as a philosophical inquirer, I want to ask my old friend Don the next time I see him: Does he want to start a band?

A man who can plan his work and work his plan to this level is a model of what it takes. We need examples like his to help guide us into a deepened appreciation of the importance of focus and concentrated effort for any challenging form of success. Good things rarely just happen. We make our own breaks. We bring them about by planning and acting in the right way at the right time. Sometimes we just need to forget the odds and follow our hearts full speed ahead. Good fortune comes to those who prepare for it and who are moving in its direction. In this chapter, I want to lay out a simple but powerfully structured proposal for attaining the sort of focused concentration that we need to move toward and attain our goals. And, if I can get away with employing another much-used type of rhetorical device here, I've developed a little acronym that I think will help.

HOW TO PLAN FOR SUCCESS

If you want success in anything, you need to PLAN:

*P*repare for your journey.
*L*aunch out in action.
*A*djust as you go.
*N*etwork with those who know.

By looking at each component of a master PLAN, we'll be able to see how a focused concentration on what it takes contributes to success.

Prepare for Your Journey

Any success worth pursuing is a journey, a process, an adventure. And any journey undertaken intelligently requires preparation. It's not a good idea to enter a marathon without preparing for it. The most satisfying successes in marathon races are built by weeks or months, sometimes even years, of preparation. Finding the right shoes, learning to stretch, eating right, running a few miles a day at first and then building up distance over time. Reading some books of advice, talking to seasoned marathoners, going over the course in advance. These and other activities prepare a person for the grueling physical and psychological challenges of running the big race. They make it much more likely that the first-time marathoner will experience the satisfying success of finishing the course. Preparation lays the groundwork for success.

Is it possible to succeed at something without preparation? I think the simple truth is: no. It is possible to attain some success at some activities without conscious, intentional preparation. It's also possible to win the lottery with your first ticket purchase. But it's

114

not very likely. Any success requires some preparation. Whenever anyone attains any real success at any activity, there was something in his or her background that prepared the way for that success. There is never any success without preparation. Likely success requires thoughtful, conscious, intentional preparation. Many kinds of success also seem to depend on luck. But as a seventeenth-century manual of success I'll draw on often in this chapter, *The Art of Worldly Wisdom*, by Baltasar Gracián, put it: "Readiness is the mother of luck." The most consistently lucky people happen to be those who are the best prepared.

> A wise man will make more opportunities than he finds.
>
> *Francis Bacon*

Another music-business story. This time, right out of the newspapers. Truth is sometimes stranger than fiction. A musician named Fish was crossing the street in New York City when he was suddenly hit and knocked to the pavement by a limousine. The lead singer of The Who, Roger Daltrey, jumped out of the limo, ran over to the crumpled-up pedestrian, helped him off the street, and asked if he was OK. The stunned Fish was all right, but was worried about a demo tape he had in his pocket. Daltrey invited him into the limo to listen to the tape, just to make him feel better, and was amazed by what he heard. The music was, in Daltrey's words, "incredible, absolutely incredible." As a result of that encounter, Fish and his band, The Raw Poets, got a record deal, with Daltrey singing on a few tracks. Asked at a later time if he had any advice on success for other young hopeful musicians, Fish replied, "Get hit by a limo with a famous star in it."

What luck! But without the right talent and preparation on the part of this luckily unlucky pedestrian, this strange situation could not have presented quite the same opportunity it ended up providing for his future in music. Fish was ready for the big time, and he was ready to take advantage of the breaks that came his way. Just another case of the power of preparation. As Friedrich Dürrenmatt wrote in his book *The Physicists:* "The more human beings proceed by plan, the more effectively they may be hit by accident," which, in the case of Fish, uses a particularly appropriate metaphor to convey this very important truth.

I have seen the power of preparation in my own life. When I was in college I decided that I wanted to become a thinker and a doer, a philosopher who could make a difference in this world. I took courses and read books that would prepare me for this goal. I entered the best graduate program I could find for pursuing my goals. I talked to wise people. I worked hard in two departments at Yale to become only the second person ever to earn a Ph.D. jointly in Religious Studies and Philosophy, so I would make sure I had all the Ultimate Questions covered. I prepared for years to teach and to write, to discover and learn and lecture.

I took my first full-time job at the University of Notre Dame because it was clear to me that they were committed to becoming the best place in the world for my scholarly specialty. I knew that to be able to have the kind of impact for good I wanted to have in the world, I had to be at such a place.

As soon as I arrived on campus, I began to write and publish numerous scholarly essays and books, seeking to pioneer new work in my field. Like any thinker and writer, I spent countless hours in the solitary confines of my study, hammering out the work that I felt was distinctively mine to do. But to have the broad impact I deeply wanted to have, I realized I couldn't do it alone. So I began to orchestrate joint ventures along with my own independent work: an international research conference; two book projects bringing together newly commissioned essays from some of the most prominent, established world-class practitioners in my field; national seminars; and the founding of a new series of books established to encourage the production of original, single-author volumes from scholars around the globe on topics whose exploration I wanted to encourage. I wrote letters, went to meetings, and made phone calls almost every day to establish new networks of communication among active scholars across the country. With each step in the process, I sought to do good. And with each step in the process, I prepared myself for the opportunity to do even more good.

A specific example. For some time I had been aware of the need for a certain kind of book to be published. So I set myself a goal. One of the most prestigious publishers in the world, Oxford University Press in England, had a famous series of books called *Oxford Readings in Philosophy.* Each was an anthology, a collection of some of the best previously published work in a certain field, or on a focal topic, selected and edited by an established, recognized, leading scholar in the field. I decided I wanted to edit a book for that series on a central topic whose further scholarly exploration I wanted to promote. I wanted to put together a book on the concept of God. But I was much, much younger than most of the other editors for that series at Oxford. Yet all my hard work in my first few years of being a philosopher at Notre Dame had put me in a position to do a good job at such a task, as well as to be able to make a credible claim that I could do it. I was a very active member of the best philosophy department in the world, where there was a great deal of new and exciting work being done on the topic of my interest. But I realized that more preparation was needed before I approached Oxford with my idea.

I wrote up a proposal for the book I envisioned, explaining the need for it and describing what it would be like. And I came up with a plan. I sent copies of this proposal to most of the established, well-known philosophers around the country who taught on what would be the specific topic of the book and asked them, if they agreed with me on the need for such a text and on the appropriateness of my editing it, to write me a letter of support saying so. These were the very same people I had invited to the large research conference I had organized, the scholars whose own contributions of exciting new essays I had solicited for previous books, and the people I was in contact with on a regular basis. They knew me and my work, and were prepared to be favorably disposed to this new idea.

Letters of strong support came streaming in through the mail each day. When I finally sent a letter of inquiry to Oxford, offering them my project if they were interested, I included copies of all the letters, from all those prominent college and university teachers who would establish the potential classroom market for the book. I was fighting long odds with this publisher, and knew I had to prepare the strongest case I could. When the editor in charge of all philosophy publishing at Oxford wrote me back, she explained that with the proposal I had written, and with the unprecedented stack of letters of support I had included, I gave her no choice—she *had* to accept the project for publication, and she did so with great enthusiasm. Success. From proper preparation.

Nothing succeeds like excess.   *Oscar Wilde*

I have elaborated this story because in a very simple way it shows a lot about the role of preparation in success. Consider how all the pieces of the puzzle fit together. First I chose what I thought of as a lofty goal and a difficult challenge, the publication of a certain kind of book with a famous and highly regarded company. For my age and relatively junior status in my profession, it was a stretch, but it was also a goal for which my education, interests, and previous accomplishments had in many ways already prepared me. But I knew I had to prepare in addition a specific plan of attack, or it would be unlikely that I would be successful with that publisher at that time. So I backed up and thought through some strategy. A publisher wants to sell books. If I could convince them that there would be a big market for my book, they would surely be interested. But I couldn't just *tell* them that there was a need for this sort of book. Why should they listen to me and take my word for it? And in addition, even supposing that I could convince them that a book on a particular topic should be included in their well-known series, it was a separate task to persuade them that I was the right person to do it.

By brainstorming over what it would take to make this all happen, I hit upon the idea of first approaching all the great teachers who would use such a book. If I could sell them, they could collectively help me sell the publisher. So I set myself the preliminary goal of selling them on my idea. For this I needed a great written proposal describing my book idea. One more goal, and the most immediate yet. I set to work on writing the proposal. In a very short time I had it finished. Success Number One. I sent it out with personal cover letters. The responses poured in. Success Number Two. I put the package of proposal and support letters in the mail to Oxford. And, in a matter of weeks, I had the response I wanted. Ultimate Success. Preparation paved the way. Preparation made the difference: my general life and work preparation, and then my specific preparation through the setting and reaching of intermediate goals. It took a lot of work, but as an old Danish proverb tells us: "He who would leap high must take a long run." I was able to focus my concentrated efforts on what it would take to

119

reach my final goal. And, with the results of those efforts, I hit my target. Bull's-eye. And then, of course, the publication of the book itself became one more contribution to my more ultimate personal goal of being the kind of philosopher who can make a difference for good in this world.

> When schemes are laid in advance, it is surprising how often the circumstances fit in with them.
>
> *Sir William Osler*

Everything we do can be, in one way or another, preparation for what we can contribute in this life. The good we do, and even the mistakes we make, can prepare us for greater good. But I cannot stress too much the importance of deliberate, thoughtful, specific, creative preparation for any success we hope to attain.

Every great football coach at the University of Notre Dame has stressed the importance of preparation for each game. A good politician prepares elaborately for his election campaign. A careful lawyer meticulously prepares for trial. A mountain climber prepares for her challenge. A teacher prepares for his class. We need to come to a greater appreciation of the importance of preparation for the larger projects in our lives.

Prepare to make the most of who you are! Prepare to become the best that you can be! Prepare to do what you are uniquely capable of doing, and then prepare to enjoy the tremendously satisfying feeling of real success in your life that will result.

Preparing for your journey toward the realization of any goal, just like your initial process of goal setting, can be a tremendous exercise in self-knowledge. It requires some solitude. It benefits from silence, and concentration. Find a place to sit quietly and think. Or find a place to walk alone and reflect. And then write down your thoughts. What is your heart's desire? What do you want to see happen? How do you imagine your future? What will it take to make that dream a reality? What will get you halfway there? Set some preliminary goals, some stepping-stones along the path. Working toward them and achieving them will prepare you for your bigger goals. And even these preliminary goals may have to be approached in steps. Analyze what it will take. Focus. Concentrate. And consult, if necessary, with other people you trust.

Do not allow yourself to be distracted from these steps of preparation. What is there in your life up until now that you can build on to move toward those preliminary goals? What has to be changed? Where does it seem that you have to start from scratch? There will always be something good in your past that you can build on. There is always something in the immediate future you can do to bring your more remote goals just a little closer to realization. What is the next step, and how can you best prepare to take it?

When we go beyond dreaming into the actual work of preparing for our journey, many of us face a problem. We suddenly become much more aware of our limitations than of our strengths. "If I were just more attractive." "If I just had a better education." "If I were just smarter." "If only I had been born into more resources." "If I just lived in a different part of the country." "If I just knew the right people." "If I didn't have so many responsibilities right now, so many claims on my time." There are endless "ifs" and "if onlys." These are the limits that bind us. The limits that hold us down. *If* we let them!

We all have limits. But there is no living, breathing, thinking, acting human being without strengths as well, strengths that can be built on in preparation for success. Henry Kissinger once said that the American presidents he has known have all been people who had learned not to dwell on their limitations but to find their strengths and draw on them in their quest for success. Some limitations are only apparent. Some are only temporary. A little effort and persistence will push them back. But some of our limits are just part of what defines us as the distinctive individuals we are. We all do have limits, and so that is nothing to be embarrassed about. But most people overestimate their limits and underestimate their strengths. There is nothing to be gained by this common distortion, and much to be lost. We all must learn to shift our focus. Prepared to deal with our limits, we must prepare to deal from our strengths as we chart a path to the success we need.

Whatever your goals are, PLAN! Prepare for the journey: analyze, visualize, prioritize, and strategize. Study the area of your aspirations. Take advantage of the expertise of others. Chart your course with the help of books, magazines, newspapers, and personal interviews with anyone who might be familiar with what it takes to realize goals such as yours. What's been done before? Has it worked? What's being done now? Is it promising? What's never been tried before? Why not? Where can you get your first foothold for real progress to take yourself to the next level?

Many people think that the key to success is to work hard. And that is important. Very important. But it's more important to work smart. The ancient Greek mathematician Archimedes invented the lever and the pulley. Overcome with a sense of the importance of the principles of leverage, he was known to go about saying, "Give me a place to stand, and I will move the earth." The ruler Hiero one day challenged the boastful thinker to put up or shut up. The sailors of Syracuse needed help to beach a large ship in their fleet. What could the great Archimedes do about that? Well, we are told that by ingeniously devising and arranging a series of pulleys and cogs, the mathematician was able by his own otherwise unaided strength to lift the great vessel out of the water and place it onto dry land. For Archimedes, working smart was every bit as important as working hard. As the great philosopher Descartes once said, "It is not enough to have a good mind. The main thing is to use it well."

"It just shows what can be done by taking a little trouble," said Eeyore. "Do you see, Pooh? Do you see, Piglet? Brains first and then Hard Work."

From Winnie-the-Pooh

Intelligent preparation can make hard work much easier. In our preparations for any new task we need to figure out what the cogs and pulleys are that can give us the leverage we need. And where is our place to stand? We need to figure out how to work smart toward our goals. How to make the most of what we have, what we are, and what we know. Knowledge itself is leverage. And with the right knowledge of what we need, even the smallest of subsequent preparations can lead to great results.

I have a friend who is a very creative woman. At fiftysomething, she has done many things successfully. She's been an artist in several media, an organizer, a counselor, a university administrator. Now she's a writer. And a very good one. Every day she would walk several blocks from her house onto the university campus to gain access to a personal computer to do her writing. One evening it occurred to her that she would be getting a lot more done if she made the investment in herself to buy her own computer, so that she could compose at home whenever the inspiration struck. She made the financial commitment and went out and bought what she needed, and that has allowed her to take her writing to the next level. By making the investment, she proved to herself that she took herself seriously as an author. And she made the process of writing much more convenient. A small thing in some ways, but an important step along the way.

Little things mean a lot. The least card in a winning hand is more important than the greatest in a losing hand. Big dreams can be daunting when we face the light of day and actually prepare to work toward making them a reality. We gain confidence and we gain control when we realize that what we first need to focus on are the little things necessary to get moving in the right direction.

Allow me to quote a Zen sage, Jiantang, who once reported: "An ancient worthy said, 'Those who plan for what is ahead first check out what is near at hand. Those who strive for the great must be careful about the small.'" And without becoming overly Zenful here, I should follow up with the words of Lingyuan, who said: "When you cut and polish a stone, as you grind and rub you do not see it decreasing, yet with time it will be worn away. When you plant a tree and take care of it, you do not see it increase, but in time it gets big."

Prepare for your success in little ways and you'll eventually see results in big ways. It's almost magical.

Launch Out in Action

Preparation is so important. Be prepared, but then: TAKE AC-TION! Beware of the threat of *Analysis Paralysis,* otherwise known as Preparation Hesitation. It's possible to spend so much time preparing for a trip, you'll never get to take it. It's important to be able to think through the best means for attaining the goals you desire. It's crucial to be able to analyze your situation, your strengths, the challenges you'll need to meet, the obstacles you'll face, the full range of requirements for realizing your dreams.

Careful analysis will break big goals down into smaller, more manageable components that can then be added back up to great success. But you've fallen into analysis paralysis when you're afraid to move until you've thought things through again, and yet again in case, maybe, just maybe, you've missed something important. Neither analysis nor preparation is an end in itself. It is a means toward the end of attaining your goals. It cannot be allowed to take on a life of its own that eclipses any real movement toward those goals. Calisthenics, running, weight training, and stretching are important to football players and basketball players. But if that's all they ever did, they would have ceased to play their sport. Likewise, all strategy and no action makes for a pretty dry exercise.

He who desires but acts not, breeds pestilence.

William Blake

Action! Action! Action!

Demosthenes (when asked the three most fundamental elements of his art)

There are two kinds of people in this world: those who watch things happen and those who make things happen. The world has more than enough spectators. We need more actors, more participants, more catalysts, performers, agents of change, movers and shakers, doers, givers, contributors, and initiators.

According to *The Art of Worldly Wisdom*, "the wise do sooner what fools do later." Overpreparation is almost as bad as underpreparation. Establish readiness, then seize the day! The moths of time eat away the fabric of our lives unless we take action and seek to make things happen. Don't wait for opportunity to knock on your door. Get out, take action, and knock on doors yourself. That's how opportunity is to be found. If you'll forgive me one more little sloganistic rhyme: Don't hesitate, initiate!

Bill Moyers, as a college student at North Texas State University, had the chutzpah to write Lyndon Johnson a letter and offer to help him in an election campaign. The young Mr. Moyers wanted to help get out the vote in Texas. That act of initiative propelled him into public life. In a surprisingly short time he was press secretary for the President of the United States, and then a network news commentator, and then perhaps the biggest force ever to hit public broadcasting in this country. For years Bill Moyers has been in a position to accomplish immense good. And it all began with a letter from the blue. It all started with initiative. Action.

I've experienced this often in my own life. My parents raised me to "have initiative" and to take the initiative when things need to change, when things need to happen. When you see something wrong, I was told, say so. When you can fix what's wrong, then fix it and move on. When you see an opportunity, take it. When you have an idea, speak up. Then try it out. The squeaky wheel gets the oil. Nothing ventured, nothing gained. If you don't ask, you don't get. Take a chance, make something happen. If not now, then when? If not you, then who?

We have a limited amount of time in this world to do the good we are here to do. It makes no sense just to float along. To wander. To procrastinate. It makes no sense not to take action. We need to make good use of the time we have.

By-and-by never comes. *Saint Augustine*

Tear thyself from delay! *Horace*

Many of the most important relationships in my life have developed because I took some initiative that took courage, however small a measure. I didn't just go with the flow, I took a risk. I launched out in action with a phone call, or a letter, or a one-on-one conversation. And it hasn't usually been very easy. But it's often been very worthwhile.

Don't ever let yourself off the hook with the easily excusing query "Who am I to do this?" If you have some preparation in your life for making a contribution, make it. Maybe somebody else could do better, but maybe they won't even try until they see you giving it a shot. And maybe then they'll sign on to help *you*. And maybe, as you take the initiative and act, you will enhance your own preparation and ability to contribute even more so that, in the end, you will have made yourself the right person for the job.

Once you plan your work, you do need to launch out and work your plan. Again, *The Art of Worldly Wisdom* tells us that "the mediocre people who apply themselves go further than the superior people who don't," and then adds: "Work makes worth." No work was ever accomplished without effort. So take the initiative! Make the effort! Get to work! It's worth it.

Adjust As You Go

Some preparation must precede intelligent action. But a lot of planning, preparing, and strategizing toward reaching your goals can only be done once you're under way. Like the "smart bomb" or heat-seeking missile that's able to adjust its course as it zeroes in on its target, we all need the flexibility of mind to be able to alter our plans and adjust our focus as we move in the direction of realizing our goals.

It is sometimes said that a bad plan is better than no plan at all. But that's true only if the plan we have gets us moving and we are able to adjust as we go to change the plan, refine it, and make it better. If we are out in the world doing things, right or wrong, the world will be giving us all sorts of feedback. This is often new information not available at the beginning stages of our initial preparations for success. It is information we produce as we act. It can fill out our original strategies, giving us new details we had no sight of before, or it can indicate to us that we need to switch direction altogether, in big ways or in small. We find in the first-century *Moral Sayings* of Publilius Syrus the remark that "it is a bad plan that admits of no modification." A truly bad plan indeed.

One of the little ironies of life is that at the outset of any new adventure we never know as much as we would like to know about exactly where we're going and precisely what we ought to do to get there. We learn as we go. And if we're willing to adjust course, we can benefit immensely from what we learn. There is information we can't process unless we're engaged in the process of working toward our goals. It is information sparked by our efforts striking obstacles in our path. And it is a view of new possibilities we see only as we move in the direction of our dreams. Some things that glittered from a distance may dull as we approach, and other things that might have seemed dull from far off may begin to sparkle brightly as we draw near.

> Our life is like a journey on which, as we advance, the landscape takes on a different view from that which it presented at first, and changes again, as we come nearer.
> *Arthur Schopenhauer*

Because of this, we need to be open to adjusting course as we proceed forward in life. One of the surprisingly successful groups of people in recent American life have been the survivors of Nazi concentration camps in the Second World War. In a book by Dr. William B. Helmreich, *Against All Odds: Holocaust Survivors and the Successful Lives They Made in America*, this group is compared with European Jews of the same age who came to the United States before the war. With less education on average, the survivors were nonetheless more successful in their careers and enjoyed higher incomes. They also contributed more of themselves in voluntary community work. In trying to identify the qualities that set them apart and made them such successful people, after having lived through such trauma, Dr. Helmreich specified that high on the list were a readiness to take the initiative in a new endeavor, and an ability to adjust and adapt to changing circumstances.

Twentieth-century biology has also continued to teach us that as adaptation is life, life is adaptation. There is certainly no shame to be attached to a positive change of course. Yet so many people seem to find it very difficult to alter their plans in light of new information. They forge ahead with a faulty plan too stubborn or proud or embarrassed to admit that they are wrong and that they need to rethink either their goals or their strategy, their means to those goals. But as Baltasar Gracián put it so succinctly three centuries ago: "There is one way to see the light—as soon as possible."

It is not a mark of weakness but of strength to rethink one's path or policies. The wise person understands that the best plans are based on incomplete knowledge. And the alert person picks up more knowledge as he puts his plans into action. It only makes sense to revise our plans in light of our ongoing experiences. The person who cannot do this is more often than not trapped by his own insecurity. He will not experience the satisfying success of which he's capable unless he can give up the illusion that excellence is the same thing as omniscience, and make the most of his limited perspective by being ever open to new insight and the changes it can evoke. As we seek to live our dreams, continual feedback is available to us if we will only look for it.

Expect the unexpected. This is one of the best pieces of advice about life that anyone can ever give, or live. This world of ours is so complex and dynamic, ever changing at an increasing pace, that it would be quite surprising if we weren't surprised on a regular basis by the things that come our way. We have to be prepared for the unanticipated turns and twists of events that take us places we hadn't planned to go. We have to be prepared for detours on our path to success. There is rarely ever a perfectly straight line to get us from *A* to *Z*. We'll have to detour a bit off to the left, and then off to the right. But with a clear vision of our goals, we can work the detours into our plans as we go.

We should not be frustrated by the inevitable. And surprises are inevitable. Some changes in our plans are unavoidable. We never know in advance everything that life will throw our way. A bumper sticker on a construction worker's truck shouted out to me one day that SHIT HAPPENS. Too bad that it was parked in my driveway. And that it offered a fairly accurate commentary on the daily turn of events during the remodeling work we were having done. The bumper sticker in its own blunt way stated a common truth in the world of human affairs. And it's a truth we all need to be reminded of, although I have to admit that if I were being wheeled into the hospital for surgery, I'd sure hate to see this little announcement posted over the operating room door. In that sort of context, the truth could literally hurt.

With a clear vision, strong confidence, a good plan, and a tactical flexibility that will allow us to make adjustments as needed, we can deal with anything life throws our way. And the importance of both vision and confidence for this cannot be exaggerated. People without a clear vision of what they want and of where they're going often allow complications, difficulties, and detours to misguide and sidetrack them. People without sufficient self-confidence sometimes let surprises stop them in their tracks. And that's too bad. We should not allow the unexpected to throw us. A surprise is not necessarily a setback. And even a setback is not always bad. In fact, a setback or delay in our plans may even generate an unexpected kind of good for us.

I say this having experienced its truth more times than I can count. After writing the first complete draft of these paragraphs on unexpected setbacks and detours, I lost all the handwritten pages. This was a particularly ironic and unexpected setback. For three days I looked everywhere for the missing pages at work and at home. I couldn't find them, although I did find lots of other stuff. Stuff I had forgotten I had, and other stuff I thought I had lost a long time ago. But all this searching took up time I had planned to use in continuing on with my writing. Detour. Delay. I worried. The first flutterings of panic began to tickle my insides. But then I reminded myself of the perspective those pages contained. "Physician, heal thyself," I heard myself saying. I calmed down. A little. A friend heard about my problem and took it upon himself to search through a very large full dumpster outside my office building, opening up big black plastic garbage bags and digging through mounds of refuse and paper. Within a couple of hours he knocked at my office door and produced the slightly wrinkled and now ever so aromatic sheets of paper I had lost. It had been quite an effort on his part, and quite an experience for me. Along the way I learned some lessons and gained some insights I would have missed if things had gone smoothly and I never had lost those pages. Lessons that have helped me with my book. Insights that have helped me with my life.

What seems very bad at the time can indeed turn out to be very good in the end. A detour is after all nothing more than a different way to get where we're going. We just can't usually see it as such unless we have that goal clearly in view and we understand the unavoidable unpredictability involved in any interesting journey. It may take us a little longer than we had planned. But then again the detour may end up being the scenic route, allowing us to see things we might not otherwise have been able to appreciate. And traveling it may enhance our skills. In my own life I have often found myself arriving at a destination and thinking, "It didn't go according to plan. Thank goodness." In any of our lives, clear vision, strong confidence, and adaptive planning can keep detours from being dead ends and can keep us on the best possible track for the attainments that are right for us.

How big are your problems? How severe are the difficulties you face in your own life as you work toward your goals? It's truly amazing how much an answer to either of these questions is a matter of perspective. To a great extent our problems are only as big as we make them. Our difficulties are only as serious as we perceive them to be. One day when walking into the administration building at Notre Dame, the edifice with the famous golden dome, I saw one of the older football coaches, a wonderful man I hadn't seen in many months. I asked him how he was. With a big smile, he growled out, "I'm doing pretty well, Tom, how about yourself?" We began walking from the ground floor up the very steep and extremely long flights of stairs to the fourth floor, carrying on an energetic conversation the whole way. When we arrived at the top, I was nearly out of breath, but the coach seemed fine, apart from a barely noticeable limp.

I said, "Coach, I see you're walking with a little limp. Have you had a leg injury?"

He shrugged and replied, "No, Tom, it's nothin' really. A couple a months ago, I had a little trouble and they had to take out a lung.

I'm OK now, though. I just got this little hitch in my walk from the whole business. I'm fine." Big smile again.

This, I said to myself, is a pretty tough guy. Three bazillion stairs, with nonstop conversation. I'm twenty years younger, I'm barely making it, and he just lost a lung. But what impressed me more than his incredible physical stamina was his extraordinarily positive attitude. What to most of us would be utterly catastrophic seemed to him to be *No Big Deal*. A minor inconvenience.

> Nothing happens to anybody which he is not formed by nature to bear. *Marcus Aurelius*

Sophocles long ago pointed out that "there is no success without hardship." But we can survive tremendous difficulties and overcome the worst of problems if we approach them with the right attitude. Do we think of ourselves as victims or as victors? Life is full of problems. Do we see ourselves as problem solvers? Can we transcend the troubles we often have to face? I think we can. We all have the resources for rising above trouble, for learning from the difficulties we face, and for making whatever alterations in our plans our new circumstances call for. Like the coach, we can keep going through even the toughest adversity. And we should.

Even the worst failure is not always what it seems. One surprising piece of advice sometimes given by highly successful people is this: "Fail soon, fail often." This does sound odd, but the explanation is simple. Anyone not experiencing failures is not launching out into new territory. Everyone who takes the risks necessary for real growth will occasionally fail. And we typically learn more from our failures than from our victories. So if to grow you must fail, and if to learn much you must fail much, then fail soon, fail often.

Of course, success is better than failure. Especially in the end. But in the end any real success likely will have arisen out of many failures along the way, both large and small. So we should not fear failure. The only failure that is really terrible and to be avoided at all costs is the failure to learn from our failures. Limited people in a complex world will occasionally mis-step. The secret is to regain your balance, correct your course, and move on.

With this perspective we can avoid two of the most common obstacles to success: the fear of facing failure and the discouragement that often comes with an experience of it. Having the confidence to succeed requires having the courage to fail. And continuing along the path to our goals requires not losing heart when we seem to fall short. We need to think of successful people as successfully self-correcting adventurers, cartographers of experience who map and remap as they go, pioneering into uncharted territory. Failures are not all high walls; they are sometimes just speed bumps along life's way. They should slow us down on occasion, and cause us to take stock of what we're doing, but they shouldn't cause us to stop dead in our tracks and give up altogether. We need to keep moving forward, however haltingly at times. As Confucius once said, "It does not matter how slowly you go so long as you do not stop."

We have to learn when to slow down, when to wait awhile with patience, and when to move forward. When to try again and when to change course. Sometimes we should persist and press ahead, and sometimes we should think again about how to move toward our goals. As Mark Twain reminded us, if you don't succeed time after time after time after time, there is a point at which you should consider giving up what you are trying. But of course Twain's giving up should be both provisional and specific before it's ever final and general. If I try to accomplish something in a certain way and face repeated roadblocks, perhaps I should conclude that this is not the way to proceed right now. Or I might decide to give up altogether on trying this particular avenue toward my more ultimate goals. Another way is better. The circumstances should determine exactly how we learn from our mis-steps and to what extent we adjust our course. No utterly general rules can be given. Sometimes a small change of course or method is all that is needed. At other times a more radical departure may be necessary to secure real progress toward the realization of our goals.

The biggest failures are often the hardest from which to learn. They may require major rethinking. And major patience. In response to small mistakes, we can often adjust as we go without even realizing the degree of our improvising. The bigger the problem is, the more it takes on our part to learn from it all we need to know. We need quiet, reflective time to think. We need to stop the buzz of inner and outer complaints, frustrations, blamings, and second-guessings. We need a healthy dose of silence. Inner calm. Equilibrium. That is often the necessary condition for any powerful rethinking of our course. What has happened? And why? What should we do? And how should we do it? We need time to quietly and calmly analyze the problem, take stock of our resources, creatively reorder the possibilities, and choose our next step. An influential Hindu teacher, Swami Paramananda, once wrote: "Silence and patience go together. Silence has wonderful creative power." It also has wonderful healing power. It can allow us to recover from trouble and renew our strength. With quiet time to think, with the resources of both patience and silence, we can learn from even our biggest mistakes and greatest failures. We can make the changes that are needed.

> No matter how often you are defeated, you are born to victory.
> *Ralph Waldo Emerson*

One of the most common sources of frustration in life is the insistence on applying a tool, technique, or method that has worked well in one context to a new context where it might not be right. We see all around us people who are trapped in that mindset—"I have a hammer; everything's a nail." Sometimes we have developed elaborate or powerful techniques that just aren't necessary in our present circumstances, and that might even be destructive. As one small-town fire chief often advised his men: "Before you break down the door with your axe, try the doorknob." The flexibility to adjust as we go will allow us to use our energy more efficiently and more effectively to accomplish what really needs to be done.

One other facet of adjustment is the ability to say no. To say no to your own previous plans if you need to change course; to say no to other people when their requests or expectations would keep you from progressing and adapting your course in line with what your experience has led you to see needs to be done. You may also have to say no often to what, earlier on, you would have perceived as wonderful opportunities and markers of success. If you want to experience the best luck possible, you shouldn't eat your fill of good luck.

Longsightedness of purpose is compatible with flexibility of mind. In fact, I believe it demands it. What counted as a very good thing yesterday may be a distraction and obstacle tomorrow. If we approach life flexibly, we have the best chance of adjusting our course in a healthy and fulfilling way.

We all have a fascinating mental ability many psychologists refer to as the "reticular activating system." This is the ability to form a pattern or network of expectations that generates a net for capturing new perceptions and new ideas relevant to our goals. Have you ever gone shopping for a new car? You're thinking about an Oldsmobile and suddenly, as if by magic, you see new

Oldsmobiles all around you on your way to work and on your way home. You've never really noticed them before. If you're shopping for a Saab, suddenly Saabs are everywhere. It can strike you as extremely bizarre. But don't worry. Nothing weird or cosmic is going on. Cars of the right make and model are not just popping into existence, showing up in driveways and on roads all over town, as if to encourage or taunt you. In the course of shopping, studying, and considering, you have just successfully reprogrammed your brain to see what's been around you all along. Your reticular activating system has just locked onto Oldsmobiles, or Saabs. Out of the uncountably many stimuli your brain receives each day, you have just decided, without being consciously aware that this is what you're doing, to let these perceptions through the net. This happens with sights, with sounds, and with ideas. The seed of a thought, which might otherwise have fallen on rocky ground, now drops into fertile soil and grows into a new idea. As you move toward your goals and have new experiences, you continuously reprogram this mental experience system in such a way as to make it possible for you to be able to see what you've never seen before and to think of what's never occurred to you before. With your continually adjusted net, you are able to capture success in ways never before possible.

We cannot know everything we need to know to attain success when we first launch out in the direction of our goals. But that's all right, because our reticular activating systems will set us up to discover, learn, and adjust as we go. The process itself becomes our ally if we are alert and flexible along the way.

Network with Those Who Know

In our attempt to attain a focused concentration on what it takes to reach our goal, in our effort to PLAN a strategy for getting there, we must never forget the potential importance of other people to our quest. At each and every step we need to recognize the values of networking with those who already know what it is we need to learn, or whose past experience can help us come to the new knowledge we need for the progress we want to make.

When my father was seventeen years old, he left the farm in Cameron, North Carolina (just outside Sanford, brick capital of the world), and set off for the big city, in his case, Baltimore, Maryland. He showed up at the Martin Aircraft Company and applied for a job. When they asked him what he wanted to do, he said, "Everything."

Everything? He was told that no one had ever given that answer before. What did he mean? He explained that he would really like to learn every job in the factory. He'd like to go into a department, learn what was done there, and when the supervisor determined that his work was as good as anyone else's, go on to a different department and start all over. The personnel people agreed to this unusual request, and by the time young H. T. Morris was twenty, he had made his way through the whole factory and was working in experimental design for a fantastic salary. He could do in two or three days what it took most people a week to accomplish, and because of his exceptional achievements he even had the strange honor of seeing the United States government officially declare that no twenty-year-old could possibly know what Martin Aircraft claimed he knew.

How did he do it? How did he reach his goal of learning nearly every job in that huge and complex factory in three years, *as a teenager*? He explained it to me at a very young age. It was simple, he said. Whenever he went into a new department, he immediately looked around for the sages—the legends, the old guys who had been around forever and had seen it all, the masters whose reputations for knowledge and expertise were part of the oral history of the place, the stuff of rumor, the plant mythology. These were the people the novices usually avoided like a plague, afraid that next to them they'd look really bad, like the beginners they were. But what's wrong with looking like what you are? These were the people my father sought out and hung around with, asking every question he could think to throw their way. They not only told him how things worked, what needed to be done, who was the best at what, they *showed* him little tricks of the trade, shortcuts, innovations, little procedures they had developed that no one else had ever asked about. They liked this inquisitive, eager young man and wanted to help him learn.

> Some wisdom must thou learn from one who's wise.
>
> *Euripides*

My father at the age of seventeen instinctively realized the value of networking with those who know. He became an apprentice. And all those sages became his mentors. The new workers who avoided these legends had to learn from scratch, or from others who themselves hardly knew what to teach. By going straight to the masters, the young newcomer tremendously accelerated his learning process, learned only the best existent ways of doing any job, and picked up hints as to how to develop for himself even better ways of working. He made his journey a group effort, a team venture. He teamed with the best and put himself in a position to see and do what no one else could.

Most successful people love to magnify their successes through others. In the eighties, one of America's most interesting billionaires was Sam Walton, the country boy who founded the Wal-Mart chain of discount stores. One of the things he was most proud of was the number of employees he had turned into millionaires. Their success, in more ways than one, was his success.

Of course, there are some successful and powerful people who are jealous guardians of their attainments and status, who feel that they can remain at the top only as long as they keep everyone else at the bottom. There are people who have the nobody-helped-me-so-figure-it-out-for-yourself attitude. But a great many of the best people at any endeavor are eager to help another person. And this is not always just because of sheer altruism. They enjoy multiplying their own attainments by using their knowledge, power, and skill to launch another person into a level of success he or she might not otherwise have been able to attain, at least for a much longer time.

Whatever your goals might be, make it a part of your plan to network with those who know. Model your efforts on theirs, adjusting and improving as you can. This will accelerate your progress immensely and make your journey so much more enjoyable. There is a fellowship of excellence among people who really care about what they are doing. Don't miss out on the chance to partake of it and reap all the benefits it brings.

> Socrates had a student named "Plato." Plato had a student named "Aristotle." And Aristotle had a student named "Alexander the Great."

Networking of the right sort requires good conversation as well as regular association, which is, as we have noted, one of the nearly lost arts of recent times. It's said that talk is cheap. But with the right person, at the right time, it can be extremely valuable. It pays to be a conversation partner with the best people around. And to do what it takes to make this possible. Whatever your focused goals might be, it is in your deep self-interest to cultivate yourself as a well-informed individual and potential conversationalist across a broad spectrum of human interests, in art, politics, history, current events, sports, literature, and philosophy, to name just a few. The benefits of such self-cultivation are multiple. You become a better person. You develop a richer inner life. You position yourself for more creative thinking within the range of the goals you pursue. And you become a much more interesting person for others to be around. You also become a more attractive person, a person whose association and conversation will be enjoyed by others, even by those whose accomplishments are at present mostly superior to yours. And, actually, especially by such people. Of course, these are the people whose conversations and association are most important to you as you strive to reach a new level of accomplishment in pursuit of your own goals.

If your goals are team goals—goals for an office, a family, a circle of friends, a major corporation or department of a large company, an athletic team, or even a neighborhood—conversation and communication take on an extra importance. Don't try to do it alone. Leadership is not like roping a steer and dragging it to where you want it to go. Team goals, joint interpersonal goals, involve team effort. As you engage in your own planning, you need to learn of the strengths and experiences, hopes and dreams of the other people involved. You need to network with them in clear communication of where you are as a group, where you need to be, and how you think you can get there together. Great leadership is not dictatorial. It is inspirational, organizational, and conversational. It involves shared values, and it involves shared resources. You help others help you get to where you need to be. There are many ways you can help the others. And there are many ways they can help you. Network with those who know, and get to where you all need to go.

This, then, I think, is the way to PLAN:

*P*repare for your journey.
*L*aunch out in action.
*A*djust as you go.
*N*etwork with those who know.

This is the procedure for acquiring the degree of focused concentration in thought and action all of us need for the attaining of new goals, in our quest for success. It is a simple procedure in outline, but one that is extremely powerful in effect. With its use we can become masters of the third condition of success, the focused concentration we need on what it takes to reach our goals.

4

A Consistency in What We Do

Condition Four: We need a stubborn consistency in pursuing our vision, a determined persistence in thought and action.

We live in the greatest society, with the most varied opportunities and the deepest resources for success, in the history of human existence. Why, then, are there so many dead-end failures? Why do so many people think of themselves as failures? And why are so many of them right? Why do so many businesses built around good ideas fail? And why do so many that stay afloat nonetheless fail to attain the excellence of which they're capable?

A few years ago I did an informal study of the causes of personal, professional, and organizational failure in American society at the present time. What I discovered surprised me. I came to realize that one of the single most widespread and powerful sources of failure nowadays is a form of self-sabotage. Self-destructive behavior. Thought and action inconsistent with the overarching goals and purposes people have. Decisions and patterns of activity out of step with the vision that ought to be guiding their deliberation and conduct.

A salesclerk who dreams of advancement is rude to his customers, often late to work, or sloppy with his records. A spouse neglects her partner. A man who needs and wants a job spends all his time either in front of the TV or just hanging out with friends. A company trying to build partnerships of trust with suppliers and clients engages in small deceptions on a regular basis. A person who has sworn off cigarettes still keeps some packs around the house and in the car. And, of course, nothing whets an appetite like the decision to go on a diet.

THE BASIC PROBLEM

People often act inconsistently with their own dreams and values. It's truly amazing how common this is. I have come to believe that we are all implicated in this, at some time or another. Whether just in small things or in large, we all at some point act inconsistently with our own values and purposes. In so doing, we place obstacles in our own paths, obstacles that impede our progress toward the goals we mean to pursue.

Several years ago I decided I wanted to become a better writer. For months I read every book I could get my hands on that gave hints and tips on writing well. I talked to good writers. I spent time imagining myself as a successful author, producing page-turners full of scintillating prose. But for all those months there was one thing I didn't do. I didn't write at all. One of the most basic truths about becoming a better writer is that you can't do it without writing. But of course, this is true of anything. A basketball player can't become a better free-throw shooter without shooting lots of free throws. A guitar player has to practice or perform on a regular basis. A dancer needs to dance. I was doing many things in support of my goal. But in the most important way I was acting inconsistently with that goal. When I finally realized this, it astonished me. And I started writing again.

At another time I was working hard on a book during the summer months. I was writing most of each day in my office at Notre Dame, and often into the night. I was hardly seeing my little preschool-age children at all, and yet I'm a person with strong "family values." It was important to me to participate in the raising of my children, and to have plenty of time to play with them. But with my work schedule I was acting inconsistently with those values. No one had forced this schedule on me. I was freely conducting my daily life in a manner inconsistent with values dear to me. My enthusiasm for the book I was writing had caused me to forget. I was caught up in a pattern of busyness, neglecting what was really much more important to me. When I suddenly became aware of the conflict, I radically changed my patterns. I began to get up at four o'clock most mornings and arrive at my office by four-thirty or five. I worked completely uninterrupted for hours, as you might well imagine, and usually finished my day's writing by lunchtime. The afternoons I could then spend with my little toddlers. I had reestablished consistency with all my goals and values.

One more confession, and this time one that's a little tougher to make. I love good food, and I have a bit of a weakness for indulging my tastes in this area. In recent months I had been enjoying quite a few culinary delights, possibly a bit beyond the bounds of normal moderation, and, coincidentally, I was beginning to notice a little less room in various suit pants, jackets, and dress shirts. I actually found myself considering very seriously the intrinsically implausible hypothesis that dry-cleaning and laundering had suddenly begun shrinking all my clothes. Finally, no longer able to sustain this little stretch of the imagination, this little piece of attempted self-deception, I realized that I needed to alter some of my eating patterns, notch up my exercise level, and shed at least ten pounds. At least.

I set my goals, I laid out a plan, and I began to move forward with confidence. A little roadwork. Free weights. Stomach crunches. These and a few other assorted unpleasantries launched me on my way. So why is it that on my next trip to the grocery store I bought myself a box of cookies? Low-cal, low-fat cookies, but cookies. Do I *need* cookies? Did my purchasing a box help me along toward my goals in any way at all? I very persuasively reminded myself that they were *extremely small,* nearly harmless cookies, one by one. And so when I got home I sat down and ate the whole box. One by one.

This is a form of inconsistent behavior I'm still in the process of expunging from my life. How about you? What sorts of inconsistencies have you noticed within your own life? Do you see any patterns of inconsistent thought or action? Behavior out of step with your goals and values? Persistent inconsistency standing in the way of your progress?

Are you completely happy with the way you interact with family members? With coworkers? With neighbors? Are you satisfied that all your habits are appropriate, in light of what you believe to be important? Do you stick to decisions you've made about changes you need to effect? Do you spend your time appropriately? And how about your money? Are your thoughts and emotions consistent on a daily basis with your deepest values and commitments? Are you investing yourself sufficiently in things that really matter? Do you consistently live out your best vision of the life you want to live? Are you doing what you think it's best to do and avoiding what you think it's best to avoid?

If your answers to some of these questions are a little embarrassing, don't despair. We all experience times of inconsistency. We all sometimes fall into self-defeating patterns of activity or thought.

We waste time, and squander resources, and fail to honor those we care for. We sometimes disappoint ourselves. Even the best of us. In a very famous passage in the New Testament, the apostle Paul expresses tremendous frustration and perplexity over discovering this in parts of his own life. With a great deal of anguish, he explains: "For that which I am doing, I do not understand; for I am not practicing what I would like to do, but I am doing the very thing I hate . . . For the good that I wish, I do not do; but I practice the very evil that I do not wish."

This passage, in the seventh chapter of Paul's letter to the church at Rome, culminates with his exclaiming, "Wretched man that I am!" In the apostle Paul's mind, his own inconsistency is linked with frustration, anguish, and wretchedness. As an observer of his own behavior, he is appalled. In his own eyes, he's got trouble.

Early in the eighteenth century, the prominent British author and publisher Joseph Addison wrote: "Nothing that is not a real crime makes a man appear so contemptible and little in the eyes of the world as inconstancy." Inconstancy. Inconsistency. Failing to stand faithful to our own ideals and values. Failing to act in support of our own settled commitments. Whether or not it involves actual evil, it always involves acting at cross-purposes with ourselves. Insofar as success is a good thing, this sort of inconsistency is surely a bad thing.

The secret of success is constancy to purpose.

Benjamin Disraeli

It is inevitable that on any path to success, at some time or another, we'll face obstacles. We have little control over this fact. But what we do have a great deal of control over is whether or not

147

we ourselves are responsible for any of them. Are we our own worst enemies? Are we holding ourselves back? Do we drop great boulders into our paths? Are we diffusing our energies and defeating our own causes? In the eyes of Addison and the world, it is "contemptible and little" to fail to exercise control where we have it to avoid the most avoidable form of hindrance, the self-defeating and even self-destructive obstacle of self-sabotage.

THE VALUE OF CONSISTENCY

But of course not everyone seems to agree about the value of consistency in human life. And we should hear from the other side. Didn't Emerson, for example, once characterize consistency as "the hobgoblin of little minds"?

Well, actually, what Emerson said was that "a foolish consistency is the hobgoblin of little minds, adored by little statesmen and philosophers and divines." And that makes it sound like he had no problem with consistency itself; it was only foolish consistency he deplored. I'll overlook the crack about philosophers. But the next sentence from this famous passage in the essay "Self-Reliance" goes on to state quite bluntly and generally that "with consistency a great soul has simply nothing to do."

Oscar Wilde weighed in heavily with the critics here and dismissively wrote: "Consistency is the last refuge of the unimaginative." And the prominent writer Aldous Huxley is often quoted for having remarked that "consistency is contrary to nature, contrary to life. The only completely consistent people are the dead."

Is consistency a condition of success, or is it rather a property of little minds, small souls, the unimaginative, and the dead? Despite the apparent dispute here, I think the truth is simple to find.

There are two very different patterns of behavior sometimes known as "consistency." One is a proper object for Emerson's criticism, Wilde's dismissal, and Huxley's little joke. This is the unthinking or obstinate rigidity of the person who cannot adapt or adjust to changing times, differing circumstances, or varying personalities. This is the inflexibility of the unimaginative, the rigidity of the dead. Rather than serving as a facilitating condition of success, this sort of behavioral pattern is almost a guarantee of failure or mediocrity in most endeavors, as I hope was made clear in the previous chapter's discussion of adjustment and adaptation.

Unfortunately, unproductive enslavement to old, and no longer effective, ways of doing things is far too common in our world. Let me give you a fairly trivial but telling example of this from my own recent experience. I have a high-end fax machine in my office that not long ago needed servicing and repair. The technical support person representing the prestigious manufacturer came to work on it and had it fixed within an hour. Although I had a lot of work to do, I offered him my desk to write up his service report, which I assumed would take only a couple of minutes. While he wrote, I sat in another chair and read a newspaper. After about five minutes I looked over and noticed that he seemed to be busy doing some sort of artwork, hunched over the paper on my desk. I asked in a nice way what he was doing and was quite surprised at his answer.

The service report form required that he take an imprint of my machine's serial number. He explained that years ago all the machines he serviced had little metal plates with raised serial numbers. After writing his report, he would lay it over the plate and rub a pencil lead back and forth on the page to take the imprint he needed. Now the machines have totally flat serial numbers, just printed on with ink. But the technical support people still "take imprints." How? They use a pencil to artistically reproduce the way the numbers would have looked if they had been able to do a rubbing instead. So my service person was seated

149

at my desk painstakingly doing a sketched reproduction of an imprint! This is not what I would call a productive consistency in work procedures.

Great success requires creativity, imagination, and flexibility both in planning our course and in implementing those plans. But there is another side to the story. Along with a willingness to change when change is appropriate, if we ever want to succeed in achieving anything truly worthwhile, we need to be able to attain a firmness of purpose that will not waver with every changing breeze that blows our way. As former President Jimmy Carter stated in his inaugural address, quoting one of his high school teachers: "We must adjust to changing times and still hold to unchanging principles."

Inflexibility, rigidity, blind enslavement to the past, and unimaginative repetitiveness hardly deserve the name of consistency. The English words "consistency" and "constancy" derive from Latin terms that mean, basically, "standing together." Do our thoughts and decisions stand together? Do our actions stand together? Is there a constancy or fidelity of purpose to what we do? Are we keeping our eyes on the road? Are we moving forward? If our behavior is rigid and inflexible, unresponsive to changing circumstances and new information, then I do not think it can be considered consistent with any vision of life or goal worth having.

One philosophical concept for the kind of behavior pattern I want to recommend might be "teleological fidelity"—faithfulness to a goal or purpose (the Greek word is *telos*). Another such concept might be "axiological fidelity"—faithfulness to a value (the Greek is *axia*) or commitment. My decisions and actions are consistent in this sense when either they effectively move me along toward my goals, or embody my values, or at the very least do not impede my journey toward those goals guided by those values.

Constancy is the foundation of virtues.   *Francis Bacon*

The greatest philosophers have recognized the value of this sort of consistency for a full and meaningful human life. Even Emerson, despite the impression his quoted remarks give. Fidelity or faithfulness is a quality whose importance for successful living cannot be overestimated. Whenever I set myself a goal, adopt a purpose as my own, or make a commitment to a cause or to another person, I lay down a direction for present and future actions, I provide a structure for my subsequent decision making. I order my life, in the sense of giving it order. And, of course, the opposite of order is *disorder*. Whenever I act without fidelity, without faithfulness to my values and commitments, I introduce disorder into my life.

Good order is the foundation of all good things.
Edmund Burke

One of the most destructive errors in the modern world has been a tendency to think of freedom solely in terms of avoidance (freedom *from*) rather than also, and most important, in terms of teleology (freedom *to*). This common misunderstanding would hold freedom and faithfulness to be in tension with one another. But nothing could be further from the truth. The value of freedom consists in our being free from outside compulsion and artificial constraint so that we can be free to pursue goals we choose, embrace values we recognize, and make commitments that are meaningful to us. A "freedom" from all commitments, values, and goals would be the most perverse sort of freedom imaginable, a freedom from all meaningfulness. It would be a quick descent into the disorder of ultimate self-destructiveness.

The Greeks understood that we are essentially teleological and axiological beings. We all need to pursue goals and structure our lives in accordance with positive values. We need to make commitments. We can't be ultimately fulfilled without this sort of order, or structure, in our lives. This is our *nature.* We are most free, and most fully human, when we are faithfully and consistently living in accordance with the highest values we have recognized and the noblest aspirations we have embraced. This is what it takes for true success.

> Ideas must work through the brains and the arms of good and brave men, or they are no better than dreams.
> *Ralph Waldo Emerson gets it right*

Consistency of the highest sort is empowerment. Our goals and values, the commitments we make to guide our paths through life, must be embodied in our thoughts, actions, emotions, and attitudes on a consistent basis if they are to make the kind of difference for us that they are capable of making. Without consistent embodiment, our greatest visions are just dreams. Consistency of the right kind always enhances our prospects for seeing our dreams become realities. It moves us along in the direction we have chosen.

And of course this is every bit as important for organizations as it is for individuals. A simple example: If the head of a business wants to encourage teamwork and trust in the workplace, it's important that all employees be treated with respect. And it's absolutely crucial that this be done with faithful consistency. What exactly this involves may be in some ways different now from what would have been required decades ago when both the work force and social conditions may have been very different. So the sort of consistency I am concerned with must incorporate a responsive adaptability to changing circumstances and different times. But it is based on unchanging principles of fidelity to the underlying values that should structure all that we do.

> They must often change who would be constant in happiness or wisdom.   *Confucius*

A purely *past-oriented* consistency is the hobgoblin of little minds. It is most often the product of fear. Or unoriginality. Or sometimes just plain tiredness. A vision- or goal-oriented consistency is quite the opposite. Its attainment often requires a discernible measure of courage, creativity, and energy. And it's only a vision-based consistency that has the flexibility of a productive sort built in that is required for attaining difficult goals in challenging conditions. To be consistent in this sense is to engage in *whatever* behavior will consistently facilitate our goals and embody our values in the circumstances we're in, *whatever* they might be. Vision consistency in principle precludes uncreative, inflexible rigidity and the blind repetition of past behavior patterns for their own sake. It is this vision consistency that is the fourth condition of success.

THE CHALLENGE OF CHANGE

We live in a world of constant change. World politics are changing. The economy is changing. Rapid technological innovation is almost dizzying in its pace. Social conditions and lifestyle patterns are continually undergoing unexpected alterations. It's gotten to the point where we can hardly imagine what novelties will next cross our paths.

The ancient philosopher Heraclitus believed that the only constant in this world is change. And the seventeenth-century French scientist and mathematician Blaise Pascal once stated his firm opinion that we ourselves are always changing, whether we realize it or not. He cleverly added that if he ever were to change his mind about this, that in itself would just be further confirmation of his belief.

Change can be exciting. But it can also be unsettling. Even threatening. Especially change that comes upon us unexpected, or unbidden. The British author Matthew Arnold once said, "Change doth unknit the tranquil strength of men." It can be very disorienting. Change presents a challenge, and like any challenge, it can be viewed as either a problem or an opportunity. But it's only a problem if we are unprepared for it. The best preparation for handling change is a clear conception of where we're going, a confidence we can get there, an ability to concentrate on what it will take at each and every step, and a firm resolve to be stubbornly consistent in pursuing our vision.

When it comes to dealing with change, too many people fall on one extreme or the other. They are either dinosaurs who can't cope and quickly become extinct, or they're chameleons who conform to every subtle shade of difference they come across, and thus whose only distinctiveness is their ability to "go with the flow." To survive and thrive with something distinctive and different to offer the world, we need to confront the changes around us with an approach of flexible firmness. We need to be firm in commitments but flexible in methods. Otherwise, in our attempts to sail the seas of success, we'll go under when the first strong turbulence comes our way. A firmness of commitment gives us a map or chart to navigate by, but a flexibility of method gives us the responsive-ness to steer around whatever obstacles we might encounter along the way.

In many business contexts a fear of change can become paralyz-ing and self-destructive. An insistence on doing things the old way, a stubborn refusal to adapt, can produce in changing circum-stances a kind of constancy better known as "stagnation." This sort of problem can sometimes be the result of a leadership situation that the economist John Kenneth Galbraith once characterized as "the bland leading the bland." Most leaders nowadays face an ever-turning kaleidoscope of possibilities and unanticipated realities on a regular basis. New conditions, new problems, and a profusion of new techniques for dealing with those problems appear with increasing frequency. It really makes very little sense to expect to do most things this year just like they were done last year. A decision that was good six months ago may need to be reversed today. As long as people in a position of leadership retain their hold on some fundamental principles to guide their adaptations to these continually changing conditions, and clearly communicate that commitment on a regular basis to the people they lead, it is much easier for everyone in the workplace to deal with the anxiety change naturally creates, and to move forward to new productive strategies that will keep them on a trajectory in the direction of their mutual goals.

No well-informed person ever imputed inconsistency to another for changing his mind.   *Cicero*

Changing times call for creative, dynamic leadership. But they also call for responsible direction. To find our way through times

155

of change we need equilibrium, balance, and a clear sense of where we are heading. The vision consistency I am recommending and reporting as the fourth condition of success is perhaps best thought of as the behavioral tendency or attitude of a flexible firmness. It is a way of adjusting to tremendous change while still holding to something unchanging. Change is most frightening and disturbing to people when they don't have any firm ground to stand on, set goals to continue to aim at, or deep values and commitments to provide the framework for successful and enriching response to that change. A flexible firmness will allow us to make the most of the changes we encounter. A creative vision consistency is what we need.

PERSISTENT INCONSISTENCY: A DIAGNOSIS AND CURE

The right sort of consistency is an important condition of success. The least little inconsistency siphons off some of our energy, detracts from any momentum we have attained as we move toward our goals, and subtly erodes the level of commitment we have to the vision we have embraced. And all this is fairly easy to understand. An inconsistent act is clearly one that is out of step with the direction of our commitments. It brings some measure of disorder into our lives. So why do we ever act inconsistently? How does inconsistency ever get a foothold in our behavior?

In a number of ways. First, without realizing it, we may have set ourselves inconsistent goals. Some of our professional goals, for example, may deep down conflict with one or more of our personal or family goals. It's so easy to compartmentalize our lives. And it can be so dangerous to do so. One set of values at work and a radically different set of values at home is a prescription for trouble. Or even if our values aren't compartmentalized, our consciousness of consequences may be. If you think of your work only within the horizons of the office, your colleagues, and your career, it's easy to buy into goals, or set yourself targets, whose consequences for your family life you don't even imagine. Conflict and inconsistency can easily result.

It may just be impossible to get a major promotion in two years, or to get a book written in six months, while engaging in certain sorts of regular learning activities and family events with your children. You may need to rethink your goals, or the timetables for those goals, or the strategies you have adopted in pursuit of those aims. Even where there is no inherent incompatibility between two goals, a compartmentalization of thinking can sometimes lead to the adopting of time frames, methods, or strategies that undercut each other. Success comes from strength. Strength comes from harmony. And harmony requires consistency in all things. To attain the sort of deep life harmony we need between and among all our activities, we need to strive to achieve a global perspective on all the facets of our lives, resisting the temptations of compartmentalization as we set our goals and chart our courses in pursuit of those aims.

> Weave harmonies divine, yet ever new.
>
> *Percy Bysshe Shelley*

Inconsistency can also enter our lives through impulse. A sudden craving, desire, itch, or lust overtakes us and knocks us off course. We don't see it coming, and we're blindsided. Or we do see it coming and we're lured. We can certainly experience sudden, intense, passing desires inconsistent with our values, commitments, and personal goals. And we can act on them. This is a very common way that inconsistency can intrude into our lives.

157

And vision inconsistency can, ironically, result from that blind, stubborn, repetitive sort of consistency that I have characterized as hardly worthy of the name. A form of behavior might be consistent in the best sense with our values, goals, and commitments in one particular set of circumstances. But if those circumstances change and we do not, the very same behavior can become inconsistent with our most basic and governing intent. Inattention to changing conditions, or inflexibility in the face of that change, can equally well, or equally badly, introduce inconsistency of the most important kind into our lives.

Small inconsistencies should never be discounted. Inconstancy always matters. But single acts of inconsistency can most often be easily overcome. Even a cluster of actions out of step with our overall vision can usually be understood and counteracted without much difficulty. But what becomes much more troublesome in anyone's path to success is a pattern of persistent inconsistency that can sometimes develop and do great damage to his or her overall prospects of progress. This is the worst sort of inconsistency we can ever grapple with, whatever its ultimate origin in our experience. And it's worth a little extra reflection to get a better grip on why we ever confront such patterns of self-sabotage in our course through life.

> It is the nature of every man to err, but only the fool perseveres in error.
> *Cicero*

How can we understand persistent inconsistencies in our lives? Why do we continue in self-defeating or self-destructive behaviors? Not long ago an administrator from a large service organization phoned me about the possibility of my coming to speak to all their employees and executives about institutional and personal success. After giving me some details about the sort of presentation she had in mind, she said something that took me by surprise. She explained that they had often brought in great speakers from around the country, and that on every one of these occasions everybody in the room had a wonderful hour, but that the very next day it was always business as usual. The company had serious problems, she said, problems with internal behaviors and practices inconsistent with their professed values and policies, problems that persisted regardless of all the high-powered help they had been bringing in to educate and motivate the staff.

I said, "You've brought in great speakers from all over the country to help you with these problems and *nothing at all* has ever changed?"

"Well," she thought, and replied, "our vocabulary changes. We get some new lingo—the modern mantras of management. After an exciting speech or workshop all our vice presidents go around chanting, 'Service, service . . . Quality, quality . . . Leadership . . . Empowerment . . . ,' but nobody *does* anything differently. The problems we have never get dealt with. And I want to know why."

It sounded like she was talking herself out of inviting me to come and give a speech. What was the point, if speakers did no good? But I was determined to do some good. I am always committed to making a difference that counts.

Over the next couple of days I took it as a challenge to figure out what was going wrong that other speakers had not been able to address. More specifically, what causes such inconsistent behaviors and practices to persist in an organization or, for that matter, in an individual life? How can self-defeating or self-destructive behavior continue on and on? Why don't we change things that need to be changed, and that may have needed to be changed for a long time?

I love being a philosopher. The challenge I set myself here was difficult. The problem of persistent inconsistency is daunting.

Why do we continue to interact with a spouse, child, parent, or coworker in a way that gets us nowhere? Why do we persist in practices that actually erode our business? Why do we insist on doing things the old way when a new and better way is available? What I love about being a philosopher is that I can often take a deep and troubling problem like this and, on careful analysis, discover that it has a simple solution. This one took me two days. I was able to capture the simple truth about this problem in what I have come to call *The Five-I Framework for Positive Change.* It is a small map of all the possible sources and solutions for persistent inconsistency in our lives. With its diagnoses and prescriptions, we can easily see how to make the positive changes that are needed to free us from the most stubborn inconsistencies that hold us back.

Let me take some time to lay out the basic components of the framework. A full understanding of it will help us all to apply it to great effect in our lives, both personally and professionally. First the diagnosis, then the cure.

There are only three possible causes for persistent inconsistencies in our lives. Regardless of what the behavior is. Just three possibilities. First, and most obviously, there is:

IGNORANCE

We don't know that there is a problem. It may be obvious to everybody else, but it hasn't occurred to us yet. We're without a clue.

Or we could realize *that* there is a problem, and yet not know exactly *what* the problem is. Something is wrong. We can sense it. But we can't diagnose it. We feel it, but we can't quite figure it out.

We're often subject to this kind of ignorance in life. Relative ignorance. We know that we have some sort of a problem. We just don't know enough to pinpoint what it is, or even to begin to fix it. Most of us are in this position when taking our car in to a mechanic, or our bodies in to the doctor. "Something's wrong, I can tell. It makes a strange noise." We wait to hear from the expert for diagnosis and treatment.

> I am not ashamed to confess that I am ignorant of what
> I do not know.   *Cicero*

We can sometimes know *that* we have a problem, know *what* the problem is, and still be utterly ignorant as to how to bring our actions into consistent harmony with our goals and values. We're trapped in a form of inconsistency, and know we are, and we can't find a way out.

Have you ever felt trapped in a situation that was clearly out of step with the direction you envisioned for your life? Let me tell you a little story. When I was a graduate student, my wife and I lived in the spacious servants' quarters of a big house in the hills outside New Haven, Connecticut. The house was on thirty or forty acres, with horses and a nice tennis court off a field behind the main buildings. Extravagant surroundings for a poor graduate student. We were very fortunate in our situation. But we owned a dog who had a knack for getting himself into unfortunate situations. He was a German shorthaired pointer. Mostly. When he was a puppy I was under the mistaken impression that he was an extremely intelligent animal. As a stray dog, at the age of about eight weeks, he had found his way to Yale, had taken up with a British theologian, and through this international mediation had eventually made his way to our place in the country where he could live in a style befitting his breed. This was the dog I mentioned in a previous chapter that we named Roo.

Well, one day a few minutes after I had let Roo out of the house,

I heard him wildly barking and making sounds like shrieks of pain. These terrible noises were coming from some distance behind the house where an old road bordered the property. As soon as I heard all the commotion, I was sure Roo had been hit by a car. Running around the house, up a hill through some orchards, and across a field, I suddenly stopped in disbelief at the sight that greeted me. The dog was fine. He was trapped inside the fenced-in tennis court and he was panicked. He was frantically running back and forth along the length of the court on the side closest to the house, scraping his nose on the fence and screaming for all he was worth. I stood still for a moment and watched it all. He was obviously as beside himself as a dog can be. Desperate to escape his unexpected prison, he was mindlessly fixated on this one section of fence. Back and forth, to and fro, scratching, scraping, screaming—he was basically just coming unglued. It was clear to me then and there that I had on my hands a very high-strung animal, and that he was not quite as intelligent as his Ivy League background had led me to believe. The court was fenced on only three sides. The length of court right behind this caged critter, whom we henceforth called Houdini Dog, was totally unfenced, completely open. There was an easy way out of his predicament, if he only would have stopped, calmed down, and turned around.

How many times do we think of ourselves as stuck in some situation? How many times do we find ourselves locked in persistent, repetitive behavior clearly inconsistent with our true goals, and aware that we're getting nowhere, when there is an easily available way out if we would just stop, calm down, turn around, and open our eyes? Our poor dog was utterly ignorant of how his behavior should have been modified at the time to attain consistency with his overall short-term goal of escape and freedom. And in our own lives, as in his, ignorance is most often imprisonment. We persist in self-defeating behaviors only because we don't know the way out.

The administrator who phoned me and posed the challenge of figuring out the causes of persistent inconsistency seemed very aware that her organization had problems, and she was able to tell me what they were. She also said that all this was widely understood in the organization. She even seemed to know how things ought to change. And, according to her, others around her knew all this as well. But the problem was that nobody was making the changes that needed to be made. If she was right, the self-defeating behavior and inconsistent practices in her company were not being perpetuated through ignorance. There had to be some other cause.

And there is a second possible cause. Something very different:

INDIFFERENCE

I love the way the distinction here was once drawn in a classroom when a teacher asked a highly intelligent but rebellious student: "Bob, what's the difference between ignorance and indifference?"

He shrugged and said, "I don't know and I don't care."

"Excellent! Exactly right!" the teacher responded. "Ignorance is 'I don't know,' and indifference is 'I don't care.'"

Of course indifference, unlike ignorance, is an attitude. It's almost the attitude of lacking an attitude. But what it is precisely is the attitude of not really caring. Lacking concern. Emotionally zero. Motivationally dead. The shining light of the Beat Generation, Jack Kerouac, is often quoted for the dismissive remarks "I don't know. I don't care. And it doesn't make any difference." Sounds like a bumper sticker. I've known people who should wear this on a button wherever they go, and whatever they're doing.

Indifference is an attitude that's often joked about. In commenting on current affairs, one political analyst recently said, "The nation is enveloped in apathy. But who cares?" Funny. But indifference can be a very serious matter. Problems of inconsistent, self-defeating, or self-destructive behavior can be perpetu-ated in our lives because, even though we're perfectly well aware that we're not doing what we ought to do, or that we're doing what we ought not to do, given our commitments and goals, and we're even aware of how we could make the changes that are needed, we really deep down just don't care. And if that's the case, then those goals we have really haven't gotten a sufficient grip on us. Those commitments are not yet rooted in our heart of hearts.

But, again, the lady whose telephone call set off my reflections on all this obviously did care about the long-term problems she was laying out to me. And, according to her, others in the organi-zation also cared. They were not indifferent about their problems. But if they weren't ignorant, and they weren't indifferent, what could possibly be the reason that the inconsistent behaviors she spoke of persisted in their business? What other cause could possibly perpetuate such problems in any of our lives? There is only one other alternative:

INERTIA

The weight of habit. We're stuck in a rut and we can't get out.

In physics, the principle of inertia is very simple. An object in motion tends to stay in motion, and as my wife would be willing to testify on a Saturday morning, an object at rest tends to stay at rest. In human life, inertia is the downward pull of habit. Repeated behaviors become patterns of life. And if they are unproductive and self-defeating, repeated behaviors can become patterns of death.

Albert Einstein, not one to avoid being blunt when he felt it was called for, once stated that "man like every other animal is indo-lent. If nothing spurs him on, then he will hardly think, and will behave from habit like an automaton."

The philosopher George Santayana even concluded from his

reflections on the subject that "habit is stronger than reason." And I think he was right. The power and pervasiveness of habit in human life is truly amazing.

> Sow an act and you reap a habit,
> Sow a habit and you reap a character,
> Sow a character and you reap a destiny.
>
> *Charles Reade*

We need habit. We depend on it. We could not possibly live without it. Life would be just far too complicated if we had to consciously think through and make explicit decisions concerning everything we ever did. I'm very glad that I don't usually have to think about whether to turn out a light when I leave a room at home I've been in alone at night. It's automatic. I don't have to think about how to use the utensils at each mealtime. I don't have to decide every morning which shoe to put on first. It's habit. So much of what we do is habitual. When we've done something successfully enough, and enough times, it naturally becomes a matter of habit. When the right conditions arise to cause the habit to kick in, we can then act without having to think carefully, or even much at all, about what we're doing. And most of the time this is a very good thing. I don't know about you, but I have only so much mental energy to go around. Too much thinking would wear out even a philosopher.

Let me give a vivid example of how habit works in our lives. If you were born and raised in the United States of America, chances are that when you walk up to a curb and prepare to cross a busy street, you look left first and then right. You don't stop and say to yourself, "Let's see. Here I am at a street. I was born and raised in America where, according to the rules of the road, traffic typically first approaches from the left, unless of course this is a one-way street running in the opposite direction. It seems to be a normal, two-way street. Therefore, before venturing forth from the curb I probably should look left, then right." At least, I hope you don't go through all this inner dialogue and deliberation. You just look left and then right. Without even thinking about it. From habit.

And this is generally a good habit to have, except, for example, when you visit England, where the traffic flow is opposite. Friends have told me that it was in London where they almost had their heads taken off by speeding buses they did not see soon enough, that they first became aware of their lifelong "look left then right" habit. A habit that served them well in some circumstances almost caused their demise in others. Habits can work like that. Some habits that were good to have in the past can then give rise to inconsistent actions as times and situations change.

Do you work in an office where things are done in a way that doesn't make sense anymore? Do you have any family habits or personal patterns of behavior that once served a purpose but no longer do so? Tradition can sometimes be a good thing. If it serves a healthy purpose. But for a good habit turned bad, or for a habit that never was good in the first place, little by way of positive recommendation can be said.

There is a tree in a small town in Indiana known as "The Shoe Tree." I once saw a picture of it on the front page of the *South Bend Tribune*. A huge old tree, it had thousands of shoes hanging by their laces from its branches. A reporter from the paper had heard about this odd tree and went looking for its story. It seems that whenever anyone in the town outgrows or wears out an old pair of shoes, they tie the laces together, make a pilgrimage to the tree, and fling them up into the branches, into whatever space they can find. When asked why they do this, all interviewed residents just looked blank and said, "We've always done it." Nobody knew why.

We are all creatures of habit. And we have habits of all kinds. Does this ever happen to you? My wife often asks me to make a quick trip to the grocery store. It's about a mile to the east of my house. My office at Notre Dame is two miles in another direction. I take the grocery list, get in the car, back out of the driveway, and drive. I'm not sure what my conscious mind does. I don't know what I'm thinking about, but the first thing I know I'm suddenly "coming to" myself as I'm turning into the parking lot at Notre Dame. I've driven two miles in the wrong direction, down a busy four-lane street, through lots of traffic and a number of stop lights, and my conscious mind has been on vacation. This bothers me. But what bothers me more is that I'm pretty sure lots of the other drivers who shared that busy street with me are then in other parts of town suddenly "coming to" themselves. How do we do it? How do we manage this without filling the streets with wreckage?

We're on automatic pilot. During those auto episodes and at a lot of other times. The cruise control of the mind. This is just one more indication of the power and pervasiveness of habit in human life. I'm sure you could tell your own stories about it.

Habit is second nature.   *Michel de Montaigne*

I've come to believe that habit is the second strongest natural power in human life. It is that potent. That's why bad habits are so hard to break. The power of inertia is enormous. When we have self-defeating or self-destructive habits, when we discover that we are victimizing ourselves with behavior patterns inconsistent with our own values and goals, with our own best vision for our lives, we often experience frustration and a feeling of powerlessness to change. And it can be tough. It can be extremely challenging. But we are never powerless. We are never without options.

I am convinced that there is one natural power in human life that is stronger than habit. And that is the imagination. We typically have the power to defeat inertia and pull ourselves out of the rut of a firmly entrenched bad habit only when we somehow get our imaginations into gear. The power of the imagination can lift us out. It can break the pattern. But to fully rid ourselves of any habitually inconsistent behavior, we need to fight habit on its own terms. We need to replace the bad habits with good habits. We need to habituate ourselves to acting differently. In the realm of habit, total, permanent eradication most often requires replacement. A new behavior repetitively and successfully engaged in will displace the old behavior that was holding us back.

A nail is driven out by another nail, habit is overcome by habit.   *Erasmus*

This is an important point. There is a level of our being that requires habit. If we stop an old habit and do not replace it with a healthier, more sensible alternative, there is a strong probability that we'll end up relapsing into the old inconsistency after a time. When we root out an old habit, we create a vacuum. And in this area, nature does indeed abhor a vacuum. We need new and better habits. It is up to us what our new behaviors will be, if we will just take the initiative and engage in an immediate, deliberate strategy of replacement.

There are stories all around us of long-term smokers who have tried for years to quit and have succeeded for a day, or a week, or longer, only to light up again. Short-term success followed by failure. Relapse into the old habit. And then they had a heart attack, or lost a lung to cancer, and quit smoking for good.

In most cases all those failed attempts were made on the basis of reason and willpower alone. Because of a magazine article, a pamphlet from the doctor's office, or the advice of a frie̅ d, they came to understand the full negative health implications o̅ ̅ ̅nok-ing. Reason told them to stop. And with a little willpower mus̅ ̅ ̅d, they tried. But reason and willpower alone were not enough long-term success. Many smokers know all the statistics and fact̅ about what they are doing to themselves. But reason alone can't activate the amount of willpower necessary to even attempt to stop.

Why do the heart-attack survivors and cancer survivors often have success where so many others fail? Simple. The catastrophe got their imaginations into gear. The severe medical crisis jump-started their dormant powers of inner vision. Their mortality became real to them. The future of their self-destructive behavior suddenly became imaginatively vivid. And with the power of the imagination in gear, they were able to break deeply entrenched long-term habits.

Isn't this the way we so often act? We persist in some inconsistent or self-destructive behavior until confronted with a crisis. A spouse leaves, or threatens to leave. An associate is investigated by the authorities. A man is arrested. A friend is killed in a dangerous sport. An important client or customer walks away. Unhealthy behavior results in a terrible disease. Or in the sudden, realistic threat of such a disease. And then, suddenly, behaviors change. Patterns are broken. Habits are overcome. But only if the crisis has finally excited the imagination, gotten it into gear, set it aflame.

The human race is governed by its imagination.

Napoleon Bonaparte

The bad news is that so many of us allow inconsistencies in our lives to persist until we come face-to-face with their disastrous results. The good news is that it doesn't need to be this way. The crisis, or catastrophe, or disaster breaks our inertia only by engaging our imaginations, and through the imagination, our emotions as well. This produces a tidal wave of willpower that can sweep away anything in its path. The good news is that we need not wait for a crisis to do the job. We ourselves can directly engage our imaginations in the effort to establish an appropriate consistency in our lives. Even when we lack the power to directly change our lives, we have the power to change our thoughts. If we begin to think about the likely results of our behavior clearly and powerfully, if we begin to picture to ourselves as vividly as possible the inevitably negative consequences of our inconsistent behaviors, we can directly engage our imaginations, which will in turn call into play our emotions and, with their help, magnify that little bit of willpower it initially took to redirect our thoughts until it becomes an irresistible force of will that can break decisively the inertial hold and imprisonment of our self-defeating and counterproductive habits.

> No one who lives in error is free.　　　　　*Epictetus*

Some self-destructive habits are reinforced by chemical dependency in the body, yielding what we call a true addiction. When there is this extra layer to an inconsistent or destructive behavior pattern, we may need the help of a physician in our efforts to change. But no doctor can medically cure us of a habit. Any physical aid we may need will at best help take care of the physical or chemical side of dependency for a while so that we can take care of the rest. Success is finally up to us. And that is both a sobering and a liberating truth.

Now, of course, the weight of habit can be compounded by various attitudes and emotions. Why do I keep doing things in the same old way although I know I'm being inconsistent with my true values, or intended goals, given my current circumstances? And even though I care? It may be that I'm too comfortable with those old patterns to change easily. I may be too lazy. I may be afraid to try something new and fail. But with a vividly enough imagined conception of what I want in contrast to where I am going with present thoughts and actions, with the right sort of healthy confidence that the same conditions of success that help others can help me, with a concentration on what it takes to break the patterns and keep them broken, I can move decisively to overcome all the weight of inertia and establish new consistency in my life.

Let me quote at some length the enormously influential first-century philosopher Epictetus on the topic of habit. In his *Dialogues*, he said:

Every habit and faculty is maintained and increased by the corresponding actions: The habit of walking by walking, the habit of running by running. If you would be a good reader, read; if a writer, write. But when you shall not have read for thirty days in succession, but have done something else, you will know the consequence. In the same way, if you have lain down ten days, get up and attempt to take a long walk, and you will see how your legs are weakened. Generally then if you would make anything a habit, do it; if you would not make it a habit, do not do it, but accustom yourself to do something else in place of it.

So it is with respect to the affections of the soul: when you have been angry, you must know that not only has this evil befallen you, but that you have also increased the habit, and in a manner thrown fuel upon fire.

He later goes on to conclude with this example:

If then you wish not to be of an angry temper, do not feed the habit: throw nothing on it which will increase it: at first keep quiet, and count the days on which you have not been angry. I used to be in passion every day; now every second day; then every third, then every fourth. But if you have intermitted thirty days, make a sacrifice to God. For the habit at first begins to be weakened, and then is completely destroyed.

We *can* take charge of our lives, in what we do and even in how we feel. As a former slave who had lived in difficult circumstances, Epictetus realized that we all can master what we do have some small control over, and that this inner mastery can have great results for our lives. He also realized that the inner life, the life of attitudes, passions, thoughts, and feelings, is of crucial importance to how we live and to what we are able to accomplish. It is hard enough sometimes to spot and deal with inconsistency in our outward actions. But what is even more difficult for most of us is to monitor the inconsistencies of our inner lives. Epictetus' example of anger is well chosen. A disposition to easily and frequently experience and express feelings of anger is one of the most common obstacles to proper progress in life. It's not that we necessarily must conclude that there is anything inherently wrong with anger, or with almost any other inner state we can experience. It's just that this emotion, like others, can affect us in ways that are inconsistent with our values, commitments, and goals if we are not very careful to control its manifestation in our lives. A failure to realize this, and to act accordingly, has held many talented people back from the success they deserved.

What is holding you back from a successful life? You can root out old unproductive, or counterproductive, habits and establish new helpful habits that will make a tremendous difference. But it's ultimately up to you. You can overcome any obstacle of inconsistency you face, inner or outer in form. If you act. If you take charge. If you work at it hard enough. So take that first step. Start now.

Success, remember, is the reward of toil.   *Sophocles*

Let's take a minute to review. Why do inconsistent, self-defeating, or self-destructive behaviors ever persist in our lives? There are only three possible causes:

1. Ignorance

2. Indifference

3. Inertia

This is a complete basic diagnosis of the psychology of inconsistency. Ignorance is a matter of the mind. Indifference is a matter of the heart. Inertia is a matter of the will.

For these three states of mind, heart, and will, there are two cures and, interestingly enough, two more alliterative terms:

4. Information

5. Imagination

This is the rest of what I call *The Five-I Framework for Positive Change*. The simple solution for ignorance is information. Listen to colleagues, coworkers, customers, family members. Ask for

173

professional advice. Read. And think. Open your eyes. And be honest with yourself. These are the cures for ignorance.

The cure for indifference and inertia is the imagination. Caring is not just something we undergo or experience in a purely passive way. It is something we do. With a vividly aroused imagination, we can be goaded to act *as if* we care. And since our emotions are touched by both the imagination and our actions, we'll begin actually to care, if only a little at first. But in an amazingly short time, as the result of our imagination, the new "as if" behavior, and the inevitable impact of emotion on emotion, we will, almost certainly, finally find ourselves really deeply caring. We will have new habits of action, thought, and feeling. And we will have overcome the spell of inertia. We can make this change. We have what it takes.

The Five-I Framework can help us take charge of our lives and establish the stubborn sort of consistency we need to attain the success we most deeply want. And it can be used to diagnose and deal with some of the most difficult long-term problems in any business context. During those two days when I discovered it and came to understand its power, I remember growing ever more eager to share it with the executive whose telephone call and questions had led me to explore the roots and remedies for persistent inconsistency. But in the process of telling me the depth of her problems and detailing the repeated failures of past speakers to make any real difference, she had apparently talked herself out of inviting me, or anybody else, to come and give another speech. She never called back. Which seemed, of course, plainly inconsistent with her apparent goals. But that's the way it goes. And so I never had a chance to tell her about The Five-I Framework. But I have her to thank for stimulating me to develop this simple diagnostic and treatment tool that since has helped so many other organizations and individuals around the country see how to break the bonds of long-term, self-defeating inconsistency and then begin to move unfettered toward greater excellence and success.

A WORD ON POSITIVE PERSISTENCE

In a book of letters to his young adult son called *Mark My Words,* Canadian businessman G. Kingsley Ward writes:

No one I know of has ever experienced one success after another without defeats, failures, and disappointments, and frustrations galore along the way. Learning to overcome these times of agony is what separates the winners from the losers.

The biggest difference between people who succeed at any difficult endeavor and those who do not is not usually talent. It tends to be persistence. As the philosopher Bertrand Russell once said by way of example: "There are people in show business who became major stars simply because they didn't have sense enough to quit when they should have." Many extremely talented and brilliant people give up. Who needs rejection? Who wants to face failure? Who wants to run the risk of getting knocked down again and again? It takes more self-esteem than lots of people can muster. But it's often been said about highly successful people that they are just individuals who got up one more time than they fell down.

Perseverance is a great element of success. If you only knock long enough and loud enough at the gate, you are sure to wake up somebody.
Henry Wadsworth Longfellow

If we feel good about ourselves, we don't feel so bad about difficulties that fall across our paths. We're not embarrassed to take a fall and pick ourselves back up. And if we come to understand the true nature of a successful life as a journey, during which many obstacles will need to be faced and overcome, we can develop a new and more positive attitude about the determined persistence we need to succeed.

Actions and thoughts are consistent when they stand together. Commitments are persistent when they stand through time and difficulty. Cucumbers grow fast. But you can crush them in your hand. Oak trees take a while. If we have chosen goals that are right for us, and close to our hearts, if our vision for ourselves is vivid enough, if we can feel the pull of our deepest values and commitments, and if we can take charge of our own confidence, then we can develop the kind of determined persistence it takes to stick to our journey, even when we might feel like turning back.

But don't get me wrong here. Consistency and persistence don't demand all work and no play. Persistence in any reasonable, long-term quest allows for needed rest, relaxation, and healthy diversion along the way. A little indulgence. Some time off. A persistent person can sometimes slow up. But a persistent person will not easily give up.

The Koran says "God is with those who persevere." As we persist in pursuit of our goals, we set up new habits, new patterns of thought and action, deep within ourselves. The developing of these habits allows for the releasing of energy to reach higher, go farther, dig deeper, and do more. God is indeed in some sense with those who persevere. The energy of the universe can be made manifest through the determined persistence of a human being on a worthy quest.

The ancient Roman poet Lucretius once pointed out the power potential of persistent engagement by directing our attention to the latent energy of even small drops of water, commenting that "constant dripping hollows out a stone." With persistence, with sufficient perseverance, a weaker force overcomes a greater. A reversal of power can occur. Stiff odds can be beaten. A surprising transformation can take place.

> Great works are performed not by strength but by perseverance. *Samuel Johnson*

With a stubborn consistency and a determined persistence, we husband our talents and energies and bring them to bear with intense focus on what needs to be done. It requires an exercise of will in an ongoing way. It demands a sustaining use of the imagination. But deep down beneath all our temptations and pressures and excuses, we all have the power of will. We can use it to activate our imaginations. And we can use it to launch out in appropriate action. It is in the last analysis up to us whether or not we'll chart our course with vision and persistence. It's up to us whether or not we'll marshal the determination to persist in our aims. Or stick to our values. If we're steering toward a goal that is right for us, nothing can stop our striving to persist. And this is a very good thing. For as Calvin Coolidge once concluded, "Nothing in the world can take the place of persistence."

We need a stubborn consistency in pursuing our vision, a determined persistence in thought and action. This is the fourth condition on our voyage of success.

5

A Commitment of Emotion

Condition Five: We need an emotional commitment to the importance of what we're doing, and to the people with whom we are doing it.

On my way to work this morning, as I was mentally preparing to begin writing this chapter, I met an interesting man with a fascinating story. Daniel E. Ruettiger, known to his friends, and now to me, as "Rudy," was born into a blue-collar Catholic family in Joliet, Illinois, one of fourteen children. He grew up hearing about Notre Dame football, listening to the legends and following the scores. It was clearly something that brought the community around him together. People he knew were excited about the exploits of the Fighting Irish, and had a strong emotional commitment to the school, along with what it stood for. Catching that excitement and coming to share that commitment, Rudy began to dream of one day playing football at Notre Dame.

Low grades in high school and low self-esteem made the dream seem impossible. But in 1966, on a senior retreat, Rudy had a

178

chance to visit the fabled campus. The dream was renewed. His friends told him to forget it. There was no way. He wasn't a good enough student to be admitted to Notre Dame. He wasn't a good enough athlete for their famous football team. He was a young man of more meager expectations. He should be more realistic. He should think about a job. So when he graduated from high school, he got a job and went to work in a local power plant.

After two years of this hard and thankless labor, and then two years in the Navy, Rudy found that he still had the dream of playing football at Notre Dame. Returning to work at the power plant, he shared his vision for the future with a close friend and coworker. One day this friend was killed in a terrible accident on the job. Rudy was stunned, saddened, and suddenly convinced that life is too short not to do everything within your power to live your dreams. So he took action.

At the age of twenty-three, he quit his job, moved to Indiana, and enrolled as a student in Holy Cross Junior College, a small school across the street from Notre Dame. His longtime emotional commitment to Notre Dame became a commitment to reaching his goal, living his dream, and somehow, someday playing football for the Fighting Irish. This was the first step in that direction. He was within sight of the Gold Dome. Within sight of his dream.

Rudy worked on his studies, raised his grades, and after two years was able to transfer across the street as a registered student at the University of Notre Dame. He boldly approached Ara Parseghian, the great football coach, and empowered by his commitment, talked him into letting him join the scout team, the group of young men who each week help the playing team prepare for their next opponent. Five feet, six inches tall, and weighing one hundred and eighty-five pounds, Rudy hadn't played the game since high school. But his emotional commitment and sheer determination got him into a Notre Dame scout-team uniform. For two years he practiced daily. He was living his dream. Almost. But he never actually played in a real game, or even dressed for game day. Up until the last home game of his senior year.

The Thursday before that final game in the Notre Dame stadium, he held fast to a hope that his dream would finally be able to be more fully realized—that he would at least have the chance to dress for a real game and walk onto the turf of the stadium that Rockne built as an athlete officially representing the University of Notre Dame. He wanted to wear the game uniform and at least stand with the team on the sidelines. But when he looked for his name on the list of players to dress for the game, it wasn't there.

Without Rudy's knowledge, some of the other players went to talk with the coach, who was then Dan Devine, to appeal to him to please include Rudy in this game with Georgia Tech. They had caught Rudy's emotional commitment to the team and had in turn become committed to him. They saw him as embodying the spirit of Notre Dame, and they wanted to see him in the game.

The coach agreed. Rudy was allowed to dress. Just walking through the tunnel wearing that gold helmet with the crowd screaming their cheers was enough. He says, "I was off the ground." Walking on air. But toward the end of the game, one student in the stands started yelling, "We want Rudy! We want Rudy!" and it spread. In his two seasons on the prep team, Rudy had already become something of a legend among the students who knew him or had heard of his story. Without ever having had a minute's playing time, or even a minute's bench time in that great stadium, he had fans throughout the student body. Soon all the other students joined in the chant. "We want Rudy. We want Rudy." A wave of enthusiasm enveloped the stands. And then it happened. At the age of twenty-seven, within the last twenty-seven seconds of the game, Rudy Ruettiger was sent onto the field as a defensive end. With the whole student section screaming "Rudy! Rudy! Rudy! Rudy!" he threw himself full speed into the last two plays of the game, making the final tackle for a five-yard loss. Notre Dame over Georgia Tech, 24–3. And a personal victory the scoreboard couldn't record. His teammates carried Rudy on their shoulders off the field in triumph.

> The great pleasure in life is doing what people say you cannot do. *Walter Bagehot*

Emotional commitment. An uphill struggle. Against all odds, and against all predictions. A dream come true. And a story worth telling.

When I met Rudy this morning, he was in the parking lot outside the Notre Dame stadium, seventeen years after that great game, standing next to an impressive-looking large group of trucks from North Hollywood, California, on a brisk and beautiful fall morning, watching a crew from TriStar Pictures prepare to film scenes for a major motion picture focusing on his life and his victory. For the theaters of America. And the world. *Rudy.* Beyond the dream.

There is no set limit to where your dreams can take you, with enough emotional commitment to the importance of what you're doing. In reflecting on his own story, Rudy says, "I feel what I went through and what I wanted is just an example of what you do if you have a passion and a commitment to get what you want out of life."

I met Rudy, by the way, quite simply. I knew there was a movie

181

being filmed on campus. Hollywood had come to South Bend, and all the papers had covered it. Pulling into the parking lot this morning, I had to steer around all sorts of equipment trucks, catering vans, and people outside the stadium. The filming obviously had begun. As I walked from the car toward my office, I took the initiative and said "Good morning" to a couple of folks, and then started up a conversation about what they were doing. The first person I spoke to introduced me to the director, and to Rudy. And of course, as you can see, his story fits beautifully at the beginning of this chapter I was ready to sit down and write.

I have had as one of my own recent goals the writing of this book on success. I have a clear conception of what I want to accomplish. Of what kind of book I want it to be. I sit down every morning to write with confidence. I try to work at it consistently. And I am emotionally committed to it. I am passionate about it. I prepare for each chapter, launch out in action, adjust as I go, and network with those who know. There could not be a better illustration of how this often develops than my unexpected meeting of Rudy this morning. When you are following your dreams, when you are embarked on an adventure of success, people will cross your path, and things will come into your life that you never could have anticipated. People who seem to be sent by Central Casting. Things that suddenly move the plot forward. But each of us has to take the initiative to connect preparation to opportunity. And be ready to adapt. These developments come as we go. They happen as we are in process, moving toward our goals. We intersect with them only if we are already making some forward progress ourselves, however small. It's exciting to see where that sort of passion and commitment Rudy speaks about can take us. And what they will bring us, in the most unexpected ways.

THE POWER OF
PASSION AND COMMITMENT

Walter Chrysler, the founder of the American automobile company that still bears his name, once said that "the real secret of success is enthusiasm." Ralph Waldo Emerson was even more emphatic when he stated that "nothing great was ever achieved without enthusiasm."

Enthusiasm. Etymologically, our word comes from two Greek terms meaning God (*theos*) infused (*en*), or God indwelt. God in you. God in me. Sheilah Graham once put it like this when discussing success: "You can have anything you want if you want it desperately enough. You must want it with an inner exuberance that erupts through the skin and joins the energy that created the world."

This is real passion. The heart of the erotic. Many serious thinkers throughout history have claimed that all human action is motivated by one or the other of two great forces. Some people identify them as Pleasure and Pain. But deeper down, behind the sensations of pleasure and pain, are the two more ultimate forces of attraction and repulsion that pull or push human conduct and human lives. What I mean to refer to are the two forces of *Eros* and *Thanatos*, to again provide the ancient Greek terms. Sometimes these words are crudely translated as "Sex" and "Death," respectively. We are drawn toward the one and flee from the other. "Death" is not a bad translation for "Thanatos." The operative ideas are dissipation of energy and cessation of life. But "Sex" is a woefully inadequate rendering of "Eros." I see Eros as rather encompassing the deepest energy of life, the divinely endowed, positive power of attraction, reproduction, growth, development, and flourishing.

Do you know people who truly love life? Who are in love with life? Who are passionate about what they do? Who embrace and savor almost every moment? Who twinkle, or glow, or smolder? These are people who embody the erotic. This is Eros, the power that can lie behind sexuality, behind friendship, behind great art, great music, successful business endeavors, and creative attainment in all human affairs.

> Energy is Eternal Delight.   *William Blake*

Katharine Hepburn was once asked the secret of success. She replied, quite simply, "Energy." The prominent actor Kevin Costner is said to be "pure energy" on the set. It's no accident that so many of the best actors, musicians, artists, attorneys, teachers, doctors, salesmen, and people in every walk of life are described quite often as "intense," "energized," and "enthusiastic," passionate about their jobs and about their lives. And it's no accident that many high achievers are themselves romantics who are often perceived by others as very attractive people. It's not just that power is the ultimate aphrodisiac, as Henry Kissinger once remarked. It's that energy is. Intensity is. Enthusiasm is. Emotional commitment. That is the erotic. That is the deepest natural attractive force in this world. Nobody wants to live in an emotional wasteland. People are attracted to people who care. And emotion is contagious. Passion enflames passion. Care generates concern.

It's sometimes said that great leaders are people of great charisma. Captivating, enthralling, mesmerizing speakers, commanding presences, magnetic personalities. But no magic is required for leadership. What the leader does need is a deep emotional commitment to the importance of what he is doing, a commitment that his actions and words communicate to the people around him. If an emotional commitment is deep enough, it practically demands to be communicated, to the extent that it nearly guarantees its own expression.

One more quick lesson from etymology. The word "emotion" comes from two root words meaning "move" and "out." Emotion is a force that by its very nature moves out from the innermost recesses of the individual into experience, and then into action and speech, and by these means out into the world at large. The more emotional commitment a person has, the more this concern moves out and creates results. The great leader need not have a beautiful face, a resonant voice, or an elegant facility with words. That sort of charisma is not required. What a great leader does need is an emotional commitment to a vision and to the people who can be involved in the realization of that dream.

An emotional commitment is necessary. And a controlled communication of that commitment is important. I don't mean that a leader, or a person working toward success, needs to be always upbeat, manifestly energetic, ever cheerful. There are people whose forced enthusiasm overwhelms others in its expression, whose artificially energetic, chirpy cheerfulness is over the top and alienates as many people as it attracts. You don't need to be *always* singing, whistling, or talking in a loud, fast-paced, and jolly voice about all the wonderful aspects of the day, the job, or the people around you. But you can clearly communicate positive emotion and care by your positive demeanor. Pleasantness is certainly better than grumpiness. A well-governed cheerfulness sensitive to the feelings of others is usually a good disposition to have. A positive, tactful, forgiving, understanding attitude of high expectations and confidence can work wonders. Greet people with a smile and a good word whenever you can. But you need not force yourself to go to unnatural extremes to communicate your emotional commitment to the job or to the people with whom you are involved. A naturally arising and controlled communication of that commitment will best display your real care, and will have the best results. If you are sensitive to the needs of others, just be yourself. It will be a natural tendency of your commitment to express itself in appropriate ways.

I've sometimes heard people in business settings say things like this: "Everybody in my office is a zombie. They're all sleepwalkers. Nobody really cares about anything. They're all just going through the motions. It's an emotional desert." But then a new manager is hired. She shows up with enthusiasm. She obviously cares deeply about what she's doing. And it's contagious. The other people in the office take notice. They begin to wake up. And they begin to care.

People are attracted to people who care. This seems to be a universal truth. And it has a simple explanation. We all have a need to engage with the erotic, to plug into the energy of life, and to feel it flowing through us in our jobs, as well as in our relationships. Without the erotic, sex is dead, friendship is flat, any job is routine, or exhausting, or both, and life itself seems boring. In other words, things are intolerable. And nobody wants that.

We *need* an emotional commitment to the importance of what we're doing, and to the people with whom we're doing it. This is the fifth condition of success.

ENTHUSIASM, ENERGY, AND SUCCESS

There are basically five different reasons why nothing great was ever accomplished without enthusiasm. First, as we have noted earlier, no great success is ever attained in this life without the surmounting of obstacles. In every life there are challenges. Some people view challenges as problems, others view them as opportunities. This marks one big difference between those people who give up and those who move up. We need to understand the positive role obstacles can play in our development. Challenges push us. They stretch us. They make us develop our potential. But you can't leap a hurdle without energy, so successful people value energy. They understand and embody the power of enthusiasm. Their commitments are not just intellectual, they are deeply emotional. And this is necessary for the sustained effort of surmounting roadblocks and outlasting adversity. Without an intensity of inner drive, without a deep emotional commitment, it is very difficult to persist in the pursuit of a dream.

Secondly, without the motivation that comes with enthusiasm, we'll never dig deep enough to discover and develop all the talents we have that can lead us to the greatest accomplishments of which we are ultimately capable. Developing our talents is itself sometimes an arduous task. Without enthusiasm for what we are doing and what we are becoming, it could be at times an exhausting and dispiriting task. It takes energy. And sometimes great energy. We often need to push ourselves to find what we're capable of doing, and what we're capable of being. With genuine enthusiasm, with the right sort of emotional commitment, we can ride a wave of energy that seems to come from far beyond our own limited resources. We can be carried by it to destinations we could not otherwise reach—destinations within ourselves and destinations outside ourselves. This is the force described by Sheilah Graham as "the energy that created the world." Enthusiasm. God with us. The fuel of greatness.

> It is energy—the central element of which is will—that produces the miracle of enthusiasm in all ages.
> Everywhere it is the mainspring of what is called force of character, and the sustaining power of all great action.
> *Samuel Smiles*

There is a third reason why nothing great was ever accomplished without enthusiasm. Great success requires great risk. It doesn't come cheap. Sometimes, financial risk. Often, social risk. Occasionally, physical risk. And, always, emotional risk. We need to be willing to try things we've never tried before. Maybe even things nobody else has ever tried before. We can't always play it safe if we want to play to win in life.

In my classes at Notre Dame I'm always trying new things—tricks, gimmicks, dramatic enactments, wild concrete illustrations of abstract philosophical ideas—that if they work will be great; and if they fail—well, then I'll look like a complete idiot.

For instance, I'm a storyteller in the classroom. I love a good story, and the more outrageous, the better—especially if it's true—because the more outrageous a story is, the more memorable it will be as an illustration of whatever philosophical point I'm trying to make to my class. If I ever just invent a story, or create a fictional example to clarify a point, I'll always make it clear to my students that it's a concocted illustration to convey a truth. But I like most of all to illustrate truth with truth, so I prefer to use examples from out of my own life. But whether the story reports a real-life incident or is just the product of the professor's fevered brain groping for a way to make a philosophical concept more vivid, telling a story always involves at least some small degree of risk. The students may not *like* the story or they may not get the point. Humor is also a risk, in similar ways. What's funny to me might just go right by a particular group of listeners. I'm not saying that this has ever actually *happened*, but it's *possible*. It always *could* happen. And so the attempt to use humor in a classroom lecture, or in a workshop, or in an after-dinner talk always involves the taking of some chance.

> During the first period of a man's life the greatest danger
> is: *not to take the risk.*   *Søren Kierkegaard*

But those are the little risks. I try to make my lecture hall at
Notre Dame an innovative place. A Philosophical Happening. For
students who give good answers to questions I pose, I throw out
candy bars. To illustrate a point in moral theory, I may toss out a
dozen Frisbees and give the class a minute's target practice. To
bring a discussion of life after death down to earth, I re-create for
the whole auditorium the reproducible perceptual components of
a Near-Death Experience, as recounted in the morning talk shows.
In the midst of a normal lecture, my students can be suddenly and
unexpectedly participants in the dramatic reenactment of this
ultimate existential adventure where, by a striking manipulation
of room light accompanied by mock-dramatic narrative, they can
imaginatively experience themselves leaving not only Philosophy
101 and the campus of Notre Dame, but even the confines of their
physical earthly bodies, floating in metaphysical space and speeding down a long dark tunnel, only to discover a Being of Light at
the end of that tunnel who is . . . me in disguise. Hoots, groans,
and laughs. A few Notre Dame jokes later, these student voyagers
are theatrically returned to the body as the room lights come back
up. It's crazy. It's corny. But when it works, it works great. It's fun.
And it's memorable.

To illustrate a point, I may do the equivalent of a two-minute
stand-up comedy routine, or, equally incongruously, take my
favorite electric guitar out of mothballs and suddenly blast them
out of their seats with a wild and deafening sixty-second solo.
After two lectures on the complexities of the mind-body problem, highlighting the logical principles and difficult arguments

on each side of the issue, I like to illustrate the prospects of *Artificial Intelligence,* that contemporary scientific project that aims at the creation of intelligent thinking machines—computers or robots who are more than hardware with programmed software, but actually candidates for silicone-based personhood. I introduce to the class what I present as the latest product of the nation's most innovative AI lab—but an object that is clearly just a long, black tape player standing on one end, wearing a cardboard face mask with novelty-shop nose-glasses, a hat, and a tie, and holding his own electrical cord in one of his taped-on cardboard tube arms: The robot of the future come to the present, Dr. Aristotle Corder, better known to his friends as "Ari Corder." Wheeled out across the stage on a rolling cart, Dr. Corder begins to go into a prerecorded monologue using every corny electricity and computer joke known to man. He says he came from humble beginnings. He was born in a shack—a Radio Shack. But he quickly explains that his mother once almost made it into the Big Time. Before the singing group The Mamas and the Papas became famous, he says, she sang with Mama Cass—she was one of the *Cassettes.* And he grew up rough, with a troubled youth. He was once even arrested, he explains, "on a battery charge."

"I know, I know," he says, "not everybody likes electricity jokes. Whenever I tell them, I get a lot of *static.* But they are about *watts* happening, *current* events, you might say. But some people think electricity jokes are re*volt*ing, so . . . so *Ohm* not going to tell any more."

You get the picture. In a four-minute blitz of bad jokes, forgetfulness, apparent irritation, and conversational interaction with me, this black box conveys the comic illusion of the long-sought and clearly overestimated "thinking machine." He gives the history of computers in less than two of those four minutes. And he gives the students a vivid psychological break from the more intellectually demanding aspects of the fifty-minute class period. His antics and mine lead to what I always hope will be a lively sense of what's at stake in the sometimes arcane debate over the claims, promises, and potential implications of Artificial Intelligence.

Why do I do such things in the classroom? I lie awake much of the night before I'm going to try out any such pedagogical gimmick and ask myself exactly this question. If it falls flat, I'll look really, really stupid, and I'll be totally embarrassed in front of hundreds of people. If it works, it will provide one of those special moments when education and entertainment, philosophy and fun make memorable contact. The students will see our intellectual grapplings in a new light; they'll catch a glimpse of the playfulness that can be an important ingredient in the life of the mind; they'll have an unexpected and, hopefully, illuminating experience; and they'll remember at least some of what we did and talked about that day years later.

> And what he greatly thought, he nobly dared. *Homer*

It's worth the risk. Because I *care* about my students. I'm emotionally committed to the importance of what we're doing together. I'm committed to helping them see the excitement of ideas, and to helping them become more philosophically reflective about every aspect of their lives. So I'll take the risk to make it memorable. I'll suffer through the insomnia, the occasional nervous stomach, and the second, third, and fourth thoughts. Some nights before the trial run of a new teaching device of this magnitude, my wife has watched my High Anxiety for hours and finally

191

has asked, "Why do you *do* this to yourself?" I most often answer, simply, "I have to."

Without the emotional commitment, I'd never take the risk. I'd never take all the extra time and all the extra chances of falling flat. With the commitment, I have to. Now, I don't for a minute want to imply that a teacher who doesn't spin yarns, tell jokes, and engage in occasionally outrageous theatrics is not emotionally committed to the importance of the classroom. Or that anyone else has to show commitment in such unusual ways. I'm just giving what *I* have to offer. I'm trying to be creative and effective in my own way. Others may bring to their work very different gifts. And very different styles. But the common thread is that if we don't feel what we're doing *from the heart,* we'll hesitate to risk doing anything very new or very different, even if we sense that it could be important for the attainment of our goals.

Some measure of risk is always involved in the distinctive deployment of our unique talents into the world. And without a strong emotional commitment to what we are doing, without a deep enthusiasm for our tasks, we won't take the risk.

The fourth reason why enthusiasm, or a strong emotional commitment, is typically necessary for greatness is that, without it, we can easily be tempted to settle for nothing more than a basic, minimal competence in what we do, at best. The world actually most often seems to be filled with plain old incompetence, punctuated here and there by a somewhat higher state of mediocrity. Buy almost anything. Hire nearly anyone to do practically anything, and you'll see what I mean. And mediocrity is not just to be found where it might be expected. Even the world of high-end merchandise and allegedly first-rate service is plagued with it, to the extent that our overall dynamic of expectations has for the most part been thrown into reverse: There's no longer a general, firm presumption that things will be done right, and a commonly felt need for a special explanation to be provided when they go wrong. People seem nowadays to just assume that things will be done fairly badly. Some special explanation is called for only when the contrary occurs and things are actually done well.

I have to admit that my eyes have been opened about this only in the past few years, through a series of events worth retelling, if you'll indulge me here for a minute. I bet you've had your own comparable, eye-opening experiences along similar lines. Maybe many.

When my daughter, Sara, was younger, she once picked out for her room some pretty bedroom furniture at a major department store. I had no idea what lesson I was about to learn as I placed our order. The first hint came weeks later when the delivery man stood on the curb at the back of his truck and said, "Let's uncrate this stuff here and look it over real good before we lug it upstairs." So there in the front yard we unloaded everything, unboxed it, and gave it all a good once-over. So did the neighbors. The headboard of the bed we had ordered for Sara looked all right, and the foot railing did too. It would be more than a year before it started to come apart. The desk and desk chair we ordered seemed fine. The long dresser passed muster. But the tall chest had a big crack on its right side. Reject. Back on the truck it went. Weeks later a replacement arrived. Within seconds the neighbors had spotted a small crack in the wood on one side. Back into the truck once more.

> A fault is sooner found than mended.
>
> *Ulpian Fulwell (1580)*

Half a month passed, then another truck brought a third dresser, obviously finished by a drunken, blindfolded person in a hurry. The white paint barely covered the wood in spots. It was so uneven I couldn't believe it. Jackson Pollock does a dresser. Splotches "Я" Us. As the weeks passed, broken drawers, long scratches, uneven trim, and more problems than I can list made us regulars on the delivery schedules of most local trucking companies. Finally a dresser with only a small flaw in the paint came to rest in Sara's room.

The lesson? One expressed long ago by Cicero when he said, "Everything splendid is rare, and nothing is harder to find than perfection." I have to admit that the saga of months in search of a product without glaring flaws took me by surprise, and was more than a bit depressing.

That little series of experiences changed my perspective, and caused me subsequently to examine everything I buy much more carefully than I ever had before. And, of course, with eyes wide open, it didn't take me long to realize that shoddy workmanship is all around us. We nowadays seem to be awash in a vast sea of sloppiness, incompetence, and carelessness. Everywhere. But there are some products and services in our world advertised to be quite different.

I have always written my books and articles by hand, with a pen on lined notebook paper. My first few scholarly books were produced with cheap, twenty-five-cent ballpoint pens. But a few years ago I gradually began to see advertisements in various magazines for extraordinarily beautiful and very expensive fountain pens said to be writing instruments of rare quality. I picked up a couple of catalogues from high-end pen stores. I was entranced by the photographs and impressed by the descriptions. The promises of true craftsmanship, attention to detail, artistic design, and meticulous production evoked a nostalgic image of a former time when people took a special pride in their creations and a man's reputation, the moral fiber of his character, turned on how well he did his job.

When I contemplated my first fountain pen purchase, I longed to enter whatever small part of that world survived in our own day. Of course, Rolls-Royce made similar claims to excellence in the realm of automobiles. As did such firms as Patek Philippe for their wristwatches. It didn't take much by way of financial self-knowledge for me to realize that my best shot for contact with the world of flawless quality would be with fountain pens. I was ready to put away the disposable ballpoint and take up a true work of art, a writing instrument that would itself embody the high ideals, care, and attention I try to put into my own work. I wanted an Excalibur of ink, and on the basis of all the ads, that's just what I expected.

> Things are not always what they seem.　　　*Phaedrus*

So the cheapo disposable went into the telephone-table drawer, and I shelled out *one hundred dollars* for a big, beautiful, black-barreled famous-name fountain pen, with a fourteen-carat-gold nib. I was ecstatic, metaphysically inebriated with the joy of owning such a rare jewel, until I got home and discovered a large scratch on the barrel. Factory installed. What a shock! But of course, the store gave me a new one, once I had time to drive across town again with the bad news. Imagine my surprise when I found that the new one skipped. Badly. And you can probably guess that this discovery was made only when I had once more returned home.

I tried to write with it. And it had its virtues, I suppose. Smooth strokes could produce cut-on-the-dotted-line children's pictures. What they couldn't produce was smooth lines. I wrote the company. A cut-along-the-dotted-line complaint. Weeks later they wrote back: "Send it in." So I did, UPS. A few more weeks later they sent it back. I unpacked the box with great eagerness and nearly breathless anticipation. I held my restored pen gently, untwisted the cap, and put nib to paper. It still skipped. Just as badly. Maybe worse. My Bic never skipped. This extremely handsome artifact did.

Over the next several months I got to know all the UPS drivers in the area. Maybe I was dealing with the wrong pen company. I decided to up the ante and spend *more than two hundred dollars* (on sale!) to buy another famous maker's top-of-the-line pen, said to be the ultimate product of "perfect engineering." It was admittedly an item of captivating visual elegance, but it also skipped. I was utterly dismayed. But after only one cross-country repair, this was corrected. It wrote with perfect smoothness, but clicked loudly through each stroke.

Time passed, and one day another brand of pen arrived as ordered. With tax and shipping charges, we now had passed the *three-hundred-dollar* threshold. Opening the package in the front yard (which, I had learned, was the place for this sort of thing), I was almost speechless taking in its beauty of design and finish. Until I turned it over and saw two glaring flaws in the cap. Sitting down to write a letter of complaint to this third and equally renowned pen company, I found that I would not be able to do so with their product. It stubbornly refused to yield its ink, except in minute and sporadic doses. So I picked up another pen and clicked off a note describing my problems. Two repairs later, it finally worked. I won't even tell you about the fourth pen, from yet another prominent maker, that arrived looking like it had been chewed on by a beaver, leaving an irregular row of teeth marks in the barrel. A phone call, a letter, and more contacts with UPS finally brought a sincere apology for a pen that "should never have been shipped or sold," in the words of the manufacturer, and a replacement that works and looks just fine.

So, what did I learn from all this? Well, I learned that Cicero knew what he was talking about. I learned one reason why shipping companies like UPS do so much business. And I learned how pervasive a lack of care and commitment really is, even where you would least expect there to be a problem.

I won't even begin to tell you about how this lesson has been reinforced and magnified in my history of automobile purchases and dealer service trips. It's just too depressing. And I've recently built a new house. But please don't get me started on that. The point has been made. We've all experienced it.

By the work one knows the workman.

Jean de La Fontaine

What's the explanation for all this? Often it's quite simple. The people involved just don't care. Too many people don't really care enough about what they are doing at work. They are not emotionally committed to the importance of what they are doing. And so they don't do it well. They're inattentive, careless, sloppy. Going through the motions. Waiting for the weekend. Doing time but not much else.

And it cannot be blamed on the job. For any job that is done badly by dozens, hundreds, even thousands of people, there is someone out there, and sometimes more than one person, sometimes several, doing it well. Very well. It's never the job. It's always the person doing the job. Is that person emotionally committed to the importance of the job, the process, the goal? Is it a matter of the heart? If the answer is no, then chances are no greatness will be found in the results. No excellence. Nothing even very distinctive. If the answer is yes, then very good things are to be expected. A commitment that comes

197

from deep within is one of the most powerful forces in our world. Its importance is every bit as great as its rarity.

> Man is only truly great when he acts from the passions.
>
> *Benjamin Disraeli*

So the inner passion of a strong emotional commitment is a facilitating, liberating, and immensely productive force in the life of any individual. With it we conquer challenges; without it we stumble. With it we develop ourselves; without it we languish. With it we are willing to take risks when needed; without it we just play it safe. With it we strive for excellence; without it we settle for much, much less. These are four very good reasons for its importance. But there is a fifth, and more social, reason as well, as my earlier remarks on leadership may have hinted already.

EMOTIONAL COMMITMENT AND OTHER PEOPLE

No great success was ever attained alone. No one in this life ever accomplishes anything worthwhile flying completely solo, start to finish. Satisfying success is always in some way, and most times in many ways, a social product, a result of people working together. Whatever our dream is, whatever our goals are, we cannot do it alone. We did not come into this world to do it alone. We were created as social beings—beings intended to exist together and to work together in relationships. We were created to journey toward personal fulfillment with other people.

But unless other people are attracted to you and your goals, you can find yourself going it alone far too much of the time. What will attract others to you? And to your projects? What will work to prevent this unhealthy aloneness? Simple: Energy. Enthusiasm. Passion. Your emotional commitment to the importance of what you're doing. And your emotional commitment to those other people. People are attracted to people who care. And people are attracted to care about what other people they are attracted to care about. Especially when those other people also care about them. This is just part of human nature. There is a somewhat complexly chiasmatic slogan now making the rounds among teachers, as a claim about our students. It reminds us that "they won't care what we know until they know that we care." And this is universal.

Rudy Ruettiger's friends, family, and neighbors were committed to Notre Dame football. And they cared about him. He was then attracted to them, committed to them, and so, as a consequence, became committed to Fighting Irish football. The players and other students at Notre Dame were struck by his unwavering commitment, and so in turn became committed to him. His dream became their desire. And through their new commitment to him, and actions for him, his dream became a reality.

People help people they care about. And people care about people who care. As long as what you care about is truly worth your care, your commitment of emotional energy will attract and hold both the attention and assistance of people around you, people who will help you attain your goals, people who will themselves accompany you on your journey of success.

If it's worth doing, you can't do it alone. But if it's worth doing, it's worth caring about. And if you care deeply enough about what you're doing, your commitment will be contagious, and you won't be doing it alone. That's as close to a guarantee as we have.

In May of 1987, I was surprised to receive a freshman teaching award. Three months later the new academic year started. When I walked into the Hesburgh Library Auditorium and greeted my new class of three hundred first-year students for Philosophy 101, I was surprised again. There were more large bodies in front of me than I had ever seen before in a classroom. After class I called the athletic department out of curiosity, identified myself, and asked how many varsity athletes were in my class. The woman I spoke with put down the phone for a couple of minutes, checked a list, and said, "Professor Morris, you have fifty-five varsity athletes in that class this semester."

"Fifty-five? Wow, I've never had more than five or ten athletes in any previous class, to my knowledge," I replied, A worry crossed my mind. "Do I suddenly have a reputation here that I don't want to have?"

"Oh no," she said. "At Notre Dame we don't put varsity athletes in classes with the easiest professors. We have a very different policy. We try to put as many of them as we can, as early in their careers as possible, in classes with professors who have won teaching awards, hoping that these faculty members will be able to get them as excited about their academic work as they are about their athletic endeavors."

On hearing this I said, "Well, I'm proud to be at a place that operates like that. I'll enjoy having them in class and introducing them to the wonders of philosophy."

Out of the thirty-one entering first-year football players that year, I had twenty-nine in that class. Each semester, for the introductory philosophy course, I give three exams and five or six paper assignments, on the basis of which grades are awarded for the course. On the first exam in that particular semester, twenty-six of the twenty-nine football players went down in flames, with grades the likes of which I had never seen in all my years of teaching. We didn't actually have to dip down into the negative numbers, but one young man did work for an hour and end up with a score of zero, on a standard scale of a hundred possible points. I had never seen this happen. Usually there's a point to be gotten *somewhere*. His colleagues managed to find seven, or thirteen, or twenty. Total.

Forty-eight students failed that exam. Athletes and nonathletes. A first philosophy exam can be a very difficult experience. Epistemology and metaphysics don't always come naturally to firsttimers. But I had never had more than a dozen students fail any given test before. What was I going to do? I couldn't lose this many of them. I cared about these students. I wanted them to learn. I was committed to the importance of philosophy for their overall educations. I was committed to them. But I couldn't just *give* them passing grades by changing my standards. Philosophy is what it is. You learn it or you don't. Mastering the material of my course requires as much care and precision as succeeding in mathematics, or chemistry, or physics, or any other demanding discipline.

I hit upon an idea. I decided to form a club for any student, athlete or nonathlete, who had made a grade below C on any previous assignment. I called it "The Below C Level Club." And I scheduled meetings for every Thursday night, review sessions that would go over the main ideas presented in class on Monday and Wednesday, to prepare my struggling students for small discussion groups on Friday. And for the next Exam Day. Our motto was "Come keep your head above water. Come to the Below C Level Club on Thursday nights."

With small children at home, I was not a night person anymore. But football practice didn't end each day until about eight at night. Then the players had to eat. So we started at nine. The students showed up in surprisingly large numbers. Coaches even came, to make sure their players were there. I led those review sessions with all the energy and enthusiasm I could muster. The quarterback told a local newspaper writer doing a story on my class that "Professor Morris must sit in his car and psych himself up before each review session. He comes in with so much *energy.*" I lectured, I quizzed, I answered questions, and I preached—about life, learning, habits, attention, concentration, self-discipline, success in the classroom, and then about life some more. I stayed as long as it took. And then I drove home completely worn out.

They could tell that I cared. I cared about philosophy. I cared about our class that semester, our joint enterprise together. And I cared about them. My caring, my energy, my enthusiasm, my emotional commitment were *contagious.* Those students very quickly began to care too. They began to reflect back some of my energy. And they began to understand more of what I was teaching them. They started to really study. And they began to do much better in the course. On the second exam, no one failed. No one. People who had made a D on the first test were up to C+ and B level. Students who had stared down the barrel of an abysmal F were making C level grades. It was astonishing. It was also very gratifying.

These were people who on the field or on the court were heroes. Back home, their names and faces had dominated their school newspapers, their local sports pages, and even area television. They were achievers. They were stunning successes, recruited nationwide. And they were going to Notre Dame with championship dreams. Then, suddenly, they were confronted with failure. A failure that could threaten to unravel all the rest of the fabric of their lives. A result that could pull the rug out from under all their hopes and dreams.

It would have been easy for many of them to give up. There is a certain psychology of "face-saving" that can click into operation at a time like this. It's natural to be tempted to quit trying so that at the end, when you do fail, you can at least say, "Well, look, I really didn't even try. I blew it off. Big deal. Who needs it?" To fail is bad, this mind-set has decided. To really try and then still fail is much worse. So the danger was that, confronted with a threat of failure in the philosophy classroom, these students would give up, and guarantee that failure.

But they didn't give up. They caught my commitment. And they succeeded. I was so proud of them. And I felt great about what I had been able to do to help them.

One day not long after the results of that second exam were in, there was a knock at my office door. It was an investigative reporter from a major national newspaper. He said, "Professor Morris, I hear that you have all the freshman football players in your big philosophy class."

"Well, I have twenty-nine of the thirty-one freshman players," I replied.

"And I hear that all of them failed your first test."

"Actually, twenty-six of the twenty-nine failed that first exam," I responded, as we stood at my door.

"I've also heard that all of them are, all of a sudden, now doing *very well* in your course."

"Oh yes," I enthused, "grades have skyrocketed on our second exam. No one is failing. They're all doing much, *much* better. I'm really proud of them."

He appeared skeptical. "Would you mind if I had a look at that second exam?" OK. It was clear to me now why he had come. He suspected that something fishy was going on. He figured that in the second test I was helping keep the football program on track, and perhaps bending a little, maybe with questions like "Discuss the concept of good in the phrase 'Good tackle.'" No problem. I opened a drawer and produced a copy of the exam. I handed it to him and watched him read aloud, in a voice of incredulity: "Present two versions of Saint Anselm's Ontological Argument for the existence of God. Lay out three of David Hume's criticisms of the Teleological Argument." Long pause. Scanning other parts of the test. "Football players can *read* these questions?"

"They not only can read them, they can *nail* the answers. These are the future philosophers of the NFL." I explained how my commitment had become theirs. How my passion for teaching had sparked a fire in them for learning. And how it is that this should be no surprise. Because I wouldn't be in teaching at all unless I had enjoyed the wonderful experience of having teachers along the way who had a passion and commitment for what they were doing and for what I was learning. An emotional commitment to the importance of what we're doing will sustain us in our journey, and it will spark others to join us in that process. It will make things happen in very exciting ways.

On life's vast ocean diversely we sail,
Reason the card, but Passion is the gale.

Alexander Pope

LIGHTING THE FIRE

An old Texas proverb tells us that "you can't light a fire with a wet match." Too many people are wet matches. There's tinder all around, dry and ready to blaze, but they can't seem to produce the least spark. If you are not throwing off sparks, if you're not yourself flaming, then *why* not? In the world of my work, in the academic world, in the intellectual life, in the realm of the mind, there seem to be a lot of people who think of themselves as guardians of the truth, protectors of its purity, keepers of the flame. I'd rather be an intellectual arsonist and help to set the world aflame with the right ideas. But to do that I need to be pretty heated up myself. I need to be on fire with those ideas.

I recently came across a wise remark by a man named Reggie Leach: "Success is not the result of spontaneous combustion. You must set yourself on fire." If we do not create energy for our ideas and then convey that energy to our projects, how will they go? If we don't share energy with other people, why should they care about us and our plans? Why should they concern themselves with our goals? But how can we generate energy and care if we don't have these qualities already? Where do we find the emotion we need? How do we set ourselves on fire?

I've come to believe that successful living and successful working is a process of:

1. Self-discovery

2. Self-invention

3. Self-discipline

    and

4. Self-indulgence

In our voyage through life, we are ideally discovering talents we may never have suspected we had. As we set goals, work on confidence, strive to concentrate on what comes next, struggle for consistency, and examine ourselves for the emotional commitment it takes, we are engaged in self-discovery, a process of self-knowledge. But not everything we are, and that we will become, is in us from the start, waiting to be unearthed. We have it within our power to create, to invent, to become what we will, compatible with the most basic talents with which we have been endowed. In this life we are launched also into a journey of self-invention. What will we become? What will we build within ourselves? We are given the raw materials, at the most basic level, but it is up to us what we do with them.

How will we form and shape our lives? Our careers? Our relationships? How will we *invent* the people we will become? At the bottom of thought, attitude, and emotion there is will. At the bottom of the undeniable effects of heredity and environment there is will. We all have power, however slight, energy, however subtle, for the will to draw upon and use. The will, the volition, the basic human ability to act, inherently contains some amount of renewable energy at its core. And nothing is more fundamental in life than the power of the will.

> The man who has the will to undergo all labor may win to any goal. *Menander*

Some pessimist once said, "Life is just one long process of getting tired." Many people seem to feel that way. They feel victimized by life, by circumstances, and by people they cannot control. They feel buffeted by the forces that cross their paths. They feel worn down by the grind of everyday living. They give up. They go with the flow. And then they complain about where they end up.

Where you are and where you are going is always in part, and to a surprising extent, a result of what you do. It is not just a result of what happens to you. The initiative is yours to take. The willpower is available. Everybody has it. We just don't always draw on it. And so we forget it's there. Or we use some of it, and then fail to renew it. We fail to dream. We fail to use our imaginations, the primary natural source of inner renewal. And so we grow weak. We flounder. W.C. Fields once cautioned, "Remember, a dead fish can float downstream, but it takes a live one to swim upstream." Are you a dead fish? Or are you more like an electric eel, flashing against the current and producing current of your own? Are you alive with what you are doing? With what you are becoming?

Swimming upstream is difficult without self-discipline. Both self-discovery and self-invention necessitate some measure of self-discipline. And self-discipline requires energy. We must direct ourselves. We must on occasion push ourselves. We must sometimes deny ourselves the ease, the comforts, the small indulgences we desire. Short-term sacrifice for the sake of long-term gain and enduring satisfaction is almost a forgotten option in recent times. By an act of will, we need to be able to marshal the power to govern ourselves. Only with sufficient self-discipline can self-discovery and self-invention truly flourish.

> When your will is ready, your feet are light.
>
> *George Herbert*

But discovering your true nature and inventing your own life trajectory ought to be the most exciting exercise imaginable. It ought to be thought of as the ultimate act of proper self-indulgence. We indulge ourselves by doing something we love whenever we can. We discipline ourselves to do whatever it is necessary to do whenever we want to, or need to, remain on target, pursuing what we deeply love and value even when we don't especially feel like it. Self-discipline is a condition of real personal growth and of the attainment of real personal excellence. It takes self-discipline to persist through difficulties. But if what we are working toward is a goal dear to our hearts, that self-discipline is ultimately in service to the best sort of self-indulgence imaginable.

207

And that effort of swimming upstream we must discipline ourselves to make will be rewarded in ways we never anticipated as we discover new currents to help carry us along to our goals. Seeing this can engage our emotions and our imaginations, which will magnify our energies. Understanding it can help us set ourselves on fire.

Are you doing what you love? Are you working at something that sets you aflame? That feeds the fires of your heart? If not, why not? Make a change. Do something else. Or else just love what you do. Put your heart into it. Now.

When love and skill work together, expect a masterpiece.

John Ruskin

That's right. One way of doing what you love is simply deciding to start loving what you do. We all have some degree of control over this. If you have a job that feels tedious, hard, thankless, or boring, you need to make a change. But you don't necessarily have to change jobs. You may want to just try to change your mind *about* your job. And of course that can change your job, *from within.* Same title, same tasks, same people, same place, same pay, perhaps—but it can be a different job if you think differently about it.

There is an often-told story. Three men are hauling stones in wheelbarrows. Each is separately asked what he is doing. The first says, "I'm hauling rocks." The second man says, "I'm helping put together a wall." The third replies, "I'm building a cathedral." Who is most likely to love his job? Who is most likely to have the energy he needs? Who is most likely to have his heart in what he's doing? And who would you expect to do the best job? No question. The third man. The one who thinks of himself as engaged in a noble task of great significance. The lesson to be learned? Don't just haul rocks or even help put together walls. Build cathedrals. Take the attitude of great builders and you can build a great life.

> Greatness, after all, in spite of its name, appears to be not so much a certain size as a certain quality in human lives. It may be present in lives whose range is very small. *Phillips Brooks*
>
> Greatness is a spiritual condition. *Matthew Arnold*

There is no job that can't be given a trivial description. There's no job that can't be given a great and noble one. As a writer, I put ink on paper. Trivial description. As a writer, I try to articulate new ideas and share them with people around the world, for the greater good of us all. Noble description. Which is my description to myself of what I do? Fortunately, it's the latter. Only an ennobling conception of what we do will inspire in us the deep emotional commitment we need to do it well.

A real estate broker should think of herself as helping to provide people with living environments that will greatly enhance the quality of their time on this earth. An auto mechanic should think of himself as adding immeasurable value to his customers' lives, as he helps guarantee that they have safe, efficient transportation, thereby perhaps even enhancing the quantity of their time on this earth. Do you work in an office? As a teacher? Providing a service? Wherever you are, and whatever you do, as long as you are involved in providing some product or service that can benefit others, you can create and maintain in your own mind a noble conception of your role in the world. You can inspire yourself to draw deeply on the resources you have to attain the success you deserve. And you can inspire in your coworkers the same thing.

> There is no trade or employment but the young man following it may become a hero.
>
> *Walt Whitman*
> (Or the young woman, Walt!)

You don't need to be physically strong or beautiful, financially wealthy or powerful, intellectually brilliant or socially connected. You may have thought up until now that your contribution to this life is small. But think again. Small things can have great consequences. Little things can carry great meaning. With the right attitude of mind, we can see that and be deeply moved by it.

In chapter two I referred to a striking claim once made by the great psychologist William James, namely, his statement that "the greatest discovery of my generation is that a human being can alter his life by altering his attitudes of mind." That is the key. On the job, get your imagination in gear. How does what you do hook in with what others do and experience? What's the Big Picture behind the smallest of your challenges and efforts? What are the loftiest values and ultimate aims you are serving? What's the most outrageously wonderful result possible for your actions, as they feed into the larger scheme of things? Use your imagination. Stretch your inner vision. What happens to us is never as important as how we think about what happens to us. What we do is only as important as how we think about what we do. So: *Think big.*

> To generous souls, every task is noble.   *Euripides*

Find specific goals to set yourself within the confines of your work, goals that you can enjoy working toward because they are yours, however great or small. Savor their accomplishment. Feel good about what you have done. And then set new goals. Be creative. Push back the normal borders of the job. Be imaginative. Be playful. Let the child in you really enjoy what you do. Cavort. Relish the process. Appreciate the little things. Then the big things will take care of themselves.

Get to know the people around you *as people.* Not just as supervisors, coworkers, colleagues, or subordinates. This is OK, but more important, get to know them as human beings with needs and wishes, loves and hates, strengths and weaknesses just like you. Build better relationships with the people around you. Show some care. Show some concern. Do something nice for them, expecting nothing in return. And then prepare for a surprise: You'll get a great deal in return.

> Doing good to others is not a duty. It is a joy, for it increases your own health and happiness.   *Zoroaster*

Take control of your current situation in a positive way. Use your willpower. Refuse to be diminished. Refuse to be down. View your labor as the extraordinarily positive thing it can be. Don't settle for anything less. Nothing is either intrinsically fascinating or un-avoidably boring. To a great extent we make anything whatever it is to us in emotion and attitude. It's up to us. As you heed these truths and follow this advice, you'll begin to set yourself on fire.

LIVING A BALANCED LIFE

The single most important thing I ever learned during all my many years of formal education, I learned on the first day of the first grade at Durham Academy, in Durham, North Carolina. Once we were all seated in our little desks, our teacher walked to the front of the room and wrote a sentence on the blackboard. We had no idea why, because none of us could read. Fortunately, she then read it out loud:

Life is not what you want it to be; it is what you make it.

She explained. And I remember it to this day. We are all artists. Our lives are our greatest works of art. Is that work of art the best that it can be? Are we *making* it the best that it can be? Are we pouring energy into life? Are we living enthusiastically?

Let me at this point quote Harry Truman, who once said:

I studied the lives of great men and famous men, and I found that the men and women who got to the top were those who did the job they had in hand, with everything they had of energy and enthusiasm and hard work.

Energy, enthusiasm, and hard work. You don't often come across these terms together nowadays. Maybe stress, exhaustion, and hard work. Perhaps thankless tedium, low pay, and hard work. But how often do we associate energy, enthusiasm, and hard work? We ought to associate them, in our minds and in our own lives.

We are meant to work. We are meant to play. And we are meant to rest. Few people appreciate equally all three of these truths. Few of us integrate them well into our lives. Most people seem to think that we work only so as to buy the time, materials, and opportunities to play, and to relax. As if that's the only point of work—its purchasing power for the time and toys to take us away from work. We do it, on this view, just to purchase what we need in order to do with the time that remains what we really love. Working for the weekend. The Thank-God-It's-Friday philosophy of life. The ideal, from this angle, would be minimal work and maximal recreation, or *no work at all*—an endless vacation.

Yet when we look around the world and see men and women with no meaningful work to do, we do not find just blissfully happy and enviable people. We find many desperately unhappy people. Depressed, angry, and frustrated people. We are meant to work. We need to work. Deprived of meaningful, productive work, we are not truly ourselves. We are not what we are meant to be. Recreation without productive creation is empty.

> For too much rest itself becomes a pain.　　　*Homer*

Of course, there are also quite a few workaholics in the world. Not many of these people seem to be models of happiness either. They are driven, "nose to the grindstone." Wherever this image comes from, it doesn't promise very pretty results. These are people who typically believe that the only excuse for rest or play is to refresh us enough to return to work. We sleep to work. We eat to work. We play sports to get and keep that competitive edge for work. The ideal, from this point of view, would be minimal play and maximal work, or *no play at all, no rest at all*—a twenty-four-hour workday. A seven-day work week. Year-round.

Every life needs balance. We need work. We need play. We need rest. We need the kind of love for what we do that generates energy and enthusiasm. And we need a better integration of all these things.

Too many people compartmentalize their lives. They divide things up. Time for work. Hard work. Time for play. Energetic play. Time for love. Enthusiastic love. Then time for rest, from all the rest.

We need more flow, more interweaving, more continuity in our lives. We need to learn to integrate play into our work, into even our hardest work. It's difficult to bring emotional commitment and energy into an environment where we have no fun at all. We need balance. And we sometimes need to integrate even rest into our work time. The busiest hands don't always accomplish the most, and don't usually produce the most important, creative results. Recreation and positive creation often go hand in hand. Learn when to take a break. Let your unconscious mind savor and slow-cook some ideas. Let go. Relax. Gain some perspective. Slow down. Stretch out. Breathe deep. Go blank. And then return to your task. Often, this little bit of refreshment, the smallest change of pace, will give you a burst of ideas and energy, a creative, passionate solution to a problem, and a renewed vigor for work so that you will end up getting more done faster than if you had plodded continually along or if you had kept dashing tirelessly, or more likely, exhaustedly, toward your goals.

What is without periods of rest will not endure.   *Ovid*

Energy, enthusiasm, and hard work. They can go together. And they should. Energy requires rest, if it is to be sustained. Enthusiasm needs play. And hard work requires love. Do what you love by loving what you do. Are you emotionally committed to the importance of what you're doing? Right now? Regularly? Don't wait any longer. Commit now. It's up to you.

"But wait," you might protest, "a lot of my job is routine, mun-

214

dane, tedious, boring. How *can* I be *emotionally* committed to all this?"

One sage once said that there are no boring activities, only bored people. Now, maybe this is an exaggeration. But the truth is, life is not what you want it to be, it is what you make it. Our jobs, our activities, our routines are wet clay waiting to be molded by us. What will we do with them? How will we think about them? What will we feel for them? It is up to us. It is, finally, a matter of *will.* How will we use our basic willpower that we do have in our own lives, or on the job, as we set and act to reach our goals? How will we envision what we do? How will we direct our own attitudes? How will we choose to invest our energies? Will it be boring? Will it be fascinating? It is, indeed, up to us. And that's a liberating truth.

We can endow our activities with interest, with energy, and with emotion. We can give our day the fire we need. We have that power. It will take imagination. And sometimes it will take some effort. But this effort will have effects that will lift us up, further spark our imaginations, and give us more energy. And they will make the next level of emotional commitment a bit more effortless. Our emotional energies will communicate themselves. People will be attracted to us and to our projects. Others will join in. And we will see results.

One of life's many ironies is that selfishness is self-destructive. We need to care about ourselves and our own projects. But we should never care only about ourselves. Self-interest is fine and healthy as long as it's not our only interest. In fact, the greatest sages have recognized that an appropriate self-concern is the ultimate basis for any proper concern for others. Our natural love of self can teach us how to love and care for others. And it should. It can seem a bit paradoxical at first, but only if we truly care about the people around us will we most likely be able to attain all the great success of which we ourselves are capable.

> A person totally wrapped up in himself makes a small
> package. *Harry Emerson Fosdick*

How then do we come to care genuinely about the people around us? For some, this comes naturally. For others, it requires a conscious effort of attention. If you find altruism to be a bit difficult, if caring about the people around you doesn't come naturally, don't despair. There are steps you can take to turn this around. Begin to include others in your plans. Make an effort to attend to them and their needs. Act *as if* you care, as sincerely as possible. This is just another application of The Action Approach to Attitude we discussed in chapter two. Pretty soon, as a result of your actions of caring, you will genuinely care. And with the help that will eventually be forthcoming for you as a natural response to what you have done for others, you will be able to do much more in moving toward your own goals than you ever could have accomplished alone. With your help, those people around you will also enjoy the very same benefit. And so the whole process will leave everyone better off than before. This is real progress along the way to the most satisfying form of success possible. An exciting prospect indeed.

> He that lives not somewhat to others, liveth little to
> himself. *Michel de Montaigne*

The fifth C of success, condition number five: We need an emotional commitment to the importance of what we're doing, and to the people with whom we're doing it.

6

A Character of
High Quality

*Condition Six: We need a good character to guide us and keep us on
a proper course.*

High achievers nowadays talk a lot about goal setting. But they
sometimes seem to talk as if it doesn't really matter *what* goals we
have, as long as we have goals. Targets to shoot at. Dreams to
pursue. Any target. Any dream. But not all goals are created equal.
Good goal setting requires good judgment, and good judgment
ultimately is a function of good character.

We live at a time when many people are beginning to say they
suddenly see that, for years or even decades, they've been chasing
the wrong things. This can be a startling realization. For some
people it's depressing. For many more it's liberating. It's revelatory
and life changing. In any case, it embodies a realization that not all
goals are equal. We are much better off if we are pursuing goals
that are really right for us, dreams that genuinely merit our time
and efforts. True success is not just attaining goals. It is attaining
goals that are worth attaining. Without the right orientation, it's

217

unlikely that we'll follow the right paths and make the right choices. We need a good character to guide us in our choice of goals.

Character is the moral core of personhood. It ought to be thought of as the foundation of personality. As Stephen Covey and others have begun to point out in recent years, too much of the success literature of our century has been personality-oriented when it should have been character-based. A beautiful house built on a bad foundation cannot provide for secure and stable long-term habitation. Nor can an attractive personality veneered over a bad character provide for any sustainable and fulfilling form of success.

Character is destiny.   *Heraclitus*

When we refer to a person's basic moral character, we refer to an integrated set of his or her most fundamental characteristics or tendencies related to moral perception, moral judgment, attitude formation, emotion, and action. Good character is usually the result of nurture—example, training, correction, and habituation. Bad character is often the result of neglect. Good character is the main wellspring of ethical perspicacity and sound decision making. Bad character is the primary source of moral error. Good character is a prerequisite for proper and fulfilling goal setting over the long run. Bad character is a guarantee of nothing but trouble and ultimately self-defeating action. I am convinced that true success cannot be attained apart from a process of ethical character development, for a number of reasons.

MEANS, ENDS, AND TRUE SUCCESS

For true success, it matters what our goals are. And it matters how we go about attaining them. The means are as important as the ends. How we get there is as important as where we go. This seems to be a nearly forgotten truth in our highly competitive society.

Everybody wants to be a winner. Nobody wants to be a loser. It was once the worst kind of insult and severest sort of condemnation to be called a scoundrel, a cad, a louse, a liar, untrustworthy, unscrupulous, unethical, immoral, or just plain evil. In more recent days, the most dreaded affront and reproach seems to be "loser." A label to be avoided at all costs. The lowest of the low. The realm of outer darkness.

> Those who know how to win are much more numerous than those who know how to make proper use of their victories.
>
> *Polybius*

"Winning is not everything," Vince Lombardi once said, "it's the only thing." Victory or nothing. This is one of the most famous quotations of modern times used as a slogan of success, almost a battle cry, by people willing to do *whatever* it takes to win, regardless of the costs and consequences for themselves and those around them. In later years, the great coach Lombardi became very frustrated with how his well-known remark about winning had come to be interpreted and used in such a way as to justify almost any form of behavior, however unethical. He even once complained: "I wish to hell I'd never said the damned thing. . . . I meant the effort. . . . I meant having a goal. . . . I sure as hell didn't mean for people to crush human values and morality." But with a fixation on winning, on attaining their goals at any cost and by any means, a great number of people committed to achievement have bulldozed their way over important, genuine human values and swept aside the whole of morality without any apparent hesitation or regret. They are people who believe that the ends justify the means, and that the end of all ends is to win.

Alfred Hitchcock once summed up a fairly common attitude along these lines when he said:

> There is nothing to winning, really. That is, if you happen to be blessed with a keen eye, an agile mind, and no scruples whatsoever.

And this, of course, expresses perfectly the mind-set of the endlessly manipulative gamesmanship that in recent years has been masquerading as success. It is no surprise that in our time the most neglected condition of success may be our condition six: the necessity of a good character to guide us and keep us on a proper course. The kind of character that will give us sound guidance in our choice of goals and of the means to those goals.

But wait a minute. Is good character really a condition of success? Can't a total jerk be a tremendous success? Aren't there great numbers of completely unscrupulous people in fairly high places in the modern world? Haven't we been told for a long time that "nice guys finish last"? How then can I plausibly identify good character as a condition of success?

I won't deny for a moment that a bad person can achieve some good results in a bad way and prosper as a result. In a limited field of endeavor, for a limited time. But those good results and that prosperity will be tainted by bad consequences that may not be easy to see at first, but that will be more significant in the long run.

A scoundrel can indeed sometimes meet all his goals, get rich, and become famous in the process. He can take pleasure in the results of his misdeeds, and even enjoy the doing of them. But can he be happy? Really happy? Truly satisfied? Fulfilled as the best he's capable of being? I don't think so. Happiness is not the same thing as pleasure, or superficial enjoyment. It is deeper, and broader. As is true satisfaction. And fulfillment. They very often involve pleasure and enjoyment, but these simpler and more immediate psychological states are no guarantee of those more profound and lasting conditions we all seek. The focus of my concern in this book is ultimately the deepest, most fulfilling sort of success we are capable of attaining, what I have called "true success." By that I mean success that is deeply satisfying, that involves making the most of our potential, and that is sustainable over the long run, the sort of success that contributes to all forms of health and human flourishing. A person may for a time *have* a measure of worldly success without good character, but without this condition no one can really *be* a success, in the fullest and deepest sense.

EXCELLENCE AND ETHICS

The ancient Greeks had a very interesting word: *arete.* It can be translated into English in two different ways. It can mean "excellence," or it can be rendered as "virtue."

Confusing. These days most people seem to think that excellence is one thing, and virtue is something totally different. Excellence has to do with success, attainment, achievement, and superiority. Virtue, by contrast, is widely thought to be something associated with an old-fashioned idea of ethics connected to a certain quaint, traditional conception of personal morality having no relevance whatsoever to anything related to questions of excellence. This common perspective could not be more wrong.

221

> Virtue is to the soul what health is to the body.
> *La Rochefoucauld*
>
> Virtue is harmony. *Pythagoras*

One day I was visited by a young executive who wanted me to come into his company and give some presentations on success and ethics. He came into my office, sat down, and said, "Look, I'm not really sure how to say this, but you need to know something up front. In our company, we have a strong values statement that is given to each new employee, at every level. We have taken an official stand on the importance of ethics and ethical conduct. But I suspect that the values statement we hand out goes right into people's files and never gets read or thought about again. In our corporate culture, our dominant concern is excellence. We think about excellence and talk about it on a regular basis. Everybody also seems to agree that ethics is important. But we don't ever really talk about it. There even seems to be an unexpressed worry in the backs of many people's minds in the company that there may be some sort of deep conflict between ethics and excellence, in the final analysis. And if push comes to shove, we're committed to excellence. We have to be. The market demands it. You see what I mean?"

I did. And I think this is a common worry in many business contexts. Morality is noble, but business is business. Our goals have to be met. The bottom line is important. Success has to be attained and then sustained, come what may. And excellence is our standard. If ethics gets in the way, well, that's unfortunate, but we do what we have to do. My visitor wanted me to speak to his organization on the importance of ethics but was a bit apprehensive about the reception this topic might face if not presented in just the right way. Could I do anything to defuse this deep-down concern about the possibility of a conflict between ethics and excellence?

I explained right away that, far from allowing that ethics and excellence might ultimately conflict, I am convinced on the contrary that we all have an ethical obligation to strive for true excellence in our personal and professional lives, and that the highest sort of excellence cannot be attained apart from a properly ethical point of view.

1. The Obligation of Excellence

If we play a role in a business that provides a good product or a good service for people, we have an ethical duty to attend to the bottom line and maintain a healthy, survivable business. People depend on us for those products, or services, or for their own employment and livelihoods. We owe it to them to do our best. We owe it to ourselves to make the most of what we are, and to become the best that we can be. And if we are not now associated with the provision of some good for the world, we ought to be. All this is part of what I think of as the ethical obligation of excellence.

I also explained to my guest the perspective of the ancient Greeks and suggested that in our own day we need to realize that, at bottom, genuine human excellence and proper human ethics are one. They are inextricably united and cannot ultimately conflict. Any belief to the contrary is just based on a misunderstanding of what excellence really is, or of what ethics is, or both.

What is excellence? *The Oxford English Dictionary* defines it as "surpassing merit." Some dictionaries present it as "the condition of being better than others," "unusually good quality," or "superiority." Etymologically, our word comes from two Latin roots that mean "to rise out from." Competitively, excellence is the quality of rising out from the crowd, or standing above others in merit, or superiority of attainment. Personally, it is the attribute of quality rising out from one's own potential. I can attain my own personal excellence as a guitar player by maximizing the development of my talents, given the constraints of my other commitments and interests, regardless of whether the end result would be counted as excellence by competitive standards applied across all guitarists. I need not be *the* best to do *my* best. Personal excellence then, of course, does not guarantee competitive excellence, although it is most often required as a step along the way to any goal of a more public superiority. Nor, on the other hand, is competitive excellence always a sure sign of personal excellence. This is an important point that is not as widely recognized. In an area where the competition is not very tough, a person can rise to the top, for at least a while, regardless of whether he or she is attaining true personal excellence. Sometimes a very talented individual can stand out on the basis of no more than a partial development of personal potential. A situation like this can easily lull a person into a sort of subtle stagnation, where any further growth of talent and skill is stunted as a result of too much easy external success. But external success devoid of any internal drive toward true personal excellence is an inherently unstable situation. We can never guarantee that we'll have poor competition in the market or on the athletic field. And, for our own developmental good, we shouldn't even wish for this. So if we strive for any sort of enduring competitive excellence, we'd best concentrate on personal excellence as the way to move in that direction.

But once we have made the distinction between personal excellence and competitive excellence, a deeper set of truths needs to be articulated. The ethical obligation of excellence is not an obligation to be better than everybody else at anything that you do. It's not essentially competitive in nature; it's personal. I am strongly inclined to think that the most fundamental ethical obligation of

224

excellence each of us has is an obligation to be the best that we personally can be at each and every thing that we do, across a broad range of interests and activities, given the legitimate constraints of our most basic natural endowments, the opportunities we've had to develop, and the other commitments it is equally good that we have.

I don't mean by this that every time I step onto a tennis court I have an obligation to go all out, playing with all the intensity I can muster. My partner and I may just want to do some lazy, easy hitting and talking. But if that's our goal, I believe I should be the best lazy, easy hitter and court conversationalist I can be. I should truly relax. I shouldn't try to make the situation something it's not. But if the goal on another occasion is competitive play, I should then be as competitive as I can be.

I've tried to state what I believe to be our most basic obligation to personal excellence with all the caution befitting a philosopher. Sometimes the most important and practical truths are subtly nuanced and are not easily captured in short, snappy statements. That's just one of the reasons why political sloganeering and posturing can be so dangerous. Our greatest insights won't all fit onto bumper stickers or into quick sound bites for the evening news. I believe I have an ethical obligation to be the best I can be in everything I do, across a broad range of activities, compatible with the realities of my situation. And I think this is an obligation had by everyone else as well. But the qualifying phrase or phrases in each of these statements of the obligation should not be overlooked. The realities of my situation—my basic talents, opportunities, time commitments, and other legitimate interests—limit what I'm ethically required to do. I can cook for my family several times a week without incurring an obligation to take culinary courses, to read cookbooks, and to spend hours shopping for the finest ingredients my budget can tolerate. I can toss a Frisbee now and then without any obligation to strive mightily to hone my Frisbee-throwing talents to their ultimate refinement. I've got other things to do. And so do you. The obligation of excellence I'm talking about does not demand *unreasonable* dedication to superior performance in everything we do. It just requires of us that we make the most of our time and talents in a balanced way as we live our lives. We should care about whatever we are doing. We should invest ourselves *wholeheartedly* in anything we choose to do, but that investment should be made *wisely* as well. A healthy human life involves many commitments, many interests, and many values. In any activity in which we are involved, we ought to be the best that we can be, consistent with the preservation of all the other commitments, interests, and values we properly have. That is the obligation of excellence.

There is nothing noble in being superior to some other man. The true nobility is in being superior to your previous self.   *Hindu proverb*

Any goal of competitive excellence should ultimately be for us just a means to pursue personal excellence. We benchmark against others in competitive situations. We push them to push us to become the best that we're capable of being. But if we're pushing them properly, then they are being pressed to become the best that they're capable of being. All parties to a competition ideally develop beyond what would be expected without the competitiveness.

A good parent tells a child in any competitive situation, "All I ask is that you do your best." And this is not a cop-out. It's not a willingness to settle for some second-rate consolation prize. It is, in itself, the ultimate goal of the competitive situation. It's not the adversarial win that's the real good, it's the personal win. That's why cheating is not only wrong, but is also ultimately self-defeating. It embodies a deep misunderstanding of the real nature of any competitive contest. It is literally a perversion.

A failure to grasp the real relations between competitive excellence and personal excellence has led in our culture to innumerable instances of competitive wins bought at the price of great personal losses. And there are many different ways this has been manifested. In too many corporate quality and excellence programs in the recent past, it seems like a concern for people has been sacrificed to the concern over products or services. The quest for excellence has been far too narrow. Companies have been tempted to neglect the real human needs of their people and fixate on the competitive advantages of their product or service. This can appear unproblematic for a while. But product excellence and service excellence are not sustainable over the long run apart from a good deal of personal excellence on the part of the people providing the product or service. And personal excellence in a particular, specific activity is not sustainable over the long run in any healthy way apart from a more general, overall personal excellence of the individuals involved.

2. The Importance of Multidimensional Living

We live in a time of many unhappy people who are unhappy not because they have little, or because they suffer much, but because they live too narrowly day to day. We live in an age of one-dimensional people. We are so desperate to be successful at something, *anything,* that we often latch onto the first talent we find we have and frantically cultivate it to the neglect and exclusion of anything else. Children discover they are good at soccer, that they gain praise and self-esteem from their talents at this sport, and then devote themselves wholeheartedly to this one athletic ability, neglecting intellectual development, music, friendships outside the sport, and anything else that does not feed that one fire. Or they do this with a musical instrument. Or with an academic subject. A five-year-old who talks nothing but dinosaurs is one thing. A forty-year-old who talks nothing but sales is something else altogether.

No one has just one talent. Talents always come in clusters. Too many people fail to explore and develop their own multidimensional potential. Too many businesses encourage their people to live and breathe one and only one thing. Thin living is not conducive to true happiness. One-dimensional people do not live healthy, well-rounded lives and do not contribute to a healthy interpersonal environment. Whatever success one-dimensional development may contribute to a corporate or social environment in the short term, narrow personal excellence does not contribute to the overall health and flourishing of any large-scale environment or enterprise over the long run. People must be allowed to, and even encouraged to, develop personal excellence in a variety of forms if they are to flourish, and if their collective enterprises are to attain and sustain a level of true excellence over time.

The increasing technical narrowness and laser-thin specialization of interest and skill in modern corporate life has created unhealthy environments for human happiness and even for corporate excellence in any rich and sustainable form. We need to strive for the cultivation of a more complete human excellence in our schools and in our workplaces along every basic dimension of human life. Because of this, I am convinced that continuing education in corporate life and throughout the business world should encompass not only the new developments in areas most immediately relevant to the technical and economic sides of business, but also such enterprises as philosophical reflection on ethics and the human drama. This will contribute importantly to the creation of a truly humane corporate environment in which individuals and their business can most fully flourish.

Philosophers for more than two thousand years have identified the most basic dimensions of human life as:

1. The *Intellectual* dimension, which aims at *Truth*.

2. The *Aesthetic* dimension, which aims at *Beauty*.

3. The *Moral* dimension, which aims at *Goodness*.

The remarkable acrostic we have here is the great "I AM"—I *am* all these things: intellectual, aesthetic, and moral. It is no surprise, then, that the great philosophers have spent so much time thinking about Truth, Beauty, and Goodness. Religious philosophers throughout the centuries have added to this list:

4. The *Spiritual* dimension, which aims at *God*.

"I am all these things," it can be said, "because God is creator of all." A profound perspective on ultimate connectedness, the core of human spirituality.

Overall human excellence involves participating in and flourishing along every basic dimension of human existence. For this reason, morality, or ethics, is inextricably tied to excellence at an ultimate level. The moral dimension is one of the fundamental dimensions of a full and fulfilling human life. It must be cultivated for true excellence to be attained.

So, if I am right, there is a bridge from ethics to excellence and a path running back in the other direction as well. If your first concern is ethics, I think you will discover that there is an ethical obligation to strive for personal excellence. If your focus is excellence, I believe you will discover that it cannot be attained in any broad and sustainable form apart from attention to the moral dimension of life. Ethics and excellence go hand in hand.

3. The Essence of Ethics

We've engaged in some exploration as to what excellence is. And now we must ask the other general question we need to explore, however briefly. What is ethics? What exactly is morality? Some people use the two terms "ethics" and "morality" differently; others use them interchangeably. Those who separate ethics from morality often think of morality as having to do with personal principles for living, especially as regards the more private spheres of life. They think of ethics, by contrast, as involving more public, or professional, rules of conduct regarding standard roles we find ourselves in with respect to our interactions with others, within the confines of overarching human institutions. From this perspective we have legal ethics, medical ethics, and codes of ethics governing real estate brokers and accountants, among all the other professions.

Some people draw a distinction between personal morality and professional ethics because they believe they can act on one set of principles in private, with friends and family, and then adopt a very different set of principles at work. An old expression for this is that "we wear different hats. One hat at work. Another hat at home." But we wear them on the same head. In modern life there is too much compartmentalization of thought, feeling, attitude, and action. How we act on any occasion, in any set of circumstances, contributes toward determining who we are. We are in a deep sense products of all that we have been and done. We should not try to draw such sharp distinctions between the public and the private. There is not such a great distance, morally or ethically speaking, between friends and colleagues, the neighborhood and the workplace, the home and the office. To make and reinforce this point, I like to use "morality" and "ethics" roughly inter-changeably.

So what is ethics? What is morality? Many people seem to think of ethics, or of morality, as just consisting of lots of rules that act as constraints on our conduct, restrictions intended to keep us from doing things we might otherwise really enjoy doing. Along these lines, a contemporary comedian once remarked that good people seem to sleep better at night, but bad people appear to enjoy their waking hours more. Some critics throughout history have thought of morality as a weapon used by superior people to keep inferior people in their place. Others have seen ethics as an instrument wielded by socially inferior people to keep their superiors in check. I can use a Rodin sculpture as a doorstop or a beautiful Pelikan fountain pen as a weapon. But that doesn't tell us much about Rodins or Pelikans. To see ethics as an inhibiting set of repressive rules is to misunderstand terribly the moral dimension of life.

Let me put it simply and straightforwardly. The way I under-stand it, ethics is just fundamentally a concern for

spiritually healthy people in socially harmonious relationships.

There are both inward- and outward-looking directions in ethics. We often think only of the outward: how we relate to other people. Our duties regarding others. But we have duties regarding our-selves as well. I use the word "spiritual" here in its broadest possible sense, as designating that aspect of the inner life of any human being that is the deepest wellspring of thought, emotion, attitude, and action. Spirituality in this sense has to do with personal completeness and connectedness—connectedness among our be-liefs, our feelings, and our acts in the world. Completeness in who we are. And connectedness with a greater whole. A truly spiritual person in this regard experiences some measure of inner complete-

231

ness and inner connectedness across every dimension of life within the self, along with a strong connectedness to other people, nature, and nature's Source, however that is conceived. This is the firmest foundation for an embodiment of virtue in a life.

> The glory that goes with wealth and beauty is fleeting and fragile; virtue is a possession glorious and eternal.
>
> *Sallust*

Only spiritually healthy people, people experiencing some measure of a deeply attuned, overall positive growth toward personal excellence, can stand in deeply harmonious social relations with other people. A spiritual malaise, or incompleteness within any person, inevitably infects relations between and among persons, preventing them from being the best that they can be.

I don't mean at all to say here that any particular religion or religious belief is necessary for ethics, or that only religious people can be moral. There are people who would acknowledge no recognizably traditional religious beliefs, who nonetheless act ethically toward others. Atheism, or an irreligious worldview, may lack an array of motivations and guidelines for moral conduct, but it need not involve a general incapacity for moral sensitivity and the adherence to a strict ethical standard. Nor, of course, does an endorsement of religious beliefs guarantee moral conduct. I do not intend in my remarks here to be tying ethics to formal religion or to specific religious beliefs of any sort. I mean only to be using the concept of spirituality in its broadest sense, as I have indicated. The precise connection between morality and theology is another matter, and is outside the specific focus of our concern here, although it is in itself a subject of great fascination and importance.

What does it take to live well? This is a question of ethics. What does it take to live well together? This is another question of ethics. Both, I believe, are finally questions about character, about what moral fiber is required, what character qualities are necessary, in an individual, in order for that individual to live a good and successful life. Character is at the center of moral concern. And any concern about character is a concern about what it takes to attain any sort of overall personal and interpersonal excellence in our lives. Genuine, overall, deeply satisfying, and sustainable human excellence requires good character, and good character, in turn, is the core issue of ethics.

What is good character? Having a good character involves integrity, honesty, patience, courage, kindness, generosity of spirit, and having a strong sense of personal responsibility, among many other qualities. It's amazing to me how little we talk about such things nowadays. Basic terms of the moral vocabulary seem to most of us so familiar, but we are often hard pressed to say exactly what they mean.

A man was in a job interview. He had been employed at a number of places before and had never stayed very long at any one job. The interviewer looked over his résumé and said, "Your employment history raises a question. Are you a responsible person?"

The man replied, "Yes indeed. At my last job, whenever anything went wrong, my boss always said I was responsible."

We need a better grasp of what it is to be responsible people, what honesty requires, and what exactly integrity is. We don't talk enough about these things. We don't think enough about these things. And we suffer from this neglect. Most people do not fully enough have their bearings in the moral dimension and are easily thrown when a difficult situation comes their way. Character development is every bit as important as intellectual development and the continuing enhancement of our perceptual and performance skills as we work our way toward success. And it's easy to say why.

THE SWEET SMELL OF SUCCESS

Without building a good character, I think it is impossible to build a truly successful life. First of all, without a proper ability to assess what is really in our own best interests, we're prone to chasing the wrong dreams and acting in self-destructive ways. Without the wisdom that comes with character, we tend to pursue what seems most immediately pleasurable, what promises us good things now. We focus on the short term. And what looks best in the short term is not always what is best over the long haul. In fact, short-term gratification often interferes with long-term growth. Without the perceptiveness, self-discipline, and patience tied up with good character, it is unlikely that we will move steadily in the direction of our own most comprehensive form of personal excellence. With the formation of a strong moral character, many impediments to true personal success can be overcome.

It is impossible to live a pleasant life without living wisely and well and justly, and it is impossible to live wisely and well and justly without living a pleasant life.

Epicurus

Character also contributes in a second way to success. Most types of public success, and a great many forms of private success, require the help and cooperation of other people. But other people won't help us, typically, unless they are attracted to us, like us, and trust us. They will not join in our projects unless they are persuaded that it is a good thing to do so. If they see that our projects will lead to good *for us*, they must be persuaded that it is good *for them* to help us attain that good. Or they must be persuaded to see, more directly, a good for them in our projects. We need to be able to sell our ideas and our projects to other people. And we need to be able to sell ourselves to other people, to convince them of our value and our worthiness of their assistance, or they will not be motivated to help us in our quests. And to be done right, this ultimately requires good character on our part.

1. Ethics and Superior Salesmanship

Aristotle long ago recognized the importance of persuasion in human life. And we must all come to see the importance in our own lives of what has come to be known as "salesmanship." I define salesmanship very simply and very broadly as the ability to convince other people to enter into joint projects that are of mutual benefit. Think about it for a minute. Without the ability to convince other people to enter with us into joint projects that will be of mutual benefit, this life would be a war of every person against every other person, an image once used by the seventeenth-century philosopher Thomas Hobbes, who also described such a life as "solitary, poor, nasty, brutish, and short."

> Everyone lives by selling something.
>
> *Robert Louis Stevenson*

Salesmanship is the glue that holds society together. Without the art of persuasion, civilization would be impossible. I believe Aristotle saw this, and so he did a careful analysis of what is required for powerful persuasiveness. He laid out three conditions for what we now call salesmanship.

The first condition of persuasion, or successful selling, has to do with the *logos* of the situation, a Greek term from which we derive our English word "logic." If we want to be persuasive to other people—if we want to sell them on our ideas, or on us, or if we're selling cars or clothes or houses—we must be masters of the logic of what we're doing. We need to know all the relevant information *cold*. We need to do our homework and reason through every aspect of what we're selling, as well as the situation in which we're selling it.

My father was for the last decades of his life a real estate broker, and he was a lifelong masterful salesman. From selling himself to the Martin Aircraft Company at the age of seventeen, to building and selling radio stations, inventing and selling toys, selling advertising concepts, houses, and large tracts of land, he had throughout his lifetime a great many wonderful successes. In every case he was a master of the *logos*. He knew his stuff. He would not show a house or a piece of land until he knew all about it. He walked the land to learn the terrain: the trees, shrubs, rock formations, and water. He examined the houses inside and out. He learned their history. He knew how far a house was from the nearest gas station, grocery store, shopping mall, elementary school, Baptist church, Catholic church, synagogue, and college campus. Four and a half miles to this, three miles to that. He knew the answers to nearly any question he could possibly be asked, and, on the very rare occasions when he was stumped he knew how to get the answer.

People were always extremely impressed with my father's knowledge of what he was selling. His obvious command of all the relevant facts made him believable. It made him an authority. It put him in control of one of the three conditions of persuasiveness. But, like Aristotle, my father always recognized that there is more to selling than just information and logic. People are not just reasoning machines. People have feelings and imaginations. And this must be taken into consideration too.

The second condition of salesmanship has to do with the *pathos* of the situation, a Greek word that we have taken over, transliterated into English as a term for emotion, feeling, or passion. If we want to be persuasive, we have to master the *pathos* of the situation. First we must have within ourselves a proper emotional commitment to what we're doing. We need passion. And, of course, this was the focus of chapter five. But then we must also be attuned to the feelings, emotions, attitudes, and passions of the people with whom we need to be persuasive.

My father realized that he could not properly help a client into a new living environment, or into a satisfying investment, unless he knew some of the hopes and fears, likes and dislikes, loves and hates, dreams and dreads of that person. He had to get to know the person. He had to ask questions. And listen. With sensitivity. He had to be attentive. If we do not plug into the emotions of other people, we cannot motivate them to join in with us on our projects. We cannot most fully help them. And we cannot inspire them to enter into whatever project or relationship will be most helpful to us. If we don't know the people with whom we are working or dealing emotionally, we don't know how to connect fully with the *pathos* of whatever situation we are in.

How important this is can be seen everywhere in society. The most popular public speakers, network news anchors, sportscasters, and politicians tend to be those who emotionally "connect" with the rest of us. They seem to be real people who understand us. They care, and so we do too. They communicate, at their best, heart to heart, to use once again that ancient and central human metaphor. As we saw in the previous chapter, people are attracted to people who care. And people respond very positively to people who come across as knowing their cares.

But there is also a third condition for persuasiveness, or salesmanship. That is the *ethos*, or the ethical condition of character. However impressed other people are by our apparent knowledge, however attracted they are to our emotional commitment and care for them, however well we are able to connect with them and appeal to their emotions, commitments, and imaginations, they most typically will not be totally sold by us, they won't be fully persuaded, unless they see us as morally trustworthy in our dealings with them. What Aristotle recognized was that, all other things being roughly equal, people are persuaded by people they trust. Apart from a firm appearance of trustworthiness on our part, other people will not enter into strong commitments with us and wholeheartedly contribute to our progress toward success. To sell others on our projects, or on our products and services, we need first to sell them on ourselves as ethical, trustworthy partners and associates.

> Do you fear to trust the word of a man whose honesty you have seen in business?
> *Terence*

My father was always my own role model for business integrity. He spoke plainly, straightforwardly, and honestly. He did not ever exploit. He always kept in mind not only his own interests, but also the interests of all the other people with whom he was dealing. He didn't just want profit. He never needed to be well known. He just wanted to profit from being known for his character, his honesty, his ethical point of view and moral practices. He treated others the way he would want to be treated. At home. At church. And in business. People were so impressed with his integrity and were so relieved to be dealing with an honorable man that they came back for his services again and again. He often sold the same piece of land many times because both buyer and seller would go away pleased with how he dealt with them. Then, when the buyer later became a seller, he would come back to my father for representation, and so on, and so on. A master of the *ethos* of business, my father was a master of satisfying, sustainable success.

As I write these words, my father has been gone from this world for two months, taken out far too young at the age of sixty-nine by lung and brain cancer. During the days immediately following his death, I was approached by scores of people in my hometown telling me of the difference his life had made to them. "He was a man of true honor." "He had real integrity." "He was somebody I could *trust*." "He was the last true gentleman in the neighborhood." At the gas station, in front of a laundromat, at a convenience store, people would stop me just to say, "Your daddy was a good man. I'll miss him." I was glad my children also heard dozens of these spontaneous remembrances of praise. Their grandfather had been a man of *character*. And this had made all the difference. This is what people he dealt with remembered and what so many of them went to the trouble of telling me. He succeeded in their eyes first and foremost because of his ethical strength. His character.

A man's own character is the arbiter of his fortune.

Publilius Syrus

---

2. Appearances and Realities

To have satisfying, sustainable success in our interactions with others, to have the sort of persuasive impact in the lives of other people we both need and want to have, we must appear knowledgeable, we must appear caring, and we must appear trustworthy. We must appear to be people of character. How then can we best appear thus? Simple. By being thus. There is no other acceptable way. But a great many people in our time seek the right appearances without the trouble of establishing the realities. People bluff. They fake concern. And they strive to come across as trustworthy, without necessarily having to bother themselves with all the work that might be required for the process of building true character.

Let me quote *The New York Times,* October 26, 1992. It's impossible to make up this stuff. Reality is often more fascinating than fiction. And sometimes a lot more unbelievable. An article headlined "Fragrance Engineers Say They Can Bottle the Smell of Success," by N. R. Kleinfield, begins like this:

> It was bound to happen. Someone thinks he is about to create the Honest Car Salesman in a bottle.
>
> A year ago, one of Detroit's Big Three auto makers hired Dr. Alan R. Hirsch, a quirky smell researcher in Chicago, to devise a rather exceptional scent. The hope was that when the odor was sprayed on a car salesman, he would—yes—smell honest.
>
> It sounds absurd. In fact, after she was done laughing, Dr. Susan Shiffman, a smell researcher and professor of medical psychology at the Duke University Medical School, remarked, "I was not aware that honesty had a specific smell associated with it." But Dr. Hirsch, who refuses to name his Detroit client, is confident that he will have the Honest Car Salesman Odor devised within a year. If he succeeds, he said, the auto maker will entrust the smell to its dealers, who will spray it on their salesmen, and then customers will catch a whiff and cars will fly off the lots.

The sweet smell of success. The aroma of trustworthiness. Every bar would be well advised to keep spray canisters around for the convenience of customers. Kids wet behind the ears with this stuff might actually convince their teachers that the dog did in fact eat the homework. Politicians could try pumping it out of crop dusters over their rallies. And I'm sure that at traffic courts and around IRS offices you could smell them coming a mile away. Incredible. Absurd.

This product will be eagerly anticipated by all those people who take the biblical injunction to "avoid all appearance of evil" in altogether the wrong way—as if it doesn't matter what you're like, as long as you take care of how you appear. But this gets it backwards. The best way to appear honest is to be honest. The simplest, most dependable, and most long-lasting way of appearing trustworthy is to be trustworthy. The biblical approach is first of all to try to avoid all evil. And then, go even a step further and be so careful as to avoid even the appearance of evil. It's not a looser standard, but a much more stringent one. Only then can you guarantee your trustworthiness in the eyes of all reasonable and well-disposed people. Nothing, of course, is guaranteed to work with the unreasonable and ill disposed. But these are people to be avoided anyway, since we are all prone to become like the people we are around.

> The way to gain a good reputation is to endeavor to be what you desire to appear. *Socrates*

Plato, the student of Socrates and the great teacher of Aristotle, most powerfully brought to our attention the distinction between Appearance and Reality. Too many people in our day choose appearances to the neglect of realities. They live lives of illusion, and try to foist those illusions off on others around them. But of course this is not limited to our day. In another century, Blaise Pascal pointed out that a great many people would cheerfully be cowards if they could somehow, by means of this, gain a reputation for courage. It is the image that is valued over the substance. In our own time, we probably have far more people than ever before who chase false dreams that appear to them to define success, and then often suffer unnecessary despair because they do not attain what wouldn't really satisfy them if they had it. Plato counseled us to penetrate through appearances and connect up with realities. The best way to appear trustworthy is to be trustworthy. Cultivate *ethos,* the real ethical dimension of your life. Develop real character. It's a condition of true success.

We shouldn't expect other people to judge us just by contrived, superficial images, and we shouldn't judge others by surface appearances either. I'm afraid I have made that mistake too many times in my own life. And I have learned as a result that appearances can be quite deceiving. Let me give you one memorable example.

When I was at Yale, and my wife and I were living in the servants' quarters of a large old house out in the country in Bethany, Connecticut, about ten or twelve miles from the university, we were once invited to a big Christmas party at a neighbor's house. As I was being introduced around a large room full of people, I was called over to the side of a very elderly man who was perched on a chair in the center of the room. My host said, "Tom, I'd like you to meet a neighbor, Bob Calhoun. Bob, this is Tom Morris, a graduate student at Yale."

I said, "Hello, Mr. Calhoun, it's nice to meet you," as I bent over to shake the wizened hand he slowly raised toward me. He looked like an ancient farmer who must have been a bit bewildered by all the activity and people.

He said, "What are you studying?" Well, I assumed that because of his age and mode of dress, he knew more about vegetables and chickens than about college life, so I didn't say, "Philosophy of religion," my focus of study at the time. I was afraid he wouldn't know what that meant. Growing up in North Carolina, all the really old people I had ever known were farmers who usually had attended only a few years of school before having to work full-time. I just assumed that this elderly gentleman would know nothing of the academic life. So in answer to his question as to what I was studying, I simply said, "Religion."

"You're in the Department of Religious Studies?"

"Yes sir, I am." He knew the proper name of my home department. Maybe he wasn't quite as cut off from university life as I had assumed. He at least must have read the local papers about Yale news or have talked with someone who understood Yalie nomenclature. I started to add that I was also in the Department of Philosophy, but I didn't want to push my luck with him.

"Well," he said in a low raspy voice, "one of your colleagues came out to see me the other day to talk about a paper he was writing on Plotinus and Neoplatonism. His thesis was that from Plato to the middle Academy . . ." The rest I don't remember because I was so surprised by, and I could hardly keep up with, the ensuing barrage of ancient Greek philosophical concepts along with this old gentleman's rapid-fire account of the twists and turns of their intellectual elaboration and development over the centuries in the hands of many thinkers I had never heard of.

Not just an old farmer. An old farmer, yes. But also a retired, internationally renowned professor of Historical Theology who had taught at Yale *forever*. Don't judge a book by its cover. Or a man by his brogans.

> Think not I am what I appear.   *Lord Byron*

But I was not the only one to misjudge this old gentleman. When he retired from the classroom, he began to raise chickens and became the egg man for some of his former colleagues. Once a week he would bring eggs to their houses, often just open the door, let himself in, deposit the eggs in the refrigerator, and leave, without a word.

One day, a well-known theologian at Yale was entertaining one of the most famous intellectuals of Europe, the New Testament scholar Rudolf Bultmann. The two men were at the kitchen table arguing vigorously over a point of interpretation concerning the writings of a Greek-speaking Christian theologian who lived and worked in the early centuries of the church. Old Mr. Calhoun, dressed in his farmer's overalls, opened the back door, padded across the kitchen floor with a nod, and quietly put his basket of eggs in the refrigerator. He walked back across the room, and hesitated a moment before going out the door. At a pause in the lively argument between the two accomplished scholars, he quoted from memory the disputed passage in Greek, gave his own brief interpretation, and walked out the door. The great Professor Bultmann looked stunned. He turned to his host and said, "Public education in America must be *amazing!*"

> We should look to the mind, and not to the outward appearance. *Aesop*

3. Golden Rule Living

Others may judge us by appearances, but we should be careful about doing the same to them. Sometimes appearances are revealing. And sometimes they mislead. Refraining from judging others too quickly can be understood as just one more type of application of what I have come to believe is the paramount ethical guideline for our dealings with others, the central interpersonal moral rule, that fundamental principle recognized across the globe and throughout the history of truly civilized peoples that we call "the Golden Rule": Treat other people as you would want to be treated if you were in their place. Do unto others as you would have others do unto you.

If we live in accordance with the Golden Rule, we will not judge others on superficial appearances. We would not want to be so judged. We will not seek to deceive them by appearing to be something we are not. We would not want to be deceived by them. We will seek success straightforwardly, building our own characters as well as harmonious relations with others on the basis of our conduct toward them. Striving to free ourselves from deceptive appearances of all kinds, we can free ourselves and others from those illusions that often stand in the way of true success.

One very successful business executive recently said to me, "I don't believe in the Golden Rule. I tell my people to forget it—it makes no sense." I asked him what he meant. He said, "Look, let me give you an example. When my wife gets the flu, she wants to be attended to constantly. She wants me to bring her tea, make her toast, bring her a magazine, check in on her every few minutes. When I get the flu, I want to be left alone. Completely. I don't want to see anybody. I don't want to talk to anybody. If I take your advice and live in accordance with the Golden Rule, then when my wife next comes down with the flu, I'll have to treat her the way I would want to be treated if I were in her place. And I would want to be left alone. So I'll stay away from her. But she'll hate that. It will hurt her feelings and make her more miserable than she already is. By telling us to treat others as we would want to be treated, the Golden Rule advises us to force our desires on other people. And I don't think that is very ethical or sensible." Clever objection.

This shows us something about the Golden Rule. Not that it's no good, but that, like any general rule, it needs sensible interpretation in concrete, specific circumstances. Fortunately, for the interpretation of general rules, we have a general rule. The general rule for interpreting and applying general rules is to begin with the general and then move cautiously to the specific. Confused yet? Don't worry, this is basically a simple point, generally speaking. The Golden Rule says that this executive should treat his wife the way he would want to be treated. What does this mean? Most generally, he would want to be treated in accordance with his own legitimate desires and perceived needs, if he were sick. Therefore, at a general level, he should treat his wife in accordance with her legitimate desires and perceived needs, since she is the one who is sick. He should then seek to learn what those specific desires and needs are, and he should seek to act accordingly. To treat her as he would want to be treated, then, does not require that he avoid her since he would want to be left alone. It requires him to be as sensitive to what she wants as he would have her be to what he wanted. So he should bring her the tea and toast.

No general rule can automatically give us all the answers. Not even the Golden Rule. Good judgment is always required. That sort of perceptiveness and wisdom that is a part of developed character is needed. But, interpreted sensitively, I believe that the Golden Rule is one of the very best guides to successful interactions with other people we could possibly have. And one of the best touchstones for character imaginable.

If I am a spiritually healthy person, I am more likely to make the decisions and engage in the conduct that will lead to socially harmonious relations with others. I am more likely to be properly sensitive to the needs of others as well as to my own true needs. I am more likely to be considerate, kind, patient, honest, courageous, and humble in my dealings with others. And these are all matters of good character.

Let me say in concluding a few words about one aspect of good character I've just mentioned. Humility. This is one of the most misunderstood and neglected of the moral virtues. It may also be one of the most important conditions of the best kind of leadership. It is surely one of the most important qualities for attracting the cooperation and assistance of other people for our projects. And it may be the core of all the virtues.

The ancient spiritual classic the *Tao-te-ching* tells us that the ocean is the greatest body of water because it lies below all the rivers and streams and is open to them all. This is a model for humility. The opposite of humility is of course arrogance, or overweening pridefulness. The humble person can be extremely confident and can have the highest degree of proper self-esteem attainable. But the humble individual seeks to serve not just himself, but others as well. Because he opens himself to others, the person displaying proper humility draws the attention and efforts and goodwill of other people to himself and his projects in the best possible way. One of the happy ironies of life is that presumptuous self-centeredness is self-destructive, whereas humility and altruism are self-fulfilling. Threatening, manipulative attempts at leadership are in the long run self-defeating. Humility in our quest for success provides for the strongest sort of sustainable leadership, and facilitates the attainment of true success. It is the core of moral character and is a surprising springboard to both personal and competitive excellence.

The sixth condition of success: We need a good character to guide us and keep us on a proper course. We need the sort of character that will enlighten us in our choice of goals and the means to those goals, a personal integrity that will inspire the trust and help of others.

7

A Capacity to Enjoy

Condition Seven: We need a capacity to enjoy the process along the way.

The six previous conditions of success can seem like a lot of work. First we engage in a struggle of self-knowledge to attain a clear conception of what we want in life. What are our goals for ourselves, for work, for family, for friendships? What exactly are we aiming at in a particular activity or project? It's not always easy to answer these questions to our satisfaction.

Once we have our targets in view, we need to create within ourselves the confidence it takes to launch out in pursuit of those goals, a confidence sufficient for carrying us through those times when we face challenges and difficulties along the way. We need to attain a focused concentration on the concrete, practical steps necessary for getting from where we are to where we want to be. What is to be done now? What comes next?

As we move forward, we have to be careful to monitor ourselves and cultivate a stubborn consistency in pursuing our vision. And

248

it's vital to generate and sustain a strong emotional commitment to the importance of what we're doing. But all of this will fall far short of bringing about the full realization of the potential we have for success unless, all the while, we are working to build within ourselves the resources of a good character, the necessary foundation for pursuing the right goals in the right ways, as well as for building between ourselves and other people the sorts of relationships and interactions that will facilitate true success.

There are many people who think of success as a far-off destination to be reached through lots of very hard work. They gut it out now, striving with all their might, in the hopes that someday they will attain the success they long for and will then be able to enjoy the fruits of all their efforts. But if we think of success as a destination, how will we recognize that we have arrived there? What exact level of accomplishment will signal that it's time to relax and enjoy ourselves? Even if we think we can specify that now, our estimation will likely change as we make progress in the direction of our goals. Thought of as an ultimate destination, success can be as elusive as the horizon—as we move toward it, it moves along with us, keeping just as far ahead as ever. The more we accomplish, the more we see that could be accomplished.

> If you imagine that once you have accomplished all your ambitions you will have time to turn to the Way, you will discover that your ambitions never come to an end.
> *Yoshida Kenkō (c. 1340)*

True success is best thought of not as a far-off destination, or an end state of any kind, but as a process, a dynamic process of successful living. As we attain valuable goals that are right for us, renew our vision, move toward new goals that have then become appropriate for us, and properly attain them, while building up our own personal excellence, as well as strong, healthy relations with the people around us, we are experiencing small individual successes within an overall process of successful living. The only guaranteed way to enjoy success within our lives is to learn to enjoy the process along the way, in its many facets. Dreaming, scheming, striving, wrestling—whatever we are doing at the present moment—can be enjoyed. It need not be just endured as we wait on some future enjoyment that we think some far-off ultimate success will bring.

PHILOSOPHERS OF THE PRESENT MOMENT

One of the most interesting philosophers of the ancient world was the Greek thinker known as Diogenes the Cynic. He was not a cynic in the modern sense. The term came from the Greek for "doglike." Diogenes was said to look like a stray dog, and was referred to as such.

We are told that Diogenes uttered such profound pieces of wisdom as: "He has the most who is most content with the least," and "Dogs and philosophers do the greatest good and get the least reward." Consistent with his own philosophy of contentment and simplicity, he gave away all his possessions except a bowl for drinking water. It is said that one day he saw a young slave boy drinking water from cupped hands and gave away the bowl. This sage who is remembered throughout the ages slept in a borrowed earthen tub.

One day Diogenes was visited by a man who lived on the opposite end of the human spectrum, Alexander the Great. Alexander was his biggest fan and had come both to pay his respects as well as to receive some wise counsel. They talked at length. At the end of the visit, Diogenes asked Alexander what his plans might be. Alexander answered that he planned to conquer and subjugate Greece. Pretty impressive goal setting. But Diogenes pressed on. After conquering and subjugating Greece, what would he do? Alexander explained that he then planned to conquer and subjugate Asia Minor. And after that? After that, Alexander intended to conquer and subjugate the world. Diogenes, who was not easily impressed or dissuaded from a line of inquiry, asked what he planned to do after he had conquered and subjugated the world. Alexander the Great told the philosopher that after all that, he planned to relax and enjoy himself. Diogenes responded: "Why not save yourself all the trouble by relaxing and enjoying yourself now?"

Alexander never got the point. Many people never do. Enjoyment is not meant to be the final end state of a long and arduous process of attainment. It is meant to be woven through the tapestry of our lives *now*. In the present. And throughout the process along the way.

Those who strive and hope and live only in the future, always looking ahead and impatiently anticipating what is coming, as something which will make them happy when they get it, are, in spite of their very clever airs, exactly like those donkeys one sees in Italy, whose pace may be hurried by fixing a stick on their heads with a wisp of hay at the end of it; this is always just in front of them, and they keep on trying to get it. Such people are in a constant state of illusion as to their whole existence; they go on living *ad interim*, until at last they die.

Arthur Schopenhauer

Tom Morris

Not long ago I enjoyed reading a simple but powerful little book called *Peace Is Every Step,* by Thich Nhat Hanh. I would often read it as I walked across campus and down the halls of my office building at Notre Dame. Here I am a Southern Baptist boy from North Carolina teaching at a great northern Catholic university, and I was frequently seen strolling the sidewalks absorbed in the writings of a Vietnamese Buddhist monk. Too much ecumenism in one place for some people, but I try to find wisdom wherever I can.

Thich Nhat Hanh taught me something about enjoying the richness of the present moment. He reminded me of the importance of mental and emotional attention to the fullness of my experience. He reminded me to savor as completely as I can the one and only time in which I actually live, the moment occurring *now.* He also reminded me of the great seventeenth-century French mathematician, scientist, and religious thinker Blaise Pascal, who remarked in his *Pensées*:

We never keep to the present. We recall the past; we anticipate the future as if we found it too slow in coming and were trying to hurry it up, or we recall the past as if to stay its rapid flight. We are so unwise that we wander about in times that do not belong to us, and do not think of the only one that does. . . .

Let each of us examine his thoughts; he will find them wholly concerned with the past or the future. We almost never think of the present, and if we do think of it, it is only to see what light it throws on our plans for the future. The present is never our end. The past and the present are our means, the future alone our end. Thus we never actually live, but hope to live, and since we are always planning how to be happy, it is inevitable that we should never be so.

This is the relation to time we are so often trapped in. But we can free ourselves from this trap. We can learn to attend to the present moment, dwell fully in its actuality, and enjoy all that it contains. We can be happy now.

> For present joys are more to flesh and blood than a dull prospect of a distant good.   *John Dryden*

Thich Nhat Hanh speaks to people in a hurry. He counsels us to pause to feel the feet in our shoes, to feel the cloth against our skin, the air on our faces. He advises us to hear the sounds around us, see the many sights, the colors and shapes, and drink in the aromas. I benefited from this advice as soon as I read it, and I shared it with my family as soon as I could. My two children laughed out loud. My son rolled his eyes while repeating the phrase "the feet in our shoes," and they both together said, "Right, Dad."

Of course, what I had failed to realize is that you don't have to advise children on how to live in the present moment. They don't need hints, tips, and techniques for appreciating the enveloping immediacy of their environment. They do it naturally. Remember what it was like when you were six, or eight, or even ten years old? There was a seemingly endless expansiveness to each day. A warm sunny afternoon could feel like it would last forever. All the many activities of the day—running, throwing, catching, playing games, riding bikes—seemed to take place within limitless horizons of an unobtrusive time. And at any moment a revelatory awareness of the smallest thing could break through and captivate all conscious attention. A blade of grass. A cloud formation. A small insect on the sidewalk. Dust motes in a ray of sunlight.

Tom Morris

> If you let yourself be absorbed completely, if you surrender completely to the moments as they pass, you live more richly those moments.
>
> Anne Morrow Lindbergh

For years I have longed to recapture that glorious state of consciousness. One picture has vividly come to mind, again and again. I'm six or eight years old. It's a beautiful summer day. Bright blue sky, adorned with a few puffy cotton clouds. The warmth of the sun is lightly tingling my skin. I'm in shorts and a T-shirt, and I'm lying on my back in the close-cut grass of my own front yard. I hear the chirps and calls of distant birds, and the occasional sounds of bugs buzzing by my ears. I take in the leaves of nearby trees, but mostly I just gaze upward into that endless blue of the air above, gloriously awash in every sensation coming my way. I'm completely, utterly content.

That's a great way to enjoy a little free time outside on a beautiful day. No worries, no plans, no thoughts of future or past—just immersion in the rich, gentle flow of the present moment. How often do we adults just lie down in the grass and take it all in like this? The neighbors would dial 911. It's simply not done. Not where I live. And I bet it's not done where you live either. Drive down any residential street on a beautiful day. You won't find the front lawns littered with supine dentists, spread-eagle lawyers, or sales reps communing with nature.

But two weeks ago, I did it. After many years of wanting to and feeling like it was something a dignified adult just didn't do. I was in a big field about a block from my house throwing a Frisbee with my son, Matthew. At a certain point I said, somewhat self-consciously, "Matt, let's just lie down in the grass and look at the

254

sky." He didn't ask why, or seem to think it at all strange. To him it was apparently the most natural thing in the world to do.

> One midsummer I went out of the road into the fields, and sat down on the grass between the yellowing wheat and the green hawthorn bushes. The sun burned in the sky, the wheat was full of a luxuriant sense of growth, the grass high, the earth giving its vigor to tree and leaf, the heaven blue. The vigor and growth, the warmth and light, the richness and beauty of it entered into me; an ecstasy of soul accompanied the delicate excitement of the senses: the soul rose with the body. Rapt in the fullness of the moment, I prayed there with all that expansion of mind and frame; no words, no definition, inexpressible desire of physical life, of soul-life, equal to and beyond the highest imagining of my heart.
>
> *Richard Jeffries*

So there we were, side by side, all alone in an open field, gazing heavenward. In a matter of seconds I was feeling mystical, transcendent, one with nature and my son. We were having a subtle, cosmic, nearly religious experience. It was almost overwhelming. Then, in a thoughtful, reflective tone of voice, he spoke. "Dad, how high up into the sky would it go if I did a fart?"

Children are a bit more casual about their mysticism. The metaphysical and the mundane are more at one. I could tell I had a lot to learn, from my children as well as from my own childhood. And from a master of mental states like Thich Nhat Hanh. His book had dropped like a seed into fertile soil. The state of mind I so wanted to recapture was at least beginning to grow within me.

The day I finished the book, I found myself standing in a long line at the grocery store. Now, I'm usually a man in a hurry, and I've always hated to wait in a long line. It's such a waste of time. When I'm without a book to read, I'm typically in a state of constant anxiety, low-level frustration, and unease, looking around, checking my watch every couple of minutes, and fidgeting in place. I'm mentally rehearsing all that I should be doing, and I'm noticing everything that anyone does to slow down my progress to the cash register. Well, this particular day, having just been taught by a master of attentiveness, I was noticing all my surroundings. I was appreciating the colors, rejoicing in the shapes, and enjoying all the sounds. I raised my right arm slightly and looked upon the drape of my jacket as I felt the cloth soft against my skin. I returned my eyes to the room around me and noticed that people were glancing my way a bit strangely. I suddenly became aware that I had a very big smile on my face as I floated immersed in the joys of the present moment. Not something often seen in the checkout line.

Then, *one week later,* I was at another grocery store with my son, in another long line. Not as long as the one the previous week, but we were four or five people from the register. None of the people ahead of us could find the change they were sure they had; someone wanted to write a check, using for identification what must have been a New Zealand driver's license; the trainee clerk was all thumbs; and suddenly I heard from the head of the line those most dreaded of words to people in a hurry: "*Price check!*" I was constantly shifting my weight, looking at my watch every twenty seconds, and muttering things like "I can't believe this." When I heard the call for a price check, I groaned aloud, "Oh, no."

Matt tugged on the sleeve of my coat and said, "Dad, the feet in your shoes."

The feet in my shoes. I wasn't feeling the feet in my shoes, or the cloth on my arm, or the air on my face, or anything but frustration. How fickle we are. The previous week I had lived in present-moment-Zazen-Baptist-Bliss after reading an enlightening book, and then only a few days later I was back to my old impatient self, enjoying *nothing* about the present moment, anxious to get back to work. I listened to my son, and I suddenly realized how habituated most of us are to being in a hurry. It is indeed the most natural thing in the world for young children to live in the present. They don't have to work at it. But we adults are always rushing into the future. We have speeded up our internal biorhythms, set our inner metronomes to click at too fast a pace. Why are we in such a hurry? Why do we put ourselves under such stress? Gandhi once pointed out that "there is more to life than increasing its speed." And yet most of us with goals and ambitions rush madly forward, fueling our acceleration with self-imposed stress, in a cycle of rapidity it's quite hard to break.

DEALING WITH STRESS

Decades ago social prognosticators predicted that by now we'd all be living lives of leisure. We'd be working shorter hours, or fewer days, or both. The pace of work would be humane, and its rewards would be great. Machines would relieve us of so much of the inconvenience and drudgery of work, and we would be living in a golden age of recreational pursuits. Colleges and universities even founded departments of leisure studies and recreation administration so that we could have plenty of help in figuring out what to do with all our free time.

It hasn't happened, has it? We have not been freed up from work, except by recessionary business cycles and their attendant unemployment. We have not witnessed the dawning of a golden age of leisure and culture. Instead we have gone into fast forward. We've been computerized, faxed, and cellular-phoned into an unprecedented frenzy of activity. The pace has become amazing. And in many business contexts, people say that the pressure has become unbearable.

Some people work well under pressure. For a while. Some people seem energized by stress. Within limits. Most people need time to think, time to rest, and a pace that will allow them to enjoy the work they are doing. We don't need unnecessary pressures.

An interesting story about stress. When the highly regarded physicist Richard Feynman took his first teaching job many decades ago at Cornell University, he had just finished working on the atomic bomb project at Los Alamos. He arrived at Cornell intellectually exhausted, and he felt that he was being offered too high a salary for what he was able to contribute (the princely sum of four thousand dollars a year!). Over a period of time, he was so busy preparing notes for his classes that he had little time for research or original thought. He felt burned out, he was having no new ideas at all, and because of this he felt increasingly unworthy of his salary. Then he began getting job offers in the mail from other universities, with promises of even higher salaries. Rather than making him feel good, this just increased his stress level. One day a letter came from the fabled Institute for Advanced Study in Princeton offering Feynman an unbelievably perfect position, better than even Einstein had enjoyed. As he shaved that morning he reflected on this fabulous offer, and what struck him as its evident absurdity made him laugh out loud. He suddenly realized that these people were expecting him to be so good it was literally impossible to live up to their expectations, and that he therefore had absolutely no obligation to do so. And when that liberating thought occurred to him, he realized that the same thing was true of all the other universities bidding for his services, including even Cornell. He said:

> I am what I am, and if they expected me to be good and they're offering me some money for it, it's their hard luck.

In that one realization, he suddenly released himself from all the stress that had been building up in him as a result of the interaction of his previous successes, his present need for rest, and the ever-more demanding expectations of other people. The more the stress built, the less likely it was that he could be creative. The more time passed without creative accomplishment, the greater the stress would grow, and the cycle would worsen, until that one liberating moment shaving. Feynman decided to just be himself. He had no responsibility for other people's inflated expectations. He had no obligation to surpass his own previous successes. He was who he was. And he had a right to be just that.

Freed from all the artificial pressure, Feynman immediately regained a playful attitude toward life, and he recognized that it was just that attitude of playfulness that had given him all his previous accomplishments. Within a week he was in the Cornell cafeteria when someone threw a dinner plate into the air. He watched it wobble and noticed the spin of the Cornell medallion in the middle of the plate. He started toying with ideas about the wobble and spin of the plate, and from these humble, playful beginnings discovered the ideas for which he later received a Nobel Prize.

> Do your duty, and leave the rest to heaven.
>
> *Pierre Corneille*

Stress kills. Anxiety disrupts. The past and the future can enslave us. So can other people's expectations, and our beliefs about other people's expectations. We need to free ourselves to be ourselves, to enjoy who we are and whatever we're doing at the present time. Only then can we become all that we are capable of being. And only then can we fully enjoy the process along the way. Attentiveness, freedom, and a sense of play are so important in our quest for success. Animals play. Young children play. And we all need to play too. Playfulness allows for creativity. Enjoyment allows for achievement. And achievement enhances enjoyment. If we are not experiencing all these things on a regular basis, we need to make some changes in the patterns, rhythms, and cycles of our lives.

Our goal setting makes a great deal of difference. Are we working under vague but unreasonably demanding expectations? Or do we have specific goals that are challenging enough to be interesting, but reasonable enough to be attainable without unhealthy levels of stress and anxiety? What is our attitude about our goals and our prospects for achieving the desired results? And in what sort of frame of mind do we work toward them? What kind of atmosphere exists overall in our work environment? Are we contributing to making it an environment where enjoyment and accomplishment can march forward hand in hand? This is what is required for true success.

The emotional and attitudinal possibilities for any work situation can be laid out quite simply:

THE ABCs OF WORK

A situation that overtaxes
your talents and skills
results in:

ANXIETY

A situation that undertaxes
your talents and skills
results in:

BOREDOM

A situation that is
right for your talents
and skills results in:

CHALLENGE

The ideal for all goal setting is to pose fulfilling challenges for the individual. Challenges that stretch us without bending us out of shape. Challenges that can be enjoyed. We should never think of enjoyment as limited to those moments we can just lie in the grass and gaze at the sky. We need such moments. But we need every bit as much to be able to enjoy our work activities, the processes by which we attempt to meet the challenges we've set ourselves, or that have been set for us.

> Life affords no higher pleasure than that of surmounting difficulties, passing from one step of success to another, forming new wishes, and seeing them gratified. He that labors in any great or laudable undertaking has his fatigues first supported by hope, and afterwards rewarded by joy. . . . To strive with difficulties, and to conquer them, is the highest human felicity. *Samuel Johnson*

If we are in leadership positions we need to remember the ABCs of any work situation and create the kind of culture, the kind of climate or atmosphere, where people are provided with fulfilling enjoyable challenges, challenges that will goad and allow them to grow in personal excellence and felicity. Only in this way can group excellence or corporate excellence ever be attained and sustained over the long run. Our progress into the future must allow for a rich enjoyment of the present moment.

THE SECRET OF ENJOYMENT

I enjoy excitement. Of a positive kind. Most people do. Every now and then I'll live through a stretch of time during which exciting new developments seem to come my way every few hours, or at least every day. New ideas, new people, and new opportunities rush and tumble into my life one right after the other at a pace that is almost dizzying. "How exciting it all must be," friends say. "How enjoyable it all must be," they think. And it is. Both exciting and enjoyable. It can be like surfing a big wave or rafting down a fast-moving river. When it's all happening with a rhythm that deserves an MTV sound track, it's easy to be caught up in it all and to experience a kind of natural bliss that some psychologists nowadays call "being in flow" or "having a flow experience." It's effortless. It's exhilarating. It's great.

But if our enjoyment depends on the excitement of external events, it's doomed to be short lived. For more than two thousand years philosophers have noted that one of the few constants in life is change. Things may be jumping today, but that's no guarantee for tomorrow. It's one thing to enjoy excitement; it's another thing to need it. Can I fully enjoy a day when nothing flashy, outrageous, unusually wonderful, or wildly exciting comes my way? If I can't, I'll have a lot of bad days. We should enjoy excitement. We can even love it. But we shouldn't need it or depend on it.

Sometimes the world will bring enjoyment to us. At other times we have to bring enjoyment to the world. Our jobs are not guaranteed to entertain us. Neither are our families. Or our friends. Only we are ultimately responsible for whether or not we enjoy the life we have. Enjoyment must come from within. This is one of the most important discoveries we can ever make.

1. Fundamental Balance

Sometimes what we need in our lives is a little philosophical equanimity. Some measure of tranquility. The ability not to get too worked up about either the good things or the bad things that come our way and cross our paths. What is often referred to as balance. We need psychic shock absorbers that will allow us to ride over life's bumps and potholes without getting unduly shaken up. One realization that helps provide this is the mid-life recognition I sometimes put to myself a bit starkly:

Nothing is as good as it seems or as bad as it seems.

The cautious philosopher in me wants to be more careful and qualified than the seventeenth-century French moralist La Roche-foucauld, who to my knowledge first gave voice to this sort of sentiment, and say only that "hardly anything in this world is as good as it seems or as bad as it seems." But as soon as we allow for exceptions, we might as well not have the rule. Because whatever it is that I'm currently getting worked up about, good or bad, I'll see as certainly the exception to the rule, if exceptions are allowed. It is psychologically safer to tell ourselves without qualification or hedging that at least within the confines of this terrestrial globe, nothing is, in itself, as good as it seems or as bad as it seems. Then we are less likely to overreact.

Some things can still be great. Others can still be terrible. But it's a general truth that when faced with either the great or the terrible, we'll get so emotionally worked up, we'll see it as even better, or much worse, than it really is. When we see things in our lives as terribly, terribly bad, it's hard to enjoy anything else. And when we see them as wonderfully, wonderfully great, we may be so dazzled by them that we fail to appreciate the good of other things in our lives we could also be enjoying. A new job, a major promotion, a new love, or even the prospect of a big, positive lifestyle change can sometimes shine so brightly in our eyes that other goods around us are cast into the shadows. In allowing ourselves to be emotionally supercharged by and fixated on one thing, we can easily come to ignore friends, neglect family, and fail to attend to the many small glories sparkling all around us. Overestimating one blazing good that has appeared on our horizon can result in an unhealthy focus and an emotional imbalance that does not conduce to the full enjoyment of life in this world. In addition, if these very good things that capture our attention are just passing through, as most things are, the more we overvalue them, the more difficult it will be to see them go. And the less likely we'll be to enjoy life without them. We are most free to enjoy when we maintain some level of tranquility of spirit down deep in our hearts. This is compatible with being, on the outside, quite excitable and enthusiastic, and full of appreciative energy. But deep down we all need some anchor, some measure of philosophical equanimity to give us emotional stability and continuity throughout our journeys.

2. Two Kinds of Enjoyment

Throughout the centuries, a long line of poets, troubadours, and philosophers have claimed that the secret of life is to enjoy the passage of time. The succession of moments. The hour. The day.

And whatever transpires therein. I think a lot of people nowadays would tend to agree with this perspective. But not a lot of people seem to realize that there are basically two different kinds of enjoyment available to us in this world.

First of all, there is the phenomenon of *intrinsic enjoyment*. If I'm drinking a cold beverage on a hot day, or if I'm in a hot bath at the end of a cold, hard workday, I may be immersed in an appreciation of the immediate qualities of the experience itself. This is intrinsic enjoyment. The tingle. The taste. The feel. Enjoying a thing in and of itself. Relishing an experience on its own merits. The sensations of a kiss. The glories of a ripe pear. Whenever the idea of enjoyment comes up, I think that this is what most readily comes to mind for most people. Intrinsic enjoyment. It's an essential capacity for a complete human life.

But there is also a second kind of enjoyment, which opens up into a broader sphere of experience, and I think it is even more important for the living of a fully human life. I have come to think of it as *extrinsic enjoyment*. This is the enjoyment of a person, place, time, thing, event, or experience *as* he, she, or it connects up with a larger context of meaning or value. There is a big difference between a pleasant sensation and a pleasant sensation experienced with someone you love. There is a big difference between a beautiful day and a beautiful day shared with a good friend. To the extent that our enjoyment of an experience hooks up with or depends for its quality on connections with a larger context outside the intrinsic characteristics of the experience itself, that enjoyment is what I call extrinsic.

I have become convinced that the more an experience is connected up with a positive framework, or overarching context of positive beliefs, attitudes, and emotions, the more likely we are to benefit from that experience. If the experience is intrinsically enjoyable, then the more we connect it up with a larger framework of beliefs, values, goals, and experiences, the greater our enjoyment of it will be. By being connected up with a larger overarching framework, a neutral experience may become enjoyable. And a negative experience can at least be made less distressing. It may even be made into a positive lesson, or seen as a good opportunity for growth and learning, however uncomfortable it might in itself be.

We need to experience both sorts of enjoyment in our lives. The intrinsic ties us to the immediacy of our experience. The extrinsic connects us to the larger meanings and values of our existence. The sound of a young girl laughing is pleasant. The sound of my daughter laughing is wonderful. The sight of a boy and his dog asleep together is pleasing. When the boy is my son and the dog is our pet, the sight is precious.

Some of the most deeply spiritual people in our world connect up everything in their experience with an overarching transcendent framework of value. We all need a Big Picture for our lives, a context that will magnify the good and make more manageable the difficult as it comes into our experience. We need connections with something larger than ourselves. We all need the attitudinal and emotional resources that will allow us to bring enjoyment to our world and to our experience of the world. And as we create with other people structures of family, friendship, and meaningful work, we provide them as well as ourselves with a deeper framework for enhancing the enjoyment possible for our lives.

3. Cultivating Our Capacity for Enjoyment

How can we cultivate most fully a capacity to enjoy the process along the way as we journey through this life? There are many ways. First, remember to feel the feet in your shoes. Attend to the moment. Notice and enjoy the intrinsic delights around you.

Don't allow this wonderful world to be wasted on you, moment to moment. Secondly, connect as many of the events in your life as you can to larger frameworks of meaning. Through family, friendship, community, and work. In your thought and in your spirit.

> The grand essentials to happiness in this life are something to do, something to love, and something to hope for. *Joseph Addison*

Thirdly, set valuable goals and work toward those goals. The first six conditions of success can actually help us put into practice the seventh condition. In a recent, excellent book on optimal human experience called *Flow,* the psychologist Mihaly Csikszentmihalyi suggests that structuring our experience toward the attainment of reasonable, but reasonably challenging, goals and attending to the feedback we receive as we strive to work toward those goals can provide the most reliable conditions for the optimal enjoyment of our experience. So I'm not saying "work hard toward success. And, oh yes, by the way, also enjoy yourself." Appropriately working toward goals is the best way of enjoying yourself, and enjoying yourself frees up your deepest potential for successful work toward your goals. That's just the way we human beings are hooked up psychologically. Insofar as our efforts toward success add complexity to our lives, complexities of skills, accomplishments, interests, and relationships, we put ourselves in better and better positions to enjoy our lives. We enhance our capacity for enjoyment. And for success.

Celebrate little victories along the way. As small-scale, preliminary goals are met, attend to that fact and engage in a little self-congratulation. Be proud of yourself. Notice your progress. Enjoy what has been accomplished. And the bigger the goal that's been met, the bigger the celebration should be. Include family. Include friends. Buy the dog a treat. Show someone appreciation.

When you've had to struggle a bit in an effort of self-discovery to know what new goals to set, and you actually get through the struggle far enough to articulate an array of at least tentative new goals, consider that in itself a success worth celebrating. A new set of goals might just be your own personal Declaration of Independence. Or they may be a part of your new personal Constitution. In any case, successful goal setting can sometimes be as worthy of celebrating as successful goal attainment.

And celebrate other people's little victories with them: an account sold, an award won, an article accepted for publication, a promotion, a particularly beneficial contribution to a difficult meeting. Acknowledging and commending other people's victories accomplishes many ends. It gives you more opportunities to enjoy the pleasures of celebration. You may yourself be in a period where there won't be anything to celebrate for a while unless you celebrate the accomplishments of others. The other people whose victories you are lauding will appreciate your notice, your praise, and your good wishes. And in response they will tend to reciprocate, joining you in some of your own little self-celebrations. They may even notice things in your life worth celebrating that you tend to overlook. And they'll remember you well for your extolling of them for a long time to come. They will feel appreciated. And that matters a great deal.

> I now perceive one immense omission in my *Psychology*—the deepest principle of human nature is the *craving to be appreciated.* William James

The first letter of acceptance I received to a graduate school, my senior year at college, was a memorable occasion. My favorite professor had me read the letter to him over the phone. He asked me to come by his office later in the day. Meanwhile he went out and bought a bottle of lemon soda as a celebration. When I arrived at his office, he welcomed me with fanfare, scrubbed out two dingy, dirty old coffee mugs, and poured us both some of the bubbly, while offering a toast. It was as meaningful a gesture as I've ever had shown to me, and I remember it with affection and gratitude twenty years later.

Celebrate with others. They'll remember. New levels of connection will grow between you. New forms of communion will develop. Competition often pulls us apart. Celebration usually brings us together.

A capacity for enjoyment can also be cultivated through well-known methods of relaxation, focusing, and visualization. There are many excellent books now in print that offer effective physical and mental techniques for relaxation and meditation. It can be very helpful to master some of these exercises and have them available for use whenever needed. Employing Eastern techniques of breathing, posture, and focus for just a few minutes each day can greatly enhance your ability to enjoy the rest of your waking hours. And periods of positive mental visualization can often work wonders.

One evening several years ago I was alone in the basement of my house playing my electric guitar. Which is the only place my wife lets me do such things. I suddenly began to daydream vividly that I was on a huge stage playing in front of thousands of people. It had been many years since I had performed in front of crowds like that as a rock guitarist, and I realized within a couple of minutes that, along with the visualization, my heart rate had increased, I actually felt a bit nervous, and it was noticeably more difficult to make my fingers go where they needed to go to play some fast and complex arpeggios and runs that I could do fairly effortlessly when I was alone both physically *and* mentally. Out of curiosity I repeated this visualization briefly for a number of days as a sort of psychological experiment. It always had the same results—a low level of discernible nervousness and increased difficulty of performance. I realized that if visual imagination could make something more difficult, it stands to reason that it should be able to work in the opposite way as well. Can I stand in front of thousands of people and so vividly imagine myself alone in my basement that my hands will fly and the notes will flow? I haven't had the opportunity to try it with my guitar, since I'm no longer a professionally performing musician, but after those basement experiences I began to use visualization exercises to prepare myself for special big lectures at Notre Dame, as well as for speeches to large business organizations. It worked wonders. And continues to do so.

We employ the mind to rule, the body to serve.   *Sallust*

Mind moves matter.   *Virgil*

I have no idea what the limits of visualization are. I am convinced, however, that most of us do not come near to tapping the full resources of this power that we have. I have been able to block pain from a dentist's drill in the dead of a gray South Bend winter by vividly visualizing a white-sand beach and foamy, white-capped blue-and-green ocean water on a sunny day. Not a small task. Was it just my imagination when I got up out of the chair, caught a glimpse of myself in a mirror on the wall, and thought I detected a slight tan on my face? Of course it was! Visualization has its limits. But no one knows what they are. What else can we do with this power we all have? With it we can enhance greatly our enjoyment of our lives. I'm sure of it. And at the same time we can use it to enhance just as much the accomplishment of our lives. I'm equally certain of this.

> Aldous Huxley once said, "What we think and feel and are is to a great extent determined by the state of our ductless glands and our viscera," but I have come to believe the truth is mostly vice versera.
>
> *(Just a comment)*

We tend to enjoy whatever we are doing the most when we are most immersed in it. Cultivate the ability to focus, and you cultivate the capacity to enjoy. When your mind is on a thousand other things, a task can be unpleasant and it can seem to take forever. When you are totally immersed in what you are doing, time can seem to stand still while, ironically, the clock speeds up. On a great day of writing, when my focus is at its best, many hours can pass by unnoticed. But when I'm distracted and pulled in dozens of directions, distracted to the extent that I can't really get into gear, the clock can sometimes crawl through each hour. When we are thinking about our audience rather than our performance, it can block or detract from the excellence of which we're capable. When we're working just for the money, or for what other people think, we can sustain excellence and enjoyment only so long, if we attain them at all. The people who flourish and exult in their occupations tend to be those whose focus is on the job itself.

Insofar as it is within our ability, we ought to work hard to create an enjoyable environment for ourselves and others. An environment in which our creativity can be freed up and we can focus on the jobs we have to perform. At work, adequate compensation and benefits will free the minds of people from unnecessary worry and will allow them to attend to the task at hand. Pleasant working conditions can provide for a meaningful, humane environment where the spirit can flourish. Interesting challenges will stimulate the mind. And an ethical culture will allow for wholehearted engagement, a strong sense of trust, and a pride of involvement. If we structure a work environment with attention to all the basic dimensions of human life—the intellectual, the aesthetic, the moral, and even the spiritual—we provide ourselves and others with all the conditions for maximal enjoyment and maximal success. Anything less is in the end self-defeating. And of course this holds true for any other human relationship outside work as well. When our lives are properly structured, both our enjoyments and our attainments are enhanced.

THE AIM OF HAPPINESS

Aristotle said that all men aim at happiness. And all women too. But what counts as happiness? What brings it into our lives? Over the centuries great thinkers have pondered these questions and have offered a variety of answers.

Some have said that happiness is pleasure. To pursue happiness, we should chase pleasure. And not just the most obvious or most readily available pleasures, but more refined and rare ones as well. But is total hedonism the model of complete human happiness?

Let's do a simple little thought experiment. Imagine a normal, healthy man lying on a bed in a scientific laboratory attached by an array of electrodes and wires to an advanced generation of super-computer. Through the wires and electrodes, the computer is able to stimulate his brain in such a way as to create the ultimate in virtual-reality experiences and pleasures. Imagine that the computer is programmed in such a way as to feed our man a consistent, nonstop diet of pleasurable experience. Because of the electrical current to the pleasure center of his brain, he wants to do nothing but undergo these sensations for the rest of his days, never again actually getting up out of bed or leaving the lab. He is hooked. The ultimate addiction. And we can imagine further an even more austere version of this scenario where the man is not only physically inert on the bed but where he is also devoid of any virtual-reality experiences of sights and sounds and is being fed only the pleasurable sensations that the brain would naturally have felt if it were to have had the perceptual experiences of, say, good food, warm sun, cool water, great sex, aromatic flowers, stunningly beautiful symphonies, lovely vistas, and satisfying companionship. Pure pleasure to the max. But nothing else.

Is this our ideal of human happiness? Would the man in the lab satisfy our conception of a completely happy person? I hope not. The man in this thought experiment is utterly inert, disengaged from real life and all its values, totally passive. Now, granted, this is an extreme situation we have imagined. But that's the way a thought experiment like this works. Some thinkers suggest that happiness is just the same thing as pleasure. We imagine a situation of total pleasure, as devoid as possible of anything else. Do we then have a situation of happiness? If our deepest intuitions lead us to think not, then we must reject the suggestion that happiness is identical with pleasure.

> The many, the most vulgar, seemingly conceive the good
> and happiness as pleasure, and hence they also like the
> life of gratification. Here they appear completely slavish,
> since the life they decide on is a life for grazing animals.
>
> *Aristotle*

Others have suggested that happiness is personal peace, or inner tranquility of mind. Imagine the surface of a pond on a windless day. This should mirror the spirit of the happy individual.

This is more Eastern in tone. We can imagine a person sitting cross-legged, back erect, eyes closed, mind a blank. Somewhere in California. Thoroughgoing unperturbedness. Existential equanimity. Is this a picture of our ideal of happiness? I am inclined to think that such experiences, or nonexperiences, as the case may be, can play an important role in a life of happiness. But they are not themselves the state of happiness. And if that is right, then we can't accept the suggestion that happiness is just nothing else but peace of mind.

> It is vain to say that human beings ought to be satisfied
> with tranquillity: they must have action; and they will
> make it if they cannot find it.
>
> *George Eliot (Mary Ann Evans)*

A much more penetrating view, in my opinion, is that happiness is active participation in something that brings fulfillment. This is a more thoroughly dynamic conception of happiness. The pursuit of pleasure and the search for peace may involve a great deal of activity, but the end state sought is in each case in itself rather passive—undergoing pleasure, or being at peace. The conception of happiness as participation in something that brings fulfillment is, by contrast, an inherently active conception. It captures the dynamism and energy ingredient in human nature and, at its best, can incorporate an appreciation for both pleasure and peacefulness. A person engaged in meaningful activity can experience the deepest, most complex, most satisfying, and most enduring pleasures. Which just proves the often-stated wisdom that pleasure is better thought of as a by-product than as a goal. And the right sort of engagement in meaningful activity must incorporate the attainment of a measure of tranquility along the way. Some even say that the greatest personal peace arises out of the satisfaction experienced in successful progress toward goals felt to be valuable and meaningful in themselves.

> Happiness is a sort of action. *Aristotle*

We are inherently active beings. And as such, our greatest fulfillment must come in acting, physically or mentally exercising our talents and realizing our potential. We need to become most fully what we are capable of being. And we need to work for something larger than ourselves. This is the ultimate in personal excellence. And this is what alone brings true happiness.

We cannot become most fully what we are capable of being unless we live our lives participating in and flourishing along every basic dimension of human experience, as outlined in chapter six. We all have intellectual, aesthetic, and moral capacities that must be exercised. We all have spiritual potential that needs to be engaged and cultivated. We need to discover all our most basic talents, develop those talents, and deploy them properly into the world. We all need to grow in these ways. This is an ongoing task of self-discovery and self-definition. It is also a process of empowerment. We can call all this the activity of *self-actualization.*

> Happiness is neither virtue nor pleasure nor this thing nor that, but simple growth. We are happy when we are growing.   *W. B. Yeats*

But we also need to work for, or toward, something larger than ourselves, something that is worthy of our commitment and loyalty. We can call this, by contrast, the activity of *self-subordination.* I have come to believe that every human being has two deep fundamental spiritual and emotional needs:

1. a need for a sense of *uniqueness*

2. a need for a sense of *union* with something larger than the self

I often refer to this expression of basic spiritual need as *The 2-U Principle.* Each of us needs to feel special, important, and distinctive. We need to be appreciated as the unique individuals we are. But each of us also has a deep need to belong, to be a part of something valuable that is much bigger than our own small selves and narrow self-interests. This is part of the deep metaphysical background to sex, and friendship. This is why people identify with their town, or state, or school. It's a significant part of the potential power of families, and, when family is not available, it's a part of the lure of street gangs. It's ultimately behind patriotism.

And it's one of the fundamental wellsprings of religion, the need for spiritual community.

We are essentially social beings. We need to belong to a society of other unique beings who support each other in work, growth, and vision. We cannot be truly happy without an experience of both uniqueness and union. We cannot truly enjoy our lives if both these equally important fundamental needs are not being met.

At some deep level I think we all know this. But where a lot of people go wrong is in how they think about what it takes to satisfy these two spiritual needs. It seems to be widely believed that uniqueness takes effort, whereas union will basically take care of itself. Have you ever noticed how hard some people are prepared to work to attain a sense of uniqueness? Bizarre dress, outrageous behavior, flamboyance of all kinds—many of us seem to be willing to go to a great deal of trouble in the quest to be different, to stand apart and be recognized as unique. Uniqueness seems to be thought of as a matter of what we do. And at the same time, in the minds of many of the same people, union with something greater than the self seems to be thought of as primarily a matter of who we are, or where we are. I am a Morris. I am a Notre Dame professor. And when I was growing up, I was taught to sing, "I'm a Tar Heel born and a Tar Heel bred, and when I die I'll be Tar Heel dead." You're Jewish, or Irish Catholic, or Methodist. You're a New Yorker. Or you're Swedish. And from this identification you may derive a sense of union with something larger than yourself. When you think like this, you may be thinking of union as not dependent on *doing* anything, but as entirely just a matter of *being* something.

Whenever we take this perspective, we get things backward. Uniqueness is primarily a matter of who you are. Union depends to a great extent on what you do.

Each of us is born unique. No one else has exactly your genetic endowment combined with your experience of life. And this is true of every single person who has ever lived. As one humorist once put it, "You are absolutely unique—just like everybody else." A sense of uniqueness comes from realizing this, and is deepened immeasurably by the continuing discovery of all your individual talents and tastes.

Union, on the other hand, can take a tremendous amount of work. Good relationships don't just happen and sustain themselves throughout the years. They must be actively cultivated and maintained. Good marriages, good friendships, good teamwork in the office or on the factory floor all take work to create and preserve. And, as great religious thinkers have proclaimed about the most important union of all, God must be served. The work we do for the sake of satisfying union can sometimes be hard, but it can also be a source of the deepest enjoyments as well.

> Many persons have a wrong idea of what constitutes true happiness. It is not attained through self-gratification, but through fidelity to a worthy purpose.   *Helen Keller*

I believe that there are also two other universal human spiritual needs that are related to, and in some sense subsidiary to, our needs for uniqueness and union. First, we all need to feel useful. Each of us has a deep need to feel that we have a task to perform in this world. We need to be needed. This is one reason why unemployment, idleness, and social isolation can be death to the spirit.

I recently saw a television news report about a group of prisoners working together in a special program to help protect towns and homes in the Midwest from threatening floodwaters.

The men seemed to exult in their work, even though what they were doing—lifting heavy sandbags to build walls—was obviously very physically demanding. Some of them may never have felt so useful and appreciated before. With their newfound positive sense of usefulness, they came alive spiritually, and spontaneously began to talk of useful employment after their release from prison.

We all need a sense of usefulness. It enhances our fundamental sense of uniqueness as we draw upon our own abilities to help others. And it enhances our sense of union with others to see how our efforts contribute to some greater good.

We all also have what I consider to be a spiritual need for understanding. We need to get our bearings in this world and feel that we have some sort of a Big Picture for what our lives are all about. Without some sense of understanding, we are more than confused. We are dispirited. It should be one of the most fundamental functions of universal education to provide people with some sense of understanding concerning their roles in nature, in their immediate families, in their larger communities, and in the human family. Understanding along these lines inspires. Ignorance of these things destroys.

I want to call all of this *The Human Happiness 4-U Thesis*. I am convinced that you and I can be fully happy, and can fully enjoy the process of living and pursuing success, only if we attend sufficiently to our own deep spiritual needs and to the needs of the other people around us for:

1. a sense of *uniqueness*

2. a sense of *union*

3. a sense of *usefulness*

4. a sense of *understanding*

Human happiness cannot exist in a vacuum. The greatest enjoyments of which each of us is capable cannot arise and be sustained, I believe, unless others around us are equally well positioned to enjoy their share of happiness. And I am convinced that this is an implication of our basic human nature. It's because of the way we were created. The most enlightened self-interest must then encompass a lively interest for the good of others. We are inextricably linked. And we should always keep this in mind when we think about, and as we pursue, success.

In setting the right goals for ourselves, in choosing the right means for attaining those goals, and in attending to the Big Picture for our lives, in which we can see both our multidimensional nature and the deep and vast interconnections between ourselves and other human beings, we provide for ourselves everything within our power for that most fulfilling and universally sought-after human state of true happiness. To be moving in that direction, and doing it well, is true success.

The seventh, and final, condition for success: a capacity to enjoy the process along the way.

Epilogue:
True Success
and the Meaning of Life

Each of us has a lot to give to this world while we're here, and the world has a great deal to give back to us in return. But none of this will happen the way it should unless we are embarked on an exciting journey of success. This should involve, first of all, an inner exploration, then an outer adventure. One of the strongest temptations in life, as we look around us in this great world, is to become so fascinated by the things we see that we forget to develop who we are. Our journey must start from within. We each need to develop in self-knowledge through the setting and seeking of goals we find on reflection to be appropriate for us, goals that resonate with what our hearts tell us we most deeply need. And as we shoot for these goals, we should always seek to deploy our talents into the world for the good of others as well as for ourselves. For only in this way will we attain the highest of which we're capable.

Tom Morris

SOME THOUGHTS
ON THE MEANING OF LIFE

What is your primary goal at work? Is it to make money? If the answer is yes, I hope you work at the U.S. Mint or the Bureau of Engraving and Printing. Because nobody else's primary goal at work should be the goal of making money.

We can draw a clear distinction between primary, focal goals and secondary, or subsidiary, or peripheral goals. Finding the meaning of our lives and achieving the happiness we desire consists, in part, in finding the right primary goals to shoot for and pursuing them, in identifying appropriate secondary goals and moving toward them, as well as in knowing the difference between the two.

> Happiness is not best achieved by those who seek it directly.
> *Bertrand Russell*

In the introduction to this book, we looked at a number of things that are often misidentified as success: wealth, fame, power, and social status. A person seeking success in life should not be seeking first and foremost any of these things. None of these conditions should be anyone's primary goal in life. And for a simple reason. Wealth, fame, power, and social status can all be thought of as forms of *recognition*, possible social consequences of who we are or of what we do. But none of them should be thought of as the substance of our calling. We are in this world to concern ourselves with the *contribution* we are capable of making. When we take care of that, the proper recognition will come.

> No man's fortune can be an end worthy of his being.
>
> *Francis Bacon*

We read in the Bible that it is more blessed to give than to receive (Acts 20:35). Why? Is there something wrong with receiving? No! Absolutely not. Receiving is great. It's wonderful. But no one who seeks only to receive will receive for very long or in the most satisfying way. No one who makes receiving his or her primary goal will receive a truly fulfilling experience of life. This is another of the many great ironies of existence. If your goal is primarily to give, you'll end up continuing to receive. Which is a very good thing for you. And for those to whom you give. I believe that we are here to try to give more to this life than we take from it, a task that, if undertaken properly, is impossible. The more we give, the more we get. But that's precisely the point. And that's a good part of the meaning of life. Miss that and you miss a lot.

> It is one of the most beautiful compensations of this life that no man can sincerely try to help another without helping himself. *Ralph Waldo Emerson*

It's not wrong to want resources. It's not wrong to have as a goal the positive recognition and respect of other people. But money, fame, power, and social status should never be our primary focus. There is nothing immoral or unseemly about a balanced desire for any form of human recognition. And it's not wrong to seek as a goal the having of any of these things. What would be wrong, though, would be to fixate on any form of recognition as a primary focus of our lives.

We should focus on becoming the people we are capable of being and on doing the good we are capable of accomplishing during our years on earth. I see wealth, fame, power, and social status as something like secondary social consequences of success, when they come. The primary social consequences of success should be providing people with useful products and helpful services that will result in an enhancement of their overall life experiences. Using the same categories of primary and secondary again, the secondary personal consequences of success might be something like an enhanced self-esteem or a noble self-image. The primary personal consequence of success would be the living of a richer and more deeply enjoyable life. The attaining of personal excellence. And I suggest that our labeling of these various possible consequences of success as either primary or secondary should be mirrored in the way we set our goals, as well as in how we pursue them. We should always have as our primary goals clear focal targets of creation, contribution, and participation in life to the fullest. The positive consequences of recognition that may result can be enjoyed immensely, but should always be secondary considerations for us.

Arriving at a proper sense of the meaning of life involves having the right sorts of goals, backed up with the proper values, and moving in the right direction within the coordinates of an insightful, Big Picture map of life. It is intimately tied, I believe, to living a life of true success, within the range of the nearly boundless opportunities we can find in the world. We find the meaning of our lives and we attain our greatest happiness as we pursue true success and make the mark we are here to make.

I speak of pursuing success or of seeking success. I assume that this is something every reader of this book is doing. We all seek success. And there is nothing at all presumptuous about this. We should never feel in the least embarrassed or uneasy about it. We are hard-wired for success. It's the natural intent of our existence. To seek domination can be presumptuous, but to seek success is not the same thing as seeking domination. To seek a narrowly self-centered form of achievement, and that alone, would be inappropriate. But there is nothing selfish about seeking true success.

Whenever we try to do anything, however small or trivial, we are setting ourselves goals and moving toward them. But to set any goal and shoot at it is to want success. Success itself can never stand alone as the goal. It is just the positive process of incrementally moving toward and attaining our more specific goals. To seek true success is just to set and seek to attain the goals we believe are most deeply right for us. And even before we've successfully attained a goal, we may be successfully moving in its direction, successfully closing in on it. Success is in this sense progress in the right direction.

To the extent that we want to have goals that are right for us and that will help us make the contribution we are in this life to make, we can be said to have as a goal true success. No one can have just success as their only goal in life. That would be utterly empty. But everyone can have, and should have, what I have been calling *true success* as a formal, general, overarching goal to structure their thoughts, their energies, and their activities. The success of inner achievement, personal excellence, and moral concern moving out into the world and making a positive difference can be our aim. And it should be. In the end, living a life geared toward true success is the only sensible way to live. It is the only way to have a thoroughly meaningful and completely fulfilling existence.

THE WISDOM OF TRUE SUCCESS

In this book we have examined the one universal framework for the attainment of true success in every facet of our lives. It is worth another look in outline:

The Seven Cs of Success

1. We need a clear *conception* of what we want, a vivid vision, a goal or set of goals powerfully imagined.
2. We need a strong *confidence* that we can attain our goals.
3. We need a focused *concentration* on what it takes to reach our goal.
4. We need a stubborn *consistency* in pursuing our vision, a determined persistence in thought and action.
5. We need an emotional *commitment* to the importance of what we're doing, and to the people with whom we're doing it.
6. We need a good *character* to guide us and keep us on a proper course.
7. We need a *capacity* to enjoy the process along the way.

This overall framework of the Seven Cs is a powerful tool kit for satisfying achievement. Each of these conditions is an effective and important tool for the building of a successful life. As a philosopher, I'm thrilled to have made the discoveries that have come my way as I've thought hard about success. I've found it exciting, gratifying, and extremely useful to have philosophized at length about this fundamental and universal human concern. Perhaps you have had some of the same experience as you have read this book. I hope that my reflections, comments, and musings have helped you to develop some new insights of your own, as well as to strengthen your grip on some old insights that easily fade from consciousness if not attended to and nurtured. I hope that you'll be encouraged to philosophize more about what success really is and how it is to be most properly realized in your unique life. And, of course, most of all, it is my deep desire that the totality of what we've seen in our look at the Seven Cs will help you greatly to make real practical progress along your own journey of true success. An enhanced life should always be the practical payoff of sound philosophy.

The general framework of this book, our map of the Seven Cs of Success, is in one sense a product of my own philosophical efforts to understand. But more deeply it is a result of the wisdom of the ages. It provides a basis for a good deal more philosophizing, as well as a strategy for wise and successful living. If wisdom is more than theoretical knowledge, if it is indeed more like a knowledge of the heart, a deep wellspring for living, I am convinced that it comes to be truly possessed only by being actually lived out, put to work, tested and refined in day-to-day experience. Philosophy, as a "love of wisdom," must be, at its best, a love of living wisely, and a love of attaining wisdom about living by and through both the act of living and the practice of carefully reflecting on that lived experience.

So the Seven Cs are not just to be nodded at, smiled upon, agreed to, or talked about. They are to be embodied. They are to be used. They are to be lived. And they are to be integrated into our lives at the most fundamental level of habit. That's the place where they can best do their work. Read them over. Think about them. Analyze your life to see how they apply to you where you are now. And then put them to work. Habitually. Only then will they have the impact in your life they're capable of having. Only then will these conditions help awaken in you the wisdom, happiness,

287

fulfilling success, and personal excellence they're capable of delivering.

If this can be the result of our philosophizing together, then we are true philosophers indeed. And we have entered onto a new path of excellence. The path of true success.

Begin, be bold, and venture to be wise.   *Horace*

Acknowledgments

Many people have contributed to the process that produced these ideas. I want to thank Linda Laskowski, Pat Cressy, Don Smith, and Bill Killilea, whose encouragement and early speaking invitations first got me on the road. Thanks also to Bill Scholl, Jim Frahleigh, Todd Bemenderfer, Barry van Dyke, and all the other good people at Notre Dame who helped launch the talks in which I began to develop this material. To Ken Schanzer at NBC: You're one of a kind. To Weldon Jefferies, deep gratitude for the way you enhance my daily working environment. And a special word of appreciation to those who read an earlier draft of the book, whose questions and suggestions helped me refine the final product: Dave Boehnan, Chuck Rogers, and my attorney and good friend Tony Edens, whose assistance and support is never ending. Thanks also to Cheryl Reed for her skills in getting this from fountain pen ink to computer disk; to Kevin Coyne for introducing me to his terrific agent, Reid Boates; and to Reid for truly masterful help in finding the right home for this book. And at the culmination of the whole process, I have benefited immensely from the inspiration and sage advice of Jane Isay, the best editor and publisher imaginable. To Jane: Heartfelt thanks and praise. I salute in addition all the other successful people I know whose lives have shown me the truth and power of the principles on which this book is built.

Index

Index

Focusing, 271–72
Fosdick, Harry Emerson, 216
Freedom, 151–52
Fulfillment, 32–33, 152, 221; and happiness, 274–75
Fulwell, Ulpian, 193

Galbraith, John Kenneth, 155
"The Gambler," 113
Gandhi, Mohandas K., 257
Goals, 35–36; and business, 52; and character, 217–18; choice of, 118–20; and commitment, 53, 56, 57–58; and conscience, 101–2; and desire, 53–58; and enjoyment, 260–61, 267–68; ennobling, 52; evaluation of, 64–65; and imagination, 62–68; inconsistent, 156; inherited, 50–51; for inner self, 47–48; and intellect, 60–61; in job, 211; materialistic, 52; new, 75–76; ownership of, 51–52; personal, 50; primary, 282; professional, 156; renewal of, 68–71; risk assessment of, 64–65; secondary, 282; for self, 47–48; setting of, 37–58, 281, 285; sharing of, 44–45, 52, 76–77; stretching for, 66–67; and success, 51, 70–71; talk about, 43–45; of teams, 141; time required for high, 67–68; in work, 211; writing of, 40–43
Goethe, Johann Wolfgang von, 76
Golden Rule living, 244–47
Good, power for, 55
Good things in life, 47
Graham, Sheilah, 183, 187
Greatness, 209
Group excellence, 262
Group goals, 44, 52, 103–4, 141

Habits, 44–45, 164–69; change of, 170–75
Handshake, 105
Happiness, 31, 34, 221, 267, 272–80, 282; and money, 31
Harmony, 157
Harris, Sydney J., 66
Health, negative thinking and, 78
Hepburn, Katharine, 184
Heraclitus, 154, 218
Herbert, George, 81, 207
High goals, 66–68, 74; failure after achievement of, 70
Hill, Napoleon, 107–8
Hindu proverb, 226
Hirsch, Alan R., 240
Hitchcock, Alfred, 220
Hobbes, Thomas, 235
Holocaust survivors, 129
Home, working at, 26
Homer, 191, 213
Honesty, 241; and salesmanship, 238–39
Horace, 126, 288
Human Happiness 4-U Thesis, 279–80
Humility, 247
Humor, 101; risks of, 188
Huxley, Aldous, 148, 271

Ignorance: and information, 173–74; and self-defeating behavior, 160–62
Imagination, 58–62, 150, 174, 177, 210; and change of habits, 168–70; and education, 60; and goal-setting, 62–68; negative, 61–62
Improvement, 47
Impulse, and inconsistency, 157
Incompetence, 192–98
Inconsistent behavior, 144–48; persistent, 156–75
Indifference: and imagination, 174; and self-defeating behavior, 163–64
Inertia, 164–69
Inflexibility, 149, 153
Information, 173–74
Initiative, 126–27
Inner life, 18–19; inconsistencies in, 172
Inner mastery, 172
Inner self, goals for, 47–48
Inner vision, 59
Intellect, and goals, 60–61

James, William, 78–80, 210, 268
Jeffries, Richard, 255
Jiantang, 124
Job: goals in, 211; love of, 208–10, 214–15; self-evaluation exercise, 46–47
Johnson, Lyndon, 126
Johnson, Samuel, 74, 76, 177, 261

Keller, Helen, 278
Kerouac, Jack, 163
Kierkegaard, Søren, 189
Kissinger, Henry, 121–22, 184
Kleinfeld, N. R., 240
Knowledge, 123; and adjustment of plans, 129; and salesmanship, 236
Koran, 176

La Fontaine, Jean de, 197
La Rochefoucauld, 222, 263
Leach, Reggie, 205
Leadership, 141, 184–86, 261–62; and change, 155
Lear, Norman, 38
Learning from failure, 94, 96, 134–35
Leisure, 257–58
Life: and adaptation, 129; compartmentalization of, 156–57; dimensions of, 229; meaning of, 282–85; order in, 151; quality of, 78; self–evaluation exercise, 46
Limitations, 121–22
Lindbergh, Anne Morrow, 254
Lingyuan, 124
Lists, self-evaluation exercise, 46–49
Literature, 56–57
Lombardi, Vince, 219–20
Longfellow, Henry Wadsworth, 175
Longsightedness of purpose, 136
Losers, 219
Lucretius, 176–77
Luther, Martin, 99

Index